RELATIONAL REMEMBERING

Series Editors: Hilde Lindemann Nelson, Sara Ruddick, and Margaret Urban Walker

Feminist Constructions publishes accessible books that send feminist ethics in promising new directions. Feminist ethics has excelled at critique, identifying masculinist bias in social practice and in the moral theory that is used to justify that practice. The series continues the work of critique, but its emphasis falls on construction. Moving beyond critique, the series aims to build a positive body of theory that extends feminist moral understandings.

Feminists Doing Ethics
edited by Peggy DesAutels and Joanne Waugh
Gender Struggles: Practical Approaches to Contemporary Feminism
edited by Constance L. Mui and Julien S. Murphy
"Sympathy and Solidarity" and Other Essays
by Sandra Lee Bartky
The Subject of Violence: Arendtean Exercises in Understanding
by Bat-Ami Bar On
How Can I Be Trusted? A Virtue Theory of Trustworthiness
by Nancy Nyquist Potter
Moral Contexts
by Margaret Urban Walker
Recognition, Responsibility, and Rights: Feminist Ethics & Social Theory
edited by Robin N. Fiore and Hilde Lindemann Nelson
The Philosopher Queen: Feminist Essays on War, Love, and Knowledge
by Chris Cuomo
The Subject of Care: Feminist Perspectives on Dependency
edited by Eva Feder Kittay and Ellen K. Feder
Pilgrimages/Peregrinajes: Theorizing Coalition Against Multiple Oppressions
by María Lugones
Why Privacy Isn't Everything: Feminist Reflections on Personal Accountability
by Anita L. Allen
Discovering Feminist Philosophy: Knowledge, Ethics, Politics
by Robin May Schott
Relational Remembering: Rethinking the Memory Wars
by Susan Campbell
Varieties of Feminist Liberalism
by Amy R. Baehr

Forthcoming books in the series by

Joan Mason-Grant; Diana Tietjens Meyers; Ruth Groenhout

RELATIONAL REMEMBERING

Rethinking the Memory Wars

Sue Campbell

ROWMAN & LITTLEFIELD PUBLISHERS, INC.
Lanham • Boulder • New York • Oxford

ROWMAN & LITTLEFIELD PUBLISHERS, INC.

Published in the United States of America
by Rowman & Littlefield Publishers, Inc.
A wholly owned subsidiary of the Rowman & Littlefield Publishing Group
4501 Forbes Boulevard, Suite 200, Lanham, Maryland 20706
www.rowmanlittlefield.com

PO Box 317
Oxford
OX2 9RU, UK

British Library Cataloging in Publication Information Available

Library of Congress Cataloging-in-Publication Data

Campbell, Sue, 1956–
Relational Remembering: Rethinking the Memory Wars / Sue Campbell.
p. cm.—(Feminist constructions)
Includes bibliographical references and index.
ISBN 0-7425-3280-1 (hardcover: alk. paper)-ISBN 0-7425-3281-X (pbk.: alk. paper)
1. Autobiographical memory. 2. Women-Psychology. 3. False memory syndrome. I. Title. II. Series.
BF378.A87C36 2003
153.1'2-dc21

2003008534

Printed in the United States of America

∞™ The paper used in this publication meets the minimum requirements of American National Standard for Information Sciences—Permanence of Paper for Printed Library Materials, ANSI/NISO Z39.48-1992.

For Jan

CONTENTS

ACKNOWLEDGMENTS

In this book, I argue against a dominant current in contemporary accounts of personal memory. To do so has sometimes felt like an isolated endeavor. I am very grateful for the generous support of the many colleagues and friends who encouraged this work to completion. My colleagues in the Dalhousie Philosophy Department and the Canadian Society for Women in Philosophy provided a decade's worth of essential critical response to my ideas. I also received helpful feedback on parts of this manuscript from audiences at Queen's University, the University of Western Ontario, the Canadian Philosophical Association, the Canadian Association of Law Teachers, the Canadian Law and Society Association, the Atlantic Region Philosopher's Association, and the Engendering Rationalities Conference at the University of Oregon. Samantha Brennan was the first to suggest to me that I should do a book on this topic. Susan Babbitt, Steven Burns, Richmond Campbell, Jacqueline Davies, Sue Dwyer, Christine Koggel, Toni Suzuki Laidlaw, Duncan MacIntosh, Naomi Scheman, and Susan Sherwin have not only commented on my work but have provided the sustaining energy of discussing how my ideas engaged with their own research interests. Their contributions have been substantial.

A Webster Postdoctoral Fellowship at Queen's University provided the research space to begin this project and, perhaps even more important, the opportunity to get to know Susan B., Jackie D., and Christine K. Working with Jennifer Epp on feminist advocacy helped me think through issues in chapter 4. Research for chapter 6 was made easier by a grant from the Research Development Fund at Dalhousie and the exemplary research skills of Angela Failler. The research for chapter 7 was generously supported by the Law Commission of Canada, and a long conversation with Andrew Brook about Ian Hacking's work instigated chapter 8. An invitation to the Université de Montréal by Marie Andre Bertrand helped me conceptualize my interests in memory and gave me a clearer idea of why I've cared so much about these debates.

Parts of this work have been previously published. Invitations to contribute to various collections were an impetus to keep going during some busy years, and I thank the editors. Part of chapter 3 was originally published as "Framing Women's Testimony," in *Fragment by Fragment: Feminist Perspectives on Memory and Child Sexual Abuse*, ed. Margo Rivera (Charlottetown, PEI: gynergy press, 1999). Much of chapter 8 appeared under its present title in a supplementary volume to the *Canadian Journal of Philosophy* (vol. 25), *Civilization and Oppression*, edited by Catherine Wilson. Christine Koggel's invitation to contribute to *Confidential Relationships: Psychoanalytic, Ethical, and Legal Contexts*, edited by Christine Koggel, Alannah Furlong, and Charles Levin (Amsterdam: Rodopi Press, 2003), came at a time when I doubted that I would complete the manuscript. I was able both to do so and to give the book its title in being engaged afresh by this invitation. Ideas from "Relational Remembering: Suggestibility and Woman's Confidential Records" have made their way into chapters 1, 6, and 8. In addition, parts of chapters 2 and 5 are drawn from "Women, 'False Memory,' and Personal Identity," *Hypatia: A Journal of Feminist Philosophy* 12 (2) (1997); much of chapter 6 first appeared as "Memory, Suggestibility, and Social Skepticism" in *Engendering Rationalities*, edited by Nancy Tuana and Sandra Morgan (New York: SUNY Press, 2001); and an earlier version of chapter 7 appeared as "Dependence in Client-Therapist Relationships: A Relational Reading of *O'Connor* and *Mills*," in *No Person Is an Island: Personal Relationships of Dependence and Interdependence*, edited by the Law Commission of Canada (Vancouver: U.B.C. Press, 2002). I am grateful to all of these publishers and to the anonymous referees who made useful suggestions and demanded greater clarity. I was also especially glad to have Stan and Lili's good cat company on the sabbatical where I finished the manuscript.

Conversations with friends and family about the sociability of memory and the ways of families have, I hope, kept me grounded in a sense of how people attempt to live their pasts with insight and integrity. I have found great value in the friendship and conversation of Denise Blais, Richard Bosley, David Checkland, Deirdre Susan Crandall, Pat Elliot, Audrey Macklin, Anne McGrath, Barry Snell, Renee Sylvain, Shirley Tillotson, my incomparable sisters Katy and Lori Campbell, and many of the folks mentioned earlier. I hope we will long continue to gather a shared past. Denise B. was also an important resource for early responses to the false memory controversies. Rocky Jacobsen and Jan Sutherland have listened with exceptional patience as I've tried to articulate my concerns about memory. They have also read and critiqued everything that I've written as a professional philosopher. I am very lucky to have such smart, clear-minded, and generous companions.

Finally I would like to thank Sara Ruddick and Hilde Lindemann Nelson for their encouragement and support of this book.

1

CONSTRUCTING THE "MEMORY WARS"

How do we now think about memory? The last decade of public and scholarly interest in memory, a period often referred to as "the memory wars,"[1] has been dominated by serious skeptical worries about the reliability of women's memories of childhood sexual abuse; in addition, it has spread related uncertainty about whether autobiographical memory is too easily manipulated to be a trustworthy source of information about the past. The origin of our new memory skepticism in distrust of women's abuse memories has become so familiar that researchers sometimes locate themselves by referring to the "false-recovered-memory controversies" (Sutton 1998, 7) without giving any detail about them. John Sutton introduces a study of early modern theories of memory by writing:

> As both recovered-memory controversies and science fiction teach, the quest to *reproduce* the content of an original experience would often fail to comfort: the personal past would be tyrannical, events preserved in aspic always returning to haunt us. . . . But whatever evidence of memory malleability, suggestibility, and distortion psychologists produce in response to moral panic about repressed memories of abuse, . . . it cannot be proven that *some* memories do not sit fixed in awful archives. (6, his emphasis)

Sutton uses the false recovered memory controversies to introduce a distinction between "storehouse" or archival models of memory and more dynamic reconstructivist models, and I will return in this book to how disputes about women's memories interweave with scientific and cultural debates over how to model memory processes. What I want to note here is that Sutton frames his research by mentioning controversies that he nowhere in his book describes. He assumes our familiarity; moreover, he assumes that referring to these controversies will serve as a compelling justification for why historical research on memory models should now hold our attention.

Sutton is a philosopher, and his book is directed to a professional audience. But writers also assume a wide public familiarity with the false/recovered memory debates:

> Memory is a machine that continuously constructs and reconstructs recollections. It mixes elements: Last autumn, I ate in a certain restaurant, but was it with Peter or with John? It embellishes: Those blissful childhood summers . . . Sometimes it even invents, like the infamous false-memory syndrome, in which involuntarily formed memories seem as real as true ones. (Villedieu 1999, 42)

To think or read about autobiographical memory is now difficult without moving through the idea of false memory. The question is how critically we do so. In this book, I challenge our present understanding of the false/recovered memory controversies. I challenge, in particular, how we have come to represent both memory and women. I use this introductory chapter to review *how* we have become familiar with the memory wars, both why and in what ways. In doing so, I display the restrictive rhetorical and argumentative framework that has dominated public and scholarly imagination and that hinders our efforts to understand our lives together as rememberers.

THE SUCCESS OF FALSE MEMORY ADVOCACY

The group most directly responsible for encouraging the recent unprecedented distrust of memory is the False Memory Syndrome Foundation (FMSF), founded in 1992 as a lobby for parents whose adult children have accused them of some abuse after a period of having not remembered it.[2] The FMSF has claimed that the number of women who allege abuse on the basis of pseudomemories resulting from suggestive therapy is a serious and prevalent enough problem to deserve the label of a syndrome. "False memory syndrome" is now part of a popular and legal discourse of skepticism when women claim to have recovered memories of sexual harm. Although the official description of false memory syndrome is gender neutral and nonspecific as to etiology, those who develop the alleged psychopathology are typically women who, the foundation contends, develop the disorder as the result of suggestive theory. FMSF material states that "while some reports of incest and sexual abuse are surely true, these decades-delayed memories are too often the result of False Memory Syndrome caused by a disastrous 'therapeutic' program" (False Memory Syndrome 1994). The FMSF has used a second term, one that has been widely adopted—"recovered memory therapy"—to suggest that a large group of therapists are engaged in the project of trying to uncover abuse memories using dangerously suggestive techniques.[3]

Memory scientist Daniel Schacter writes: "Our memories belong to us. They are uniquely ours, not quite like those of anybody else. We feel this way in part because our memories are rooted in the ongoing series of episodes and incidents that uniquely constitute our everyday lives" (1996, 15–16). Because personal memories are essential to our self-conceptions as unique individuals—often the first point made about them by theorists—the FMSF has found it relatively straightforward to transform a concern about distorted personal memory into a charge of identity disorder. The foundation explicitly defines false memory syndrome as:

> a condition in which a person's identity and interpersonal relationships are centred around a memory of traumatic experience that is objectively false but in which the person strongly believes. . . . The syndrome may be diagnosed when the memory is so deeply ingrained that it orients the individual's entire personality and lifestyle, in turn disrupting all sorts of other adaptive behaviors. The analogy to personality disorder is intentional. (False Memory Syndrome Foundation 1994)

Of particular concern to FMSF members are the identities of women who reject their family affiliations and state publicly that they are incest survivors: "They are no longer someone's daughters; they are Survivors" (Pendergast 1995, 478).

Finally, throughout the 1990s, FMSF members and supporters persistently made claims about the dangerous and uncontrolled spread of the pathology, saying that it had "manifested sufficient numbers of cases to reach epidemic proportions" (Pope 1996, 957).[4] Numbers offered of therapeutically induced false memories of abuse ranged from tens of thousands (Ofshe and Watters 1993, 14) to speculations about a million cases a year (Merskey 1997, 134). The FMSF thus argued that the public and courts should regard claims of recovered memory with grave suspicion and should reconsider the wisdom of amending legislation to allow women to testify to historic abuse.

The FMSF has attempted to ignite public and legal skepticism about women's claims of historic abuse by encouraging widespread social alarm about the suggestibility of women's memories and by pathologizing women through the introduction of a new syndrome. But the creation and publicizing of this syndrome do not explain its hold on the public imagination, its success in the media and in the courts, or its acceptance by many psychologists who study memory. False memory syndrome has no official status as a psychiatric disorder. A number of researchers quickly objected to the label as "a nonpsychological term originated by a private foundation whose stated purpose is to support accused parents" (Carstensen et al. 1993, 23 quoted in Pope 1996, 959). Claims in the mid-1990s that the pathology was extremely widespread, even epidemic, were not made on the basis of any studies of women who allegedly suffered from the disorder. As lawyer Wendy Murphy points out, "no studies or research exist to suggest that anyone suffers from it" (1997). Instead numbers were calculated using information from therapists about whether they used techniques regarded as suggestive, or they were calculated by the number of calls received by the FMSF. Psychologist and ethicist Kenneth Pope writes:

> It is worth emphasizing that some therapists engage in incompetent, unethical, or well-meaning but misguided behaviors, sometimes with disastrous consequences for patients. . . . In some instances these behaviors include using unvalidated, misleading, or bizarre methods for assessing whether a patient was sexually abused as a child. . . . However, such facts alone are insufficient basis for claims that there "is an iatrogenic disease created by therapy" and that this "false memory syndrome has reached epidemic proportions." (Pope 1996, 961)

Pope contends that we need to understand the "complex factors [that] may shape the process by which announced discoveries and conclusions encounter or elude careful scrutiny" (957). He claims, quite rightly, that such factors "are themselves a legitimate and important focus of scientific questioning" (957).

I hope to make a contribution to this more complex analysis in the chapters that follow. But I also want to point to the many obvious, close-to-hand explanations for why the public has been moved to skepticism. The specter of convicting innocent (and often elderly) parents and the FMSF's warning that the syndrome could affect any family have had considerable impact. In a very well-publicized case, George Franklin, the first person to be convicted on the basis of a recovered memory, was later released. The case of Paul Ingram, who confessed to sexual abuse of his daughters, has been widely reported as an obvious case of suggestible memory and false confession that resulted in grave injustice.[5] Many women, referred to by the FMSF and themselves as "recanters," have said they were encouraged by therapists to believe not only that they had been abused but that they had suffered ritual or cult abuse when all the evidence seems to suggest otherwise (Diana Russell 1986/1999, xxvii). Moreover, a number of critics, some associated with the FSMF, have recently raised vigorous objections to the validity of the concepts of repression and dissociation, concepts used to explain how memories of trauma can be preserved but inaccessible. Finally, the alarm about suggestible memory has been bolstered by current scientific research on the reconstructive nature of human remembering. Scientists now explain that our memories do not faithfully reproduce past scenes. Instead, we combine information from various times in our past with information from the present, and with general knowledge, our imaginings, and the views of others to creatively reconstruct a rendering of our past experience.

From its inception, the FMSF's work has been supported by an impressive and very active Scientific and Professional Advisory Board that has played a key role in legitimating the foundation and in spreading concern about memory influence. Advisory board members have appeared as regular speakers at FMSF-sponsored conferences; they have been expert witnesses in court cases involving delayed recall of abuse; and they have entered the public debate via popular books on the disastrous consequences of ignoring the malleability of memory.[6] In particular, the writings of sociologist Richard Ofshe (Ofshe and Watters 1993, 1994) and forensic psychologist Elizabeth Loftus (Loftus 1993, 1997; Loftus and Ketcham 1994) have had enormous influence, and I refer to them often in this book.[7] They have told the public that because memory is reconstructive, not reproductive, false memories can be created through the suggestions of those we trust in combination with our own inabilities to distinguish imagination from memory. Loftus has offered evidence for this hypothesis by devising experiments in which people claim to remember having been lost as children when encouraged to do so by a trusted relative (Loftus 1997; Loftus and Ketcham 1994, ch. 7).

In a surprisingly short time, and due in no small part to the authority of its advisory board, the FMSF has ignited public distrust of women's recall of abuse. The institutional response to the FMSF has been widespread and profound. The media has shifted from reporting on the harm of childhood sexual abuse to extensive reporting on alleged false memory and false accusations (Stanton 1997).[8] Professional associations of psychologists and psychiatrists have expressed formal concern about recovered memory and suggestive therapy, and they have legitimated the activities of the FMSF. The American Psychological Association, for example, approved the foundation as a provider of continuing education programs (Pope 1996, 957). Numerous professional periodicals have devoted special issues to the debate.[9] Many introductory psychology textbooks now review it as well (False Memory Syndrome Foundation 2000).[10] The courts have moved to disallow uncorroborated recovered memory testimony and open possibilities for third-party negligence suits against therapists while accepting expert testimony from foundation advisors and supporters about false memory (Bowman and Mertz 1996). One now often sees the endorsement of current public, legal, and scientific attention to memory distortion and suggestibility as a vital cultural corrective.

Skepticism about women's recall has not been and will not be contained in those situations where women recover memories of abuse while undergoing therapy. Although FMSF writings have been directed at the dangers of therapy, they have also condemned a wide range of cultural influences as contributing toward false memories, including feminist activism, self-help books, and dramatized narratives of abuse. In a 1999 clinical study at the McLean Hospital, for example, Chu and colleagues found that a substantial number of a group of patients were able to find support for recovered abuse memories and that most had not recovered these memories in therapy. A respondent suggested that a plausible explanation of the study's finding is that "false memories" are more effectively induced by "subtle suggestions (including such as might arise through exposure to movies or articles about recovered memories)" than through explicit suggestion in therapy (Good et al. 2000).[11] On the assumption that the memories are false but that the women have not had suggestive therapy, different sources of distortion need to be identified.

Moreover, continuous as well as recovered memories have become the object of false memory skepticism. According to reporter Kirk Makin, advisory board member Harold Merskey has "sounded a warning note" that "some complainants . . . have reacted to legal skepticism . . . by disguising the purported origin of their recollections . . . [portraying] these memories as having been there all along" (Merskey quoted in Makin 1998b). Advisory board member Campbell Perry has also warned that therapists may now be encouraging women to simply say they have always remembered the abuse (Perry 2000). The widespread suspicion that women have not been telling the truth about past abuse creates elastic possibilities for now contesting their claims. In chapter 7, I discuss the impact of the false memory discourse on debates about the confidentiality of women's therapy records in a legal context where recovered memories were rarely at issue.

Sara Scott writes that false memory syndrome "is fast becoming a free floating explanation, bobbing up in 'ordinary' conversation, providing a mechanism by which accusations of child sexual abuse can be transformed into errors and overreactions" (1997, 33). In fact, false memory syndrome has become an expression for inaccurate memory, suggestible memory, or the plain unbelievable. On the one hand, false memory syndrome remains tethered to the work of the FMSF and is largely directed at women's memories; on the other, it has become a part of a new memory discourse centered on malleability, suggestibility, distortion, skepticism, and disbelief. These changes in how we have come to think about memory, and specifically women's abuse memories, have led to more recent FMSF claims that the epidemic of false memory is now being controlled, largely through a result of its efforts. According to advisory board member Paul McHugh: "False memory syndrome was a major epidemic of psychiatric misadventure, and we pretty much put an end to it" (quoted in Peter Freyd 2002).

Feminists have been deeply concerned about the ramifications of the false memory debate: about its general undermining of women's credibility and about its threat to the possibilities of therapeutic, legal, and public support for women with abusive pasts. Some FMSF and advisory board members have reanimated stereotypes of women as easily influenced, narcissistic, and vindictive; they have cast doubt on the competence of women therapists and counselors; and they have reinforced a public perception of feminists as zealots with little concern for evidence or fair procedures. But many feminists have felt constrained in their responses to these controversies by their own concerns about the manipulation of women by experts and the vulnerability of memory to distortion through reconstruction. These concerns have obviously not simply worried us in the abstract but via vivid reports of what seem to be incontestable accounts of implausible accusations and abuses of therapeutic practice. Moreover, because of associations with multiple personality disorder, ritual abuse, hypnosis, and sexual secrecy, the debates have often felt tinged with irrationality. As Janice Haaken writes:

> women who report dramatically altered memories of the past are viewed by men, and even by many women, as excessively emotional and as lacking rational capacities. This project of exploring the credibility of women's memories, then, takes us into deep cultural affiliations among women, emotionality and hysteria. (1998, 8)

She insightfully notes that even feminists have the tendency to distance themselves from "women's complaints that seem to have a 'hysterical' cast for fear of losing credibility" (9).

Finally the debate about false memory has been extraordinarily heated. It has involved sensationalized court cases and very public family conflict. It has also resulted in accusations of professional malpractice, of ethical violations, and of lack of academic integrity. It has been (and will remain) difficult to enter this debate both passionately and as anything other than a memory skeptic. Nevertheless, it is this very skepticism—and the charge of suggestibility that has funded it—that is the focus of this book.

Law professors Cynthia Grant Bowman and Elizabeth Mertz wonder "why it is apparently so difficult to contemplate the obvious but . . . complicated possibility that there are both accurate and inaccurate claims of remembered sexual abuse" (1996, 622). In this book, I in no way deny this more complicated possibility. Nor do I deny the claims made by clients, by feminists, by concerned therapists, by researchers, and by the FMSF that some therapists have irresponsibly and destructively influenced vulnerable clients to falsely believe that they have been sexually abused. But granting these points does nothing to assuage my critical concern about the work of the False Memory Syndrome Foundation. My research is in feminist philosophical psychology. I have been particularly interested in the importance of emotion and memory in how we come to conceive of our lives and in the use of memory and emotion to challenge the credibility and mental health of individuals and groups.

I have been thinking and writing about the views of the FMSF on and off for the last decade. I remain critical of writings that promote the idea of false memory and false memory syndrome. Even as publicity over the debate has waned, I have become increasingly disturbed by its impact, not only on how the courts, media, and public have come to regard women who talk about abuse, but also on how we have come to regard memory. These concerns are intimately entwined: I do not believe we can come to an adequate understanding of the nature and importance of memory through a distorted view of rememberers. The harmful stereotypes of women's passivity that have repopulated discussions of abuse have led many theorists to regard the social dimensions of remembering only negatively, as a kind of threat or contaminant to memory; they have led them to restrict an analysis of power relationships to a discussion of how authority figures like therapists can exercise a damaging influence over our views of the past. But, I contend that a discussion of the relational dimensions of remembering primarily in terms of the threat of memory distortion compromises our understanding of the sociability of memory.

Particularly crucial for feminists and other anti-oppression theorists are accounts of the social resources needed for successful remembering, attention to the vulnerability of specific groups of rememberers, and specific, detailed analyses of how individual and group memories are undermined and pathologized. I believe this past decade, while often distressing, has also offered an excellent opportunity to think about some of the relational dimensions to memory experience, memory competencies, and memory narratives. This work is important: the social dimensions of remembering have been largely ignored across the disciplines—certainly in my own discipline of philosophy but also in empirical psychology. Public and scientific alarm over women's memory has flourished in a context where rememberers have been presented either as isolated individuals or as corrupted by their dependencies. I shall argue that although feminists have been put in a difficult position to respond to the "discourse of disbelief" that now surrounds women's memory (Scott 1997, 33), we need to do so with a passionate critical commitment to exploring the social and political dimensions of memory experience, memory narrative, and memory challenge. We must be alert to when public debate requires vigorous conceptual analysis, and we need to defend groups of rememberers from epistemically damning stereotypes without fear that doing so will affect our own credibility. I recognize that the chapters that follow this introduction form a limited contribution through the lens of a very particular debate to a political reconceptualization of memory.

THE FRAMING OF THE "MEMORY WARS"

In August 2000, Dr. John Read, a clinical psychologist and senior lecturer in the University of Auckland psychology department, resigned his position as director of scientific affairs for the New Zealand Psychological Association. The resignation was a protest because Elizabeth Loftus, a memory researcher at the University of Washington and the most well-known member of the FMSF advisory board to the public, was invited to be first keynote speaker at the society's annual conference.[12] Although Read did not object to Loftus's speaking, he felt that her position as first keynote would give "undue prominence and credibility" to her arguments (Dixon 2000). He expressed particular concern about the use of Loftus's research on the malleability of memory to discredit the testimony of adults who claim to remember childhood sexual abuse; moreover, he pointed out that the more "mental health staff believe abuse disclosures to be false, the less likely they are to ask their clients about abuse" (Dixon 2000). He summarized his concerns by a call for New Zealanders to stay focussed on the national crisis of child abuse, specifically on issues like underfunding and the need to train psychologists to know how to ask about abuse. He implied that Loftus's position as first keynote would disturb this focus.

Loftus did eventually present as first keynote at the conference, and Read's resignation and Loftus's appearances were reported on and discussed by the New Zealand press. Because the coverage was by a number of different journalists, we have a good opportunity to assess what the public might now understand about memory and child sexual abuse after a decade of controversy. Also, while my interests are more conceptual than Read's, it is an opportunity for me to point to both the importance and the difficulty of trying to reframe a public debate. The most serious disagreement between Read and Loftus is about the ethics of attention.

Of the five pieces of coverage I accessed over the web—four newspaper articles and one National Radio (New Zealand) interview with Read—the most self-consciously balanced story welcomes people to what "have been called the 'memory wars,'" describing them "as a near internecine conflict . . . between those who believe recovered memory is a form of collective, often media-hyped, hysteria and those who say that it is possible to recover memory of events such as abuse during childhood" (Dixon 2000). We would thus understand that one of the most important issues about child sexual abuse is whether adults can recover memories of the abuse or whether those who claim to do so are being collectively affected by a kind of hysteria. That is, outside of some very determined remarks by Read in the radio interview (Hill and Read 2000), while the articles relate Read's concerns about focus, they give no coverage to the issues that Read thinks Loftus's appearance will displace. They nevertheless give considerable coverage to Loftus's research.

The press clearly privileges Loftus as the expert on memory and abuse, a privileging made unremarkable by her position as the invited first keynote. She is described as "a world authority on the memory capabilities of children" (Hill and Read 2000; in fact, most of Loftus's research has been on adult memory); a "leading American academic who specializes in memory research" (McLoughlin 2000b); and "an authority on research into memory and a researcher of false memory syndrome" (Dixon 2000). Despite Read's twenty years of clinical experience, he is not characterized as an expert or an authority.

Loftus describes her research as being about the "flimsy curtain that separates our imagination and our memory" (Dixon 2000), implying that these faculties are too close in nature for us to trust our judgment about when we are remembering and when we are imagining. According to the press, her work involves the power of suggestion to distort recollection; in addition, all the articles adopt the phrasing that memories can be "implanted" by therapists. In one interview, Loftus explains one reason why therapists attempt to "dig out" claims about abuse:

> the problem is the therapist who has only one hypothesis. It isn't the case that every bit of pelvic pain means you were abused, that every case of depression or low self-esteem means you were abused, yet those therapists are not open to entertain [*sic*] another hypothesis other than their sex abuse agenda. (McLoughlin 2000a)

Thus, if we accept Loftus as the expert on memory in the context of child sexual abuse, we would understand that the significant issue about abuse memories is their malleability by one group of people, namely therapists. Moreover, we would learn that those therapists who are responsible for distorting women's memories have a dogmatic commitment to making nearly any complaint the consequence of unremembered abuse.

The coverage, however, gives no history of "false memory" or "false memory syndrome." Schacter worries that "the notion of 'false memory' itself is too coarse for the complex relations between memory and reality" (1996, 277). And until the 1990s, the vocabulary for suspect memory experience was more varied. We are not reminded of this vocabulary and are thus in a poor position to assess the effect of its absence; that is, we cannot assess whether "false memory" marks a significant change in our discourse, one that is framing attention in ways damaging to our understanding. The term "false memory" is unsurprisingly common in the articles, as it has become almost the exclusive popular term for what we seem to remember that didn't happen. It is not marked as new or contested vocabulary, although "recovered" memory is often contested by being marked off by quotes. Similarly, only Read associates Loftus with the FMSF; and the foundation itself is not identified as the advocacy group that originated false memory syndrome. This absence has had an impact. My students know about false memory syndrome and know that it particularly affects women's memories of abuse; but they do not know about the advocacy of the FMSF. When Loftus is described "as a researcher of false memory syndrome" (Dixon 2000), the disorder is reified.

Loftus allows that people can "remember things they haven't thought about in a long time," and she uses the example of a high school reunion as a context in which memories might be triggered (Dixon 2000). But she also claims that the cases she's seen involving alleged recovered memory of abuse are "generally . . . extremely suspicious," often involving claims of "animal sacrifice, baby breeding, baby sacrifice and satanic abuse" (McLoughlin 2000a). She mentions those who claim recovered memories of sexual abuse alongside people who believe they are possessed by demons and have been abducted by aliens.[13] There is no space in the rhetoric of Loftus's presentation for recovered memory that is not suspect. Disturbingly, though again unsurprisingly, two reporters use "false memory syndrome" and "recovered memory syndrome" interchangeably, associating all recovered memory with the idea of a disorder (Clausen 2000; Hill and Read 2000). Through identifying Loftus as the authority on memory, the journalists make recovered memory look extremely suspicious and well deserving of skepticism.[14]

More importantly, though, from Read's standpoint, the press coverage presents the disagreement between him and Loftus as one about *recovered versus false memory*. But Read does not want to debate on Loftus's territory; he says he wishes that she had stayed home. He is, in fact, not interested in defending recovered memory, which is not to say that he wouldn't defend it. (He is pressed to defend it, and in the radio interview he does so.) It's to say that defending recovered memory is not his focus of interest or concern. Read is interested in more resources for uncovering and treating child sexual abuse, but he ends up occupying a set position in the "memory wars." With Loftus in New Zealand, Read does want to challenge the appropriateness of attending to people's claims of abuse through an attitude of skepticism fostered by suspicion of their memories. For Read, once Loftus is invited to speak as the first keynote, her power to influence how we attend to child sexual abuse becomes the significant issue. The logic of Read's position, however, is not fully understood. Kim Hill, the National Radio interviewer, expresses confusion about why Read would object to the *positioning* of Loftus's speaking rather than her speaking at all, referring to it as "the interesting dilemma really in your position" (Hill and Read 2000).

Loftus's own response to Read suggests that he is irresponsible and unreasonable in insisting that framing is a significant issue. She positions the "responsible" person as one who realizes that addressing the malleability of memory will not "distract attention from New Zealand's present debate over child abuse. I think they're very different [arguments] and I would think that responsible people would recognize the difference and help other people appreciate that they are different" (Dixon 2000). Moreover Loftus suggests that Read's reaction is not only excessive but somewhat dated: "I feel like I'm back in a time warp. . . . I went through these kinds of experiences five, six, seven years ago when I first started speaking out about this problem" (Dixon 2000). Another psychology lecturer affirms that the debate about recovered memory is "all a bit passé" (Clausen 2000). But these remarks indicate the success of the skepticism that Read wants to reject. He cannot seem to reject this skeptical framing, however, without thereby being positioned as an advocate for recovered memory.

In saying that many therapists have "only one hypothesis," Loftus calls into question whether they would be good scientists. In saying that different debates can surely be pursued together, she evokes a powerful model of scientific inquiry as one of free and open debate; as long as all researchers are appropriately concerned with evidence and truth, one line of inquiry will not interfere with another. Read's colleagues express a very clear desire to be seen as responsible scientists. One observer worries that to withdraw the invitation to Loftus would be to "stifle debate:" "My feeling is that if we withdrew Professor Loftus, essentially what we would be saying was there was only one side to this particular debate" (Dixon 2000). A second says, "I think we all do respect each other as colleagues and respect different points of view. In the end psychology is a scientific profession. We've got to try and examine the evidence and judge the evidence and our understanding must come from there" (Dixon 2000). A third says, "generally one wants to foster debate and look at all sides in a scientific manner" (Clausen 2000). Even if well intentioned, Read's refusal to endorse research that he thinks primarily offers a strategy for discrediting people who say they were abused, when viewed through this model of inquiry, cannot help but be seen as an unscientific and blinkered dogmatism, an unwillingness to consider "different sides" to an issue. But the temptations of this reading again indicate that Read has not succeeded in making the issue one of how to attend to child sexual abuse; instead, he ends up debating on Loftus's territory. He is positioned within a model of scientific investigation that does not consider that prior understanding may determine what counts as evidence or truth, that pursuing certain lines of inquiry may make others less possible, or that the power of science as a model of knowledge seeking may disenfranchise the perspectives of those who are not scientists.

THE CALL FOR A MIDDLE GROUND

Read's position raises difficult and important questions. The attitudes of audience faith or doubt that make it possible or prohibitive for people to speak about or explore their pasts with others have ethical, epistemic, and practical import. I share Read's concerns about how we attend to memory and child sexual abuse. Because I consider the question of framing worthy of investigation—both the genesis of our present memory skepticism and its wisdom—I reject what is frequently offered, indeed pressed, as the most reasonable position about contemporary memory controversies: the seeking of a conciliatory "middle," or common, ground. In his chapter "The Memory Wars," Schacter claims that "contrary to what some have said, there is a middle ground in the recovered-memories debate; the problem is to identify it. I believe that this is our best hope for resolving the bitter and divisive arguments that continue to rage among patients, families, and professionals" (1996, 277). The call for a "middle ground" has been a distinctive part of the way the "memory wars" are presented. I call attention to it here to briefly highlight and problematize the role of science in the current debates.

The call for a middle ground has most often been made by memory researchers, who hold a number of different perspectives on the false memory debates. The call has come from prominent researchers like Schacter, who makes a considerable effort to evaluate the memory debates fairly and from the standpoint of a comprehensive scientific understanding of memory. It has come from clinicians and researchers who want to acknowledge that while we must guard against false accusations and suggestible memory, recovered memories can be accurate. It has come from those, like Loftus, who support the work of the FMSF. Schacter's words make clear that the "memory wars" refers to the extremism of at least some professionals. To seek out a middle ground is to try to be more epistemically and ethically responsible than these people. The pledge to seek a common ground is now often made at the beginning of research on recovered memory as a way of disavowing extremism. But what and who are being disavowed by this distancing gesture, and what is being accepted?

Feminists and frontline clinicians and therapists have been those most often positioned as extremists in the memory controversies because of their insistence on raising political questions about memory.[15] I believe that rather than allow for a responsible movement toward a reasonable view, the call for a middle ground, whether accepted or rejected, positions these groups in ways that make it very difficult to respond adequately to the politics of these controversies. First, because of its symbiosis with the "memory wars," the idea of a middle ground implies that we agree that the dispute is over recovered versus false memory. Schacter writes: "I believe that the depiction of the recovered memories debate as a winner-take-all battle between advocates of recovered memory and proponents of false memory is overly simplistic" (1996, 252). I do not use "the false-recovered-memory debate" in the rest of this book because I do not want to be confined to the question of whether people can recover memories of childhood sexual abuse or whether they sometimes seem to remember abuse that didn't happen. Both of these positions seem to me beyond reasonable dispute and therefore suggest that the real issues are elsewhere. In later chapters, I interrogate the specific discourse of "false memory" without defending or even talking about the idea of recovered memory.

Second, to accept the wisdom of a common ground is to position others as extremists. While not denying the excesses of some responses to the controversies, including feminist responses, I object very strongly to two of the reasons many feminists and therapists have been positioned in this way. I reject one reason because it is inaccurate, and I object to the other because it is not an indication of extremism.

Some authors have charged that most feminists and many therapists believe that whatever women claim to remember about their pasts is thereby true of their pasts; therefore, we have good enough reason to question their objectivity. As I have said, the skepticism we bring to people's recountings of their experiences raises complex issues. The appropriateness and impact of our attitudes, for example, differ depending on who these others are and our position in relation to them. But the FMSF has tended to represent its critics as simply naive about the nature of memory, the number of poorly qualified or unethical therapists, and women's capacities for confabulation. It is important to realize that feminist response to the work of the foundation has been varied and that much of it is not naive.[16] Many feminist critics have themselves expressed caution about certain types of therapy and the dangers of suggestion and overinfluence. Some have been critical of encouraging client confrontation with a family and about a therapist's motives in encouraging such confrontation. Almost all acknowledge the possibility of a client's developing illusory memories to confirm a therapist's hypothesis about the origins of the client's difficulties. Finally, a number of feminists have called for research in women's social memory that studies the broader cultural functions of abuse narratives while acknowledging that some are not literally true.

Nevertheless, critics have objected to the work of the FMSF along several dimensions of concern: the invention of a syndrome that pathologizes women and of the legal use of that syndrome; the animation of stereotypes of women as passive and highly suggestible; the categorization of therapists who take child sexual abuse to be serious and widespread as "recovered memory therapists" who are as a group incompetent; the talk of an epidemic of suggestibility and the concomitant implication that all women who see therapists or who are even immersed in a cultural milieu that takes abuse seriously are at more than minimal risk of confabulating abuse in their pasts; the consequent participation in a general undermining of women's credibility as autonomous agents; and, finally, the effect of skepticism on victims of sexual assault and sexual abuse. My own critical stance toward foundation advocacy includes all of these concerns. I concentrate, however, on what has so far received little attention. I contend that a fear of memory suggestibility that we have not adequately analyzed is damaging to our theories of memory. Thus, the call for a "middle ground," like the "memory wars," can distract our attention from the range of alternative positions that feminists have explored and from the need for positions that challenge the current framing of these debates.

But feminists are also positioned as extremists because of what is true of feminists: that we are both political and generally impassioned about our politics. In an early call for a common ground, Lucy Berliner and Elizabeth Loftus identified themselves as a therapist and a scientist "desperately seeking reconciliation," as two people who might be thought on opposite sides: "those who care about victims and those who care about the truth" (1992, 570). They reject this description of themselves and others—that is, they say we all care about victims and the truth unless we are extremists:

> We recognize that there are some who are not interested in establishing more of a common ground. As in any field, we have extremists and charlatans. Ideology, zealotry, bias and greed have powerful distorting influences. . . . If we talk about what evokes the emotionality that so often interferes with rational discourse, then we can move past that emotionality. (570–71)

On this telling, for feminists to seek common ground is to say that we now care about truth as proved by our rejecting ideology and transcending passion. But feminists neither do nor should accept the incompatibility of passion and ideology with truth. The risk of being labeled extremist in denying that the search for truth can or should be free of one's ideological commitments is familiar to us. If we attempt to depoliticize the false memory debates, we will neglect the effects of power on the lives of rememberers and on which accounts of memory secure scientific and public allegiance.

Finally, Berliner and Loftus suggest that one thing that those of us who are reasonable can agree on is "that there are clearly some unresolved questions that are legitimate subjects for further scientific inquiry. For example: Are there as yet unexamined variables that influence suggestibility?" (573). In accepting a middle ground, one accepts not only that the current debates are about false versus recovered memory. One may also be accepting that the fact of our suggestibility is the most important issue about memory and that it appropriately belongs to the purview of scientific investigation. I have learned much from scientists, both feminist and nonfeminist, who study memory. But I shall argue that the idea of memory suggestibility requires a prior conceptual investigation that focuses on the ways in which we consistently fail to see memory as an appropriately relational capacity.

If I reject the "extreme" positions offered in the memory wars and if I reject as well the idea of staking out a reasonable middle ground, how do I locate my project in a way that makes sense? Moreover, how do I position myself in a way that can effectively resist the reader's temptation to move me to one side or the other, or to decide that I do in fact occupy a middle ground? I conceive of my project as one of philosophical excavation. In rejecting designated positions, I do not attempt to stand outside or beyond these debates. Rather I attempt to excavate some of the cultural and conceptual ground on which we are at present standing. I do so as a philosopher interested in the connections among our ideas. Many of these connections are not obvious, and I hope to make them so.

REFRAMING THE DEBATES

In the chapters that follow, I offer a feminist philosophical analysis of contemporary public skepticism about women's memories of past harm, concentrating on writings associated with the FMSF. The false memory debates have offered one opportunity to explore how people may be politically undermined when their memory competencies are challenged and how our theories of memory must change to reflect this reality. The book has two closely interrelated aims: one deconstructive, one constructive. First, I offer a specific conceptual critique of the skeptical strategies that have been used to challenge women's memories, particularly those meant to arouse alarm about suggestibility. I do not claim that we should never distrust women's memories of abuse. I do, however, vigorously contest the ways in which concerns are being framed: namely, so as to provoke an uncritical anxiety about women's memories. I focus on the introduction of "false memory" as part of a new memory discourse that allows for the reinvigoration of stereotypes of women as incapable of truth-telling because of weak identities. I examine the construction of specific narrative positions for women that undermine their credibility as testifiers. I deconstruct the figure of the therapist as deceiver in false memory writings; and I examine how suggestibility is operationalized in much current research on memory to reinforce the idea that when our memories are influenced, we inevitably come to believe what is false.

Second, I use the false memory debates to develop the thesis that current models of memory displace significant social and political dimensions to successful remembering. I analyze memory as a complex of cognitive abilities and social–narrative activities where one's success and failure as a rememberer are affected by one's social location and have profound ramifications for one's cultural status as a moral agent. I attend to the features of significance, authority, and vulnerability that characterize memory narratives; the norms of personal accountability that help determine which models of memory secure scientific and public acceptance; the distribution of narrative and interpretive positions that support certain groups and not others as testifiers to the past; and the representations of rememberers that determine whose memory we worry about and why.

I argue that casting current controversies about memory as theoretical questions about the nature and reliability of mental processes covers up and displaces what is also a public contest about women's cultural status as rememberers and therefore as moral agents. Moreover, I argue that contemporary models of memory at work in the debates are, in general, inadequate to our understanding of the harms linked to oppression and marginalization: they suggest that group understandings of the past are incompatible with the integrity of personal memory.

Our Western understanding of memory links it to the concept of moral personhood, and this concern is the focus of chapter 2. That individuals have comprehensive memory of their past has been a condition for treating them as full members of a moral community, for we can only be responsible for what we remember. The possibility that we may call into question the reliability of someone's memory as a way of undermining his or her claim to full moral personhood is a pressing concern arising from our cultural understanding of the significance of memory, but it is one that has received little theoretical analysis.

To analyze how persons can be politically undermined when their memories are contested, I adapt feminist accounts of persons as essentially relational. I argue that the cognitive abilities necessary to being a person and hence to being a moral agent develop only in relations with other persons and only with the support of shared communal practices that foster these abilities. Memory is one of the key cognitive abilities through which we develop personhood, and the kinds of activities important to the developing and maintaining of this core cognitive ability are activities involving self-narratives. Our success at remembering is not merely a matter of private experience; more important, it involves public action. I argue that the constituting of memory abilities is ongoing and that our abilities to be successful social rememberers may be undermined by depriving us of self-narrative opportunities.

The historical and current vulnerability of women as rememberers can be assessed, in part, by social restrictions on their opportunities to assume self-narrative positions that are specifically testimonial—that is, with self-narratives concerned with the truth of the past. I argue that our Western understanding of memory allows the political vulnerabilities of rememberers to be deceptively masked by the epistemic authority that we purportedly grant to memory experience. Whether we actually succeed as testifiers depends on the relational context of our speech and the attitude of our interpreters. In chapter 3, I use the work of C. A. J. Coady (1992) on natural testimony to develop an account of memory testimony and to examine the ways in which women may be narratively positioned to encourage distrust of their narratives. One of the catalysts for the FMSF's development was a change in the laws of several states that widened the opportunities for women to testify to abuse in court under a doctrine of "delayed discovery" (Brown, Scheflin, and Hammond 1998, ch. 3). Though few child sexual abuse survivors take their perpetrators to court, I argue that the FMSF has attempted to control women's testimonial positions by encouraging a quasi-legal understanding of their abuse narratives. Skepticism and challenge is the appropriate interpreter response. At the same time, I examine and call for models of natural testimony that stress that the success of testimonial speech requires generally trusting interpreters.

An alternative political strategy to fostering distrust of women's testimony is to simply represent child sexual abuse survivors as not testifying when they speak about abuse. In chapter 4, I examine a chief reason why the public has rejected women's abuse narratives as testimonial: survivors seek therapy; and therapists, from naivete or bias, overinfluence survivors' understandings of their pasts. To uncover the assumptions of this position, I consider criticisms of therapist Judith Herman's work on trauma and memory (1992). Feminist psychoanalyst Janice Haaken (1996, 1998), in sympathy with much of the FMSF critique of therapy, accuses Herman of holding an outdated archival theory of memory and thus of not seeing how therapists help coconstruct the meaning of their clients' narratives. I argue that Haaken's critique repeats the persistent unfortunate tendency of contemporary scientific accounts of memory to see interpretation and objective truth as opposites. I argue throughout this book that all memory involves interpretation and that this requisite is no bar to the objective truth of much memory narrative.

The aim of chapters 2 through 4 is to sketch a politically nuanced account of memory activity and a feminist relational account of personhood that makes evident how contesting memory can undermine one's political and moral status. In chapters 5 and 6, I continue to situate the rhetoric and strategies of the False Memory Syndrome Foundation within the model of memory and personhood that I have developed.

In chapter 5, I focus on the new discourse of "false memory," examining links between our representations of rememberers and our theories of memory. I offer a discursive analysis that illustrates parallels between the work of the FMSF in launching a novel discourse of "false memory" and the misogynist writing of Otto Weininger (1906), a turn-of-the-century Viennese philosopher. These writings exhibit a shared logic of discrediting women as rememberers. In particular, the writings of the FMSF, like the writings of Weininger, represent women as lacking the sense of self necessary for competent remembering. Particularly disturbing in the writings of foundation advisory board members Loftus and Ofshe is a personification of memory that then acts as a replacement for the subject whose memory it is. These authors' descriptions of memory as suggestible, malleable, and false come to characterize the woman who makes a claim about abuse in her past. The representation of women as highly suggestible in turn affects how we think about memory. John Sutton (1998) has argued that norms about personhood and control of one's personal past have helped determine which models of memory achieve conceptual dominance. The political use of particular versions of reconstructivist models support long-standing stereotypes of women as unreliable rememberers while increasing our general fears about memory suggestibility.

Because we are socially constituted as rememberers, our assessment of the false memory controversy cannot be a judgment about the simple truth of the past as experienced and then reported by a wholly autonomous rememberer. This figure is a fiction. None of us is free from influence; therefore, it is important to see the ways in which the idea of social influence is being used in the false memory debates.

Prominent in the remarks of those who deny the credibility of women's claims of abuse is the alternative explanation of imagining or fantasizing abuse as encouraged by therapist suggestion. Chapter 6 offers a political analysis of suggestibility, not as a pathology to which those with weak identities are susceptible, but as a kind of social alarm raised in cases of suspected problematic influence. While not denying that therapeutic influence can be harmful and manipulative, I show that the foundation's argument for women's suggestibility, with its use of the therapist as a deceiver, interestingly recalls Descartes' use of the evil demon in the *Meditations* (1641/1988). This type of argument is designed to raise a widespread and thoroughgoing skepticism about the nature of our faculties. Its intent is to alarm the public into withdrawing support for psychotherapy for women while waiting for science to discover the truth about memory.

I point out that once we allow certain skeptical worries to grip our imaginations, we have no more reason to trust science than we do to trust therapy. However, I also argue that because an alarm about suggestibility represents a complex grouping of concerns about who we become and what actions we take through our associations with each other, we must lift the analysis of suggestibility from under the jurisdiction of science. To leave the analysis of suggestibility to science encourages a widespread fear of false belief as an inevitable effect of our influence on one another, and it ignores that science itself is a product of social forces.

Chapters 7 and 8 apply and extend my analysis of memory suggestibility. In chapter 7, I use a Canadian legal controversy to explore some of the costs afforded to sexual assault victims via the false memory reanimation of women's suggestibility. Throughout the 1990s, defense counsel in sexual assault trials requested and often received access to a broad range of complainants' personal records—including psychiatric, counseling, and rape crisis center records—thereby compromising therapeutic confidentiality and reinforcing women's persistent legal vulnerability as sexual assault complainants. False memory discourse facilitated access to records in a context in which recovered memories were rarely legally at issue. In this chapter, I examine the eventual legislative and judicial response to this practice. I argue that because the Supreme Court of Canada finally brought a relational account of women's lives to its deliberations, it was able to move away from its own prior skepticism about memory influence.

I believe that the thought of women together, influencing each other's understandings and self-identifications, is a disturbing picture to many who contest women's memories. Chapter 8 situates my critique of suggestibility as a social alarm within a broader exploration of the relation between women's personal and collective memory. I argue that recognition of the harms of oppression necessitates the collective reinterpretation of personal pasts in the light of new social understandings and that it is this very possibility that is threatened by the false memory debate. I focus on the work of Ian Hacking (1995), who positions himself as a skeptical spectator to contemporary memory debates. Hacking, however, endorses recent concerns about suggestibility; he categorizes women's memory as personal in contrast to communal; and he views occasions of shared reinterpretation through new social understandings as sites of potential memory contagion. I use Hacking's work to sharpen my identification of current tendencies to theorize about memory in ways that prevent shared reinterpretations of the past from contributing to viable personal memory. I argue that such accounts foreclose on our communal ability to identify and understand the harms of oppression.

The false memory controversy raises complex questions of moral and social epistemology. How do we adjudicate our understandings of the past when the avowed experience of some conflicts with the dominant social memory of others? Moreover, because the controversy focuses on the obligations of women identified as good daughters versus their therapeutic and self-identifications as victims or survivors, the debate is also a struggle over who has the authority to determine the social identity of women. Finally, because of the social and political nature of memory, the controversy raises deep philosophical issues about the role of memory in identity and about autonomy as self-governance—concepts at the base of Western notions of moral responsibility.

My methodology in this book is straightforward. I take the concepts, values, and concerns at issue in the false memory debates—memory, selfhood, suggestibility, testimony, autonomy and so on—and I situate and analyze these concepts and values in terms of the concrete social relationships and complex institutional practices that give them their actual character. I reject the framing of the current crisis of memory as being primarily about the nature of memory processes. I instead attempt to deepen contemporary feminist insights about the social nature of the self to examine the political questions of memory, identity, and personhood made urgent by the false memory debates. Finally, I find it worth stressing once again that my point is not to get embroiled in the debate about false versus recovered memory; it is rather to argue that the debate has misshaped our appreciation of how people remember. If I dwell throughout this book on these debates, I do so to expose the distortions that shape our current understandings of memory and of rememberers.

NOTES

1. Reference to these debates as "war" is ubiquitous. See for example: Shelley Park (1999), "Reviewing the Memory Wars: Some Feminist Philosophical Reflections"; Daniel Schacter (1996, ch. 9), "The Memory Wars: Seeking Truth in the Line of Fire"; Janice Haaken, "[the] dominant discourse in the war over family recollections is a scientific one" (1998, 42).

2. For a range of diverse descriptions of the genesis and work of the FMSF see Frederick Crews (1994); Carolyn Enns et al. (1995); Jennifer Freyd (1993); Janice Haaken (1998); Miriam Horn (1993); Jann Mitchell (1993); Kenneth Pope (1996, 1997); Mike Stanton (1997). The FMSF publishes a newsletter and maintains a website: www.MemoryandReality.org or www.FMSFonline.org.

3. See Richard Ofshe and Ethan Watters (1993) for an early use of this term. Kenneth Pope (1996) points to its use in Stephen Lindsey and J. S. Read (1994). Unfortunately, it has been adopted even by authors who attempt to be careful in their assessment of the FMSF. See Janice Haaken (1998) and Shelley Park (1999). This term does not always pick out a distinctive therapy movement or school in the way it is intended. It is used indiscriminately by many authors to criticize any practice of psychotherapy that involves an interest in a woman's past.

4. Kenneth Pope (1996, 1997) provides a good survey of claims about an epidemic as well as the best critical analysis of their lack of support. See Linda Singer (1993) for a general critique of claims about social epidemics. She argues that the point of using such language is to raise fears of an uncontrolled harm to the social body that then licenses exceptional measures of control.

5. Lawrence Wright's two-part New Yorker series on this case—"Remembering Satan" (1993)—won a National Magazine Award, and the case has been widely used to support alarm about false memory syndrome. Richard Ofshe, hired as a consultant by the prosecution, argued that inadvertent suggestion and hypnosis during Paul Ingram's interrogation resulted in false memories of abuse and hence a false confession. Neither Ingram's attempt to withdraw his guilty plea nor his appeal was successful. Karen Olio and William Cornell critiqued Ofshe's analysis of the case, and they argue that uncritical acceptance and repetition of Ofshe's view have led to "an academic version of an urban legend" (1998, 1182).

6. For books directed to the public by members of the board see Terence Campbell (1994); Frederick Crews (1995); Elizabeth Loftus and Katherine Ketcham (1994); Richard Ofshe and Ethan Watters (1994); Ralph Underwager and Hollinda Wakefield (1995). For books by supporters of the FMSF who are not members of the board see Mark Pendergast (1995) and Eleanor Goldstein and Kevin Farmer (1993). The FMSF maintains a list of advisory board members on its website and in its newsletters. I identify advisors in the text.

7. In the body of the text, I generally refer to Elizabeth Loftus and Richard Ofshe and not to their coauthors Katherine Ketcham and Ethan Watters. Loftus and Ofshe appear to be the primary authors of these texts, and the Loftus and Ketcham work (1994) is written in the first person with Loftus as the narrative voice.

8. Journalist Mike Stanton describes the FMSF as "an aggressive, well-financed p.r. machine adept at manipulating the press" (1997, 45). He reports on a study by sociologist Katherine Beckett, who reviewed coverage of sexual abuse in *Time*, *Newsweek*, *U.S. News & World Report*, and *People*. Beckett reported a dramatic shift from more than 80 percent of coverage on stories of survivors in 1991 to more than 80 percent of coverage on stories of false accusations. Stanton argues that media's coverage of sexual abuse has been generally uncritical, and he condemns fellow reporters in the 1990s for relying on FMSF experts and propaganda to assess the controversies.

9. These include *Applied Cognitive Psychology* (August 1994), *Consciousness and Cognition* (September/December 1994), *International Journal of Clinical and Experimental Hypnosis* (October 1994 and April 1995), *Psychiatric Annals* (December 1995).

10. This article from the FMSF newsletter reported on a study that found twenty of twenty-four recent introductory texts reviewed the debate.

11. The study was conducted at the McLean Hospital, the teaching hospital associated with Harvard University (Chu et al. 1999). Other studies have found that recall of historic abuse is most typically not the result of therapy (Raitt and Zeedyk 2000, 147). The response to the Chu study is by Russell Powell (Good et al. 2000).

12. Elizabeth Loftus is now a distinguished professor at the University of California, Irvine.

13. This is not an unusual pairing. In his introduction to *Searching for Memory*, Daniel Schacter writes that we hear of false memories in therapy and of alien abductions (1996, 3).

14. Alan Scheflin and Daniel Brown concluded that full or partial amnesia was a robust research result across all studies of amnesia for childhood sexual abuse (1996). That memories of abuse are sometimes recovered is indisputable. See Daniel Schacter (1996, ch. 9) for some incontrovertible cases.

15. This scenario is not true in Daniel Schacter's book where Schacter seems to want to position some advocates for false memory syndrome as tending to hold extreme positions.

16. This criticism has sometimes been expressed by making a distinction between True Believers, those who uncritically accept all claims of abuse as absolutely true, and Skeptics, who are committed to scientific truth-seeking (Loftus and Ketcham 1994, 31–32).

2

RESPECTING REMEMBERERS

> If Jack succeeds in forgetting something, this is of little use if Jill continues to remind him of it. He must induce her not to do so. . . .
>
> Jack may act upon Jill in many ways. . . . He may *invalidate* her experience. This can be done more or less radically. He can indicate merely that it is unimportant or trivial whereas it is important and significant to her. Going further, he can shift the *modality* of her experience from memory to imagination: "it's all in your imagination." Further still, he can invalidate the *content*: "It never happened that way." Finally he can invalidate not only the significance, modality, and content, but her very capacity to remember at all, and make her feel guilty for doing so into the bargain.
>
> This is not unusual. People are doing such things to each other all the time.
>
> R. D. Laing, *The Politics of Experience*

The dailiness and seriousness of memory contests in our lives, our own doubts about how faithfully we remember the past, and a well-founded concern over the potential abuses of psychoanalytic and therapeutic practices have made it difficult to know how to respond to the new skeptical discourse about women's memories described in chapter 1. For this chapter, I start from the premise that we must insist on cultural respect for women as rememberers, which is not to say what feminists are frequently accused of saying: that "absolute belief in the accuracy and truthfulness of all charges is the only appropriate stance" (Ofshe and Watters 1993, 5). Nor is it to support a naive view of memory in which each seeming memory experience is a reliable representation of a past event. To insist on respect for women as rememberers is simply to claim that women share no characteristics that would preclude them from engaging competently in a range of memory activities, including performing acts of testimony. But how do we defend our commitment to women's credibility without sounding to the incredulous like "a mere holy hearing of voices" (Swindells 1989, 28)? And what principled reasons can we use to persuade others to adopt this commitment? I believe that we can find these reasons only if we concentrate our attention on the social and political dimensions of the making and contesting of memory claims and of the narrating of memory experience.

The crisis about women's abuse testimony has been presented as if it were primarily about the nature of memory processes. Is autobiographical memory too easily influenced and confused to reliably represent the past? Are there memory mechanisms that could explain an individual's suppression and subsequent recovery of knowledge of a traumatic past, or is talk of repression and dissociation the fanciful legacy of an unscientific approach to the mind?[1] The FMSF presents itself through the expert writings of academics who study memory and suggestibility. Those experts state that "this is a debate about memory" (Loftus and Ketcham 1994, xi) and that "the substantive controversy turns on the validity of the concept of repression" (Ofshe and Watters 1993, 5). Scientists have naturally tended to share the view that the debate is one about memory processes. Daniel Schacter writes, "The recovered memories controversy, though a complex affair that touches on issues of incest, family, social mores, and even religious beliefs, is fundamentally a debate about accuracy, distortion, and suggestibility in memory" (1996, 251). Even feminist critics of the FMSF write that "the critical element in the recovered memory debate is the nature of human memory. How does it work; how well are its processes currently understood; how much trust can be placed in any specific memory?" (Raitt and Zeedyk 2000, 145–46). Moreover, the FMSF's focus on memory processes and its specific criticisms of repression as a memory mechanism have shaped public understanding of what is at issue when women claim to newly remember abuse. A letter criticizing a recent New Zealand Law Commission initiative on historic abuse states: "No credible scientific research supports the fanciful notion that women can 'repress' memories of sexual abuse. It has been exposed as dangerous nonsense" (Waugh 2000).

At the same time, because the foundation's membership is composed primarily of parents whose children have accused them of abuse, and most of these adult children are women, we can also accurately describe the nature of the false memory controversies as the public contesting of the memory claims of one group—women who are claiming to remember sexual abuse—by another group—those who are being accused of the abuse. The makings of memory claims are actions with consequences. Researchers who offer the mysteries of our memory mechanisms in support of distrusting women's claims often share the foundation's beliefs that the problem of "false memory syndrome" is what women are doing in making these claims. Richard Ofshe and Ethan Watters warn that thousands of women are being encouraged "to publicly accuse, confront and perhaps sue those they believe to have been the perpetrators. . . . The inevitable result is the destruction of the families involved" (1993, 5). Harold Merskey writes that false memory syndrome includes the "propagation of hate and hostility" (1995, 6 quoted in Haaken 1998, 32).

I reject the framing of the current crisis of memory as being primarily about memory processes.[2] There is a much greater skepticism toward the memories of those who claim abuse than toward the memories of those who deny it, and this asymmetry cannot be fully accounted for by a general concern about the reliability or suggestibility of experiential memory. Moreover, in being persuaded to accept this frame, we are distracted from paying adequate attention to the kinds of circumstances, both the everyday and the legal circumstances, in which memory claims are made and contested and in which memory experience is narrated and challenged. In this chapter, I am concerned with what the nature of memory challenge can tell us about the value of memory and about what it means for persons when we fail to value it.

I argue that part of the seriousness of the current memory debates can be seen by taking into account that, in the Anglo-European tradition, memory, self, and person are historically braided concepts. It is thus possible to attack or to undermine the selfhood and personhood of others by undermining them as rememberers. I contend that on some occasions when we challenge others as competent rememberers, our intent is to undermine them as persons due various forms of respect, by calling into question how well they can function cognitively. Moreover, that there are legitimate concerns about some women's claims to remember abuse will not settle the issue of whether women are being disrespected as rememberers.

One particular group of women is the focus of the FMSF, women who typically are white, middle-class, and in their thirties and forties. These are women who have access to therapy and whose parents have the financial resources to fund the FMSF as a powerful lobby. False memory rhetoric undermines these women in a manner historically effective against this group. For example, presenting feminists as ideological extremists reinforces the "hysterical" representation of women who purportedly recover abuse memories in therapy because these women are themselves the poster children "for (bourgeois white) feminism" (Park 1999, 291). But I would hope that the discussions that follow do not speak only to this group. Because false memory skepticism has spread to contexts other than therapy (see chapter 7), all groups of women who testify to harm in the past have been affected by it.[3] Moreover, the memory debates have encouraged a general heightened suspicion of testimonial narrative. Strategies of cognitive and psychological undermining are among the staples of contemporary forms of Western political subordination (Harvey 1999). My intent in this chapter is to offer an understanding of the social dimensions of personhood that directs us to be politically sensitive to the ways in which people's cultural status as rememberers can be undermined.

In what follows, I use the work of feminist life-history researchers to make preliminary sense of the claim that in contesting someone's memory we may be attacking their sense of self. That we may be doing so approaches common wisdom for feminists, and I think it is illuminating to understand what underlies this worry. I then offer a model for understanding how one's status as a person is susceptible to being undermined by people's failure to respect one's core cognitive abilities, the same abilities that are integral to forming a sense of self. I refer to these abilities as *person-abilities* and/or *self-abilities.* Finally, I discuss remembering as a cognitive ability central to our notions of selfhood and personhood. We become good rememberers only when we are allowed and encouraged to engage in self-narrative activities. When our abilities to remember are devalued, both our sense of self and our cultural status as persons may be undermined. The full defense of this final claim requires a detailed analysis of memory challenge and is only fully supported by the arguments and illustrations of subsequent chapters. My aim here is to first identify the type and level of moral concern we should bring to our assessment of how we treat others as rememberers.

SELVES

In an excellent article, "That's Not What I Said: Interpretive Conflict in Oral Narrative Research," folklorist Katharine Borland says that "the performance of a personal narrative is a fundamental means by which people comprehend their own lives and present a 'self' to their audience" (Borland 1991, 71). Those who do oral narrative research are often acutely aware that the feminist imperative that women give their own accounts of their experience is vexed with theoretical tensions. Borland points out that "the very fact that we constitute the initial audience for the narratives we collect influences the way in which our collaborators will construct their stories" (64) and the meanings that emerge through their telling. She wishes to emphasize that in listening to a woman speak of her experiences and in later representing what she has said, we must understand our responsibilities as a collaborator, a witness, and a potential threat to her identity. Thus, Borland continues, "Our scholarly representations of those performances, if not sensitively presented, may constitute an attack on [a] . . . carefully constructed sense of self" (71).

Borland's reflections are pressured by an angry fourteen-page letter from Beatrice Hanson, Borland's grandmother. The letter questions the authenticity of the feminist narrative that Borland has used to represent Hanson's story of betting on a horse against her father's advice and winning:

> So your interpretation of the story as a female struggle for autonomy within a hostile male environment is entirely YOUR interpretation. You've read into the story what you wished to—what pleases YOU. That it was never—by any wildest stretch of the imagination—the concern of the originator of the story makes such an interpretation a definite and complete distortion, and in this respect I question its authenticity. (70)

Does Borland's representation of Hanson as the feminist she is not constitute an attack on her sense of self or her identity? How are we to understand such a strong worry in the face of the very strong voice to Hanson's rejoinder?

"Sense of self" is a vague notion, but I propose that your having a sense of self requires at least the following: opportunities to understand yourself in relation to your past, opportunities to plan and to act on your intentions, and some self-regarding emotions or attitudes. In other words, a sense of yourself depends on some of your experiences becoming your memories, some of your needs or desires becoming your plans and intentions to act, and some of your pleasures and displeasures becoming self-regarding attitudes, like pride or shame. I propose these conditions because I think they are uncontroversial. I believe that we would all agree that a sense of self, while expressible in many ways, requires a reflective awareness of the self that is partly achieved and made evident in the doubled presence of the self in expressions of memory, intention, and in attitudes such as pride.[4] Awareness of the self is evident in the grammar of these expressions. *I* remember, intend, or am proud of *my* doing something. In expressing personal memory, for example, I can mention myself twice, both as the subject of the claim and as an embedded subject of the object of the claim. To remember seeing you is to remember my seeing you. It is perhaps more difficult to understand how such activities as remembering are creative of a sense of self. Coming to understand this process requires our first understanding the cultural importance of the notion of self. Some of this understanding should emerge in the investigations of this chapter.

I have presented a sketch of the notion of *self*, one that highlights the heightened reflexivity of certain psychological activities, partly to make sense of Borland's concerns about her interaction with her grandmother. Philosophers tend to understand a sense of self in terms of a self-concept. I believe we should equally think of a sense of self as something like the site of certain activities. I have given these activities general psychological descriptions—remembering, intending, and becoming proud—and sometimes these activities have no outward expression. But more often they simply are the public activities of reminiscing about a holiday, telling someone what you intend to do that weekend, or expertly telling a story. I do not develop a sense of myself independent of what I do, reassessing my past through narrative, for example; nor do I develop a sense of self independence about how others make possible and influence my acts of remembering, intending, and becoming proud. If the sketch is accurate, it suggests that we can attack someone's sense of self when we interfere with her abilities to understand her past, her abilities to carry out her plans, or the grounds for her self-respect.

Hanson regards her granddaughter's interpretation as, at the very least, an attack on her past. It turns Hanson's father, against whom Hanson is betting, from a lifelong, if aggressive, supporter and witness to her independence into a deep political adversary. Further, Hanson's pride in her competence, to which her father was witness, is a self-regarding attitude. Borland's interpretation undermines the positive role that the father plays in Hanson's self-regard. Also, as Borland realizes, Hanson essentially repeats and intends to repeat the occasion of coming to be proud by skillfully relating the story of her competent betting to her granddaughter. Borland is meant to witness Hanson's skill at betting through her skill at storytelling. When Borland suggests that Hanson, in telling the story, unknowingly misrepresents herself and misframes the importance of her own narrative, Borland is refusing to be this witness. Hanson's remembering, intending, and coming to be proud are confuted by Borland's interpretation.

I present the encounter between Borland and Hanson to give substance to the claim that our sense of self is involved, often in complex and detailed ways, in our narrating past experience and in the reception of these narratives. What's more, we can often expect our view of the past to be challenged. The text from Laing with which I began raises the question of distance between contesting someone's memory claims in a certain way on a certain occasion and destructively calling into question their competence as a rememberer. I do not think there is a principled way to mark this distinction. First of all, Laing's passage illuminates the idea that contesting memory has many forms that are not clearly separable in practice. At one level, Borland merely challenges the significance of a story presented to her by the teller as an "amusing anecdote" (71). By redescribing it, however, as a more "significant" story of hidden meaning and female autonomy, Borland disrupts the content of Hanson's memories of her father. Second, the import of contesting someone's memory is varied and hard to predict. Hanson replies forcefully to Borland, but it may be that the force of her response reflects the degree to which she takes herself, as a elderly rememberer, to be under attack. The effect of memory challenge may be more serious for those whose competence as rememberers is often under attack. Finally, some challenges to memory do not destructively call into question someone's competence as a rememberer, but are a way of respecting and training that competence. We correct our children's memories to train them as accurate rememberers. And most of us depend on the challenges of particular people close to us to keep us honest about the past. The effects of memory challenge depend on a great many other factors about a person's situation.

Nevertheless, feminist life-history researchers worry a great deal about the vulnerability of the sense of self formed through women's memory narrations and about whether they are fully respecting this vulnerability; and I take their worry to be well-founded. If someone who tells her experience fails often enough or seriously enough to have her account credited by others or if she is unable to engage in activities that are tellings of her experience, she may be unable to establish an adequate sense of herself. What will this failure mean for her, and what will it allow others to do to her? At this point, I think it is appropriate to phrase the concern in terms of something as fundamental as personhood.

PERSONS

According to Robin Dillon, "personhood is one of those very important concepts that are difficult to pin down, an essentially contestable, ideologically malleable concept, the content of which is given to a great extent in what we (whoever the 'we' is that is doing the defining) value most deeply about being human persons" (Dillon 1992, 12). In the Anglo-European tradition, "person" is our most fundamental status category. It is on the basis of our being persons that we are granted rights, protections, freedoms, and privileges. The concept of person is discussed as if it has two aspects, one that reflects the content, one that reflects the valuing. The "we" who are doing the defining treat those and only those who we regard as having the full set of person-qualities with the kind of attitude that we regard persons and only persons as deserving. The qualities have generally been thought of as abilities to engage in certain kinds of cognitive activities. As will become clear, intending, one of the abilities key to a sense of self, is also key to being a person, and I will argue that memory, another key self-ability, is likewise a key person-ability. The attitude with which we regard persons is generally theorized as a kind of respect. We treat persons as full and equal members of a moral community. So one part of the concept seems to involve the *recognition* of others as having certain abilities or person-content worth valuing; the other involves the appropriate *response* to the recognition. In recognizing that you can formulate your own plans for how to accomplish your goals, I respond to this recognition by not interfering with your plans. The cognitive abilities are expressed in your actions. The respect is expressed in my actions. As cognitive abilities are typically expressed in our activities, attitudes like respect are also typically expressed in activities.

The distinction we can make between the content of personhood and our response to persons—what is valued versus our ways of valuing—can obscure a dangerous possibility: that by consistently disrespecting others and calling into doubt their person-abilities, we can be undermining those abilities. This undermining is sometimes the intent of such disrespect, and sometimes it is simply its effect. To establish this possibility, I wish to outline four aspects to personhood: (1) that the concept of person is normative; (2) that persons are socially constituted; (3) that social personhood admits of degrees; and (4) that, when examined more closely, the respect due to persons involves activities that in fact constitute persons as persons and do not merely recognize them as such.

1. The distinction between the content of what we value and our valuing may make it sound like we could give a value-neutral description of persons, perhaps the same description we would give of humans, and then go on to say why we value creatures who have the set of properties described. But Dillon's point—that the content of personhood is given by what those of us who are doing the defining come to value—is that the concept of a person is not interchangeable with the concept of a human. The latter concept—human—has a content independent of what we morally value. Person does not. The personhood of a human is that set of qualities through which we configure that human as a moral agent in a way that can be given a fairly precise description. A person is a being who can be held responsible and who can take responsibility for his or her actions.[5] Because of its connection to responsibility, the idea of a person presupposes moral discourse. A familiar way of indicating the independence of the concept of a person from the concept of a human has been via a thought experiment of the following sort: we would allow that nonhumans could be persons if and only if they met the description of moral agents.
2. Persons are socially constituted. By this I mean that the abilities that are necessary to being a person, and hence to being a moral agent, develop only in relations with other persons and only with the support of shared communal practices that have the development of these abilities as their goal. Annette Baier has offered a formulation of a relational notion of personhood that has been influential for some feminists, and I repeat it here: "A person, perhaps, is best seen as one who was long enough dependent on other persons to acquire the essential arts of personhood. Persons essentially are *second* persons" (Baier 1985a, 84, her emphasis). Christine Koggel identifies three separate el-

ements to Baier's use of second persons: that relationships, including dependency relationships, are a basic aspect of human lives; that "being a person is an ongoing process, the 'arts' of which are learned and developed in relationships"; and that we come to know ourselves and our interests only through relationships (Koggel 1998, 143). Feminists who endorse a relational view of the self stress that we must attend to the full range of relationships that affect our development as persons and that we must be especially attentive to the impact of unequal relationships (Koggel 1998; Sherwin 1998). I provide a fuller account of a relational model of persons in chapter 7.

In her own development of the idea of "second persons," Baier has shown a detailed interest in the way in which our cognitive abilities are dependent on our relations with others. My reflections on memory are influenced by her close attention to how we form particular cognitive abilities. In her essay entitled "Mixing Memory and Desire," for example, she offers an account of our ability to form intentions to act, a core person-ability, as dependent on communal practices of intending involving training, evaluation, and criticism. Without these practices, we would have no sense of what we are *able* to do, and we can only intend to do what we think we are able to do:

> Without community intentions expressed and executed in practices of training and criticism, there could be no distinction between what I do and what lucky results I am vouchsafed, nor therefore between what I intend to do and what I expect and want to happen, miraculously and opportunely. Since intentions are different from confident expectation of miracle, the concept of intention involves that of ability, and so of group intentions and practices as those involved in the creation, recognition, and encouragement of agents' skills and competencies. (1995b, 13)

Hanson declares: "I am *betting on my horse* and I am betting *ten bucks* on that horse. It's gonna win!" (Borland 1991, 67, her emphasis) To emphasize this moment of climax as an act of intention, Hanson relates to Borland the communal basis of her knowledge of horses: ". . . 'though I could not go *fishing* with my father on Sundays, or *hunting* with him on any other day of the week, for some strange reason, he took me with him, mornings' to watch his horses being exercised" (67, her emphasis).

3. Although it is an important plank of the ideology of personhood that all persons are equally persons, in practice we operate with diminished categories of personhood, a fact that the ideology of personhood obscures. In either recognizing or thinking that a person

lacks certain valued abilities, we withhold the kinds of respect that would be due one who had those abilities. In recognizing that a person cannot make the difference for themselves between planning their finances and the illusion that they have plenty of money to spend, we do not give them the right to control their own income. We sometimes treat people with diminished cognitive capacities as less than full and equal persons, though we may continue to treat them well and with great respect in many ways. The failure of some people to treat others as full persons has often, of course, been a matter of serious and sometimes deliberate moral misrecognition. Charles Mills has argued, for example, that our political system is a global white supremacy established and maintained by a "set of formal and informal agreements" among one subset of humans ("whites") to categorize the remaining subset (those designated as "nonwhites") as *subpersons*, as having "a different and inferior moral status" justified by supposed cognitive inferiority (1997, 11). Because personhood is partly a matter of cognitive capacities and abilities that admit of degrees, and of various kinds of recognition and valuing that also admit of degrees, there seems little basis for the claim that we all treat each other as full and equal persons.

4. That persons are socially constituted and that valued person-qualities admit of degrees seem to straightforwardly raise the prospect that we sometimes diminish the social personhood of others through our activities. If the activities through which we respect persons are the same activities through which we help constitute them and if this constituting is ongoing, then we can enhance the social personhood of others by respecting them and undermine the social personhood of others by disrespecting them. I put this forward as a possibility that is obscured by a content–respect distinction. The idea that persons are formed, recognized, and then either respected or not creates an odd, safe space for disrespecters to claim that their actions are not undermining the personhood of those they are disrespecting—that, in fact, they recognize others as persons but just don't respect them. If a part of the ideology of *person* is that we remain secure in this status, independent of what disrespecters do, then all sorts of attempts to undermine our status as persons may go unnoticed.

What I think needs a much fuller account is how this sketch affects those cognitive activities at the core of the Western notion of personhood. In particular we need an account of how the withholding of respect for certain person-abilities might affect how others can exercise and, in some cases, develop these abilities, thereby helping to create the situation where further disrespect then seems appropriate.

It is not difficult to illustrate the dynamic I have in mind with intending. Laurence Thomas, in "Moral Deference" (1992–1993), recognizes that persons can be downwardly socially constituted by others, that for the victims of oppressions, who Thomas calls "diminished social category persons," such downward constitution is a pervasive feature of their lives (238). Thomas defines social constitution in terms of a self-concept: "the way in which we conceive of ourselves is, at least in part, owing to how others conceive of us, and necessarily so" (238). I believe Thomas's notion of a self-concept is close to what I have been calling a sense of self, and I have suggested that a sense of self consists not of something like a picture, but rather it resides, in part, in our abilities to engage liberally in certain cognitive activities. Thomas points out that "one of the most important ways in which downward social constitution occurs pertains to expectations. It is just assumed, often without awareness of what is being done, that this or that category person cannot measure up in an important way" (238). I suggest that a devaluing of someone's life possibilities through the failure to expect their success will result in that person's diminished access to the cultural practices of training, criticism, and evaluation that not only create options for successful acting but are necessary for becoming, being, and remaining a successful intender. Say, for instance, that I do not show respect for your intending to go to graduate school by doing what I can to provide the training, criticism, and evaluation that would facilitate your plan. Instead, either I question your ability, or I don't respond at all. If I do so whenever you express plans for your future and if what's more, you meet this response frequently from others, you are less likely to be able to plan and act in a whole range of circumstances than someone who has been supported in their intendings. The resulting dismissals of you as lazy, shiftless, and unmotivated will further diminish your sense of self and your status as a full and equal member of a moral community, one due various kinds of respect.

As a second example, Judith Herman, in *Trauma and Recovery* (1992), discusses the difficulty that an incest survivor may have with self-protection. The past constant undermining of the child's attempt to plan and act upon plans to guarantee her basic bodily security, activities expressive of her intending, may have serious consequences for the adult intender who now needs to learn that she *can* "plan and initiate action" for her own safety "capacities . . . which have been systematically undermined by repeated abuse" (Herman 1992, 167). Some adult survivors can "barely imagine themselves in a position of agency or choice" (112) when others make emotional demands on them. The survivor's undermined ability to make judgments relating to her own safety may increase the possibility that the survivor will be further abused as an adult. The social judgment of a woman who is in repeated situations of sexual harm, namely that she must be "asking for it," will further diminish the survivor's sense of self and her status as a person deserving respect.

That the constitution and undermining of persons through respect or disrespect of their abilities are ongoing is a fact that we sometimes recognize, perhaps most commonly in Western culture, in our acknowledgment of our destructive paternalism toward old people. The dynamic of undermining and respect is positively represented in Borland's account. Concerned that she has undermined Hanson in the presentation of the latter's betting narrative, Borland negotiates with her grandmother to publish a version that includes Hanson's response.

REMEMBERERS

Some, though not enough, attention is paid to the kind of respect we accord people as intenders. Traditionally, this is the respect of noninterference, or as Marilyn Frye puts it, our recognition of people's having a legitimate domain of activity that is in part negotiated through attention to the domains of others. This kind of respect is formally summarized in talk of rights and responsibilities (Frye 1983a). I have suggested, with Baier, that other expressions of respect—training, evaluation, criticism, and encouragement—are necessary as well. Little attention is paid to the kind of respect we accord people as rememberers. I will argue that as traditional links between memory and moral agency highlight the importance of self-narrative, we can look for much of our cultural respect for rememberers to be realized in the types of narratives we allow or encourage them to engage in and in the various narrative positions we allow them to hold. Moreover, the role that memory has played in the development of the concept of a person gives us both an indication of the implications for personhood of calling into question our abilities as rememberers and a sense of what strategies others might use to undermine us.

Connections among self, memory, and person enter our tradition in their most influential formulation in John Locke's discussion of personal identity in *An Essay Concerning Human Understanding* (Locke 1690/1961). For Locke, what constitutes my personal identity, what makes me the same person over time to you, and what also gives me my sense of self is that I can remember my past actions. I can therefore be held responsible for them (448–49). Person, for Locke, is a normative concept that has taking responsibility and being held responsible for one's actions at its core. It is "a forensic term appropriating actions and their merits" (467). A person must be an actor and an intender—this, Locke simply assumes. Assuming our capacity to form and act on our intentions, Locke defends experiential memory as the cognitive ability crucial to responsibility and therefore personhood. It is "as far as any conscious being can repeat the idea of any past action" (451) with the same consciousness she had of that action at the time, and the same consciousness she has of herself at present, that she can claim those actions as her own—that she becomes "concerned and accountable" (467). It is because of my ability to remember my own past that I am a self to myself, a person to others, and a moral agent—capable of following a law and a fit subject for punishment and reward.

I accept from Locke that our abilities to remember are crucial to selfhood and personhood, though I shall take exception to his claim that, in remembering, we repeat past actions with the consciousness that we had of them at the time we acted. But the core of truth in Locke's view is not evident from his own brief treatment of memory and personhood; nor does he show how the notions of selfhood and personhood are linked through our memory abilities. Locke's claims can best be explored and defended by thinking about selves in a way that does not occur to him—as developing in and through relationships with others.

Selfhood is generally understood as a process of differentiation and individuation (Waites 1997, 89). According to Daniel Dennett, even very basic creatures have a minimal self, "a principle of organization that creates and maintains boundaries" (Dennett 1991, 358). But the more robust notion of a human self involves a capacity for self-representation to others as the primary strategy of self-differentiation (359–60). Human memory contributes to selfhood because of the kind of biological capacity it is. Human beings are able to "link their representations of objective events with their representations of themselves as experiencing observers of events" (Waites 1997, 32). We are also a social species; and in a meticulous presentation of the observations and conclusions of social and developmental psychologists, Elizabeth Waites describes how memory capacities are socialized from infancy. She discusses the importance of early attachment relations that, in her words, offer "basic interactional schemas for organizing memories about self and others" (64). Attachment regulates attention, provides "the emotional content that makes certain experiences memorable," contributes the crucial "conceptual and linguistic categories" that we use to encode our experience, and prescribes "the evaluations that help the child differentiate between what should be remembered and what forgotten" (65). As I shall presently illustrate, we are schooled as rememberers from a very young age. Waites writes that "by orchestrating attention and establishing the schemas that organize encoding and retrieval, social interactions eventually evolve into personal history" (66). As older children and as adults, we continue to be self-constituting rememberers both through our interactions with others and through the impact of an individual history of relationships on how we attend to our environment—through interests, emotions, and judgments.

Waites argues that an early concept of self also involves a "growing realization of how one's own behaviour contributes to outcomes" (1997, 70). The types of behavioral evaluations to which we respond from the time we are small children involve considerations of responsibility. As many of these evaluations take place in the context of reviewing the past, they provide the link that Locke fails to elaborate between the role of personal memory in making us selves to ourselves and at the same time persons and moral agents to others. The following example from John Middleton and Derek Edwards's study of how children are socialized as rememberers through family conversations illustrates the dynamic that Waites's work describes:

Extract 7: *Learning Remembering*

Mother: oh look / there's where we went to the riding stables, wasn't it?

Paul: yeh / er er

Mother: you were trying to reach up and stroke that horse

Paul: where? [laughs]

Mother: would you like to do that again?

Paul: yeh

Mother: you don't look very happy though

Paul: because I thought I was going to fall off

Mother: you thought you was going to fall off did you? / right misery / daddy was holding on to you so that you didn't / did it FEEL very bumpy?

Paul: yeh

Mother: did it make your legs ache? [*Paul laughs*] Rebecca enjoyed it

Paul: yeh

Mother: she's a bit older wasn't she? / you were a little boy there (Middleton and Edwards 1990b, 38–39)

In reviewing family pictures with his mother, Paul links representations of himself now and in the past with representations of past events. Paul's mother provides the schemas for Paul's developing memory. She directs his attention; comments on how Paul's emotions made the experience memorable (for the family he was a "right misery"); provides descriptions "of what he is depicted as doing" (Middleton and Edwards 1990b, 39) and thus provides the conceptual and linguistic resources for remembering; and finally, provides evaluations focused on Paul's youth, his sister's maturity, and his father's dependability. But Paul's mother also encourages Paul to take responsibility for how he has participated in the family outing. She prompts him to provide explanations for his own responses and to rethink his responses in light of what she identifies as salient. For example, Paul was a "right misery" because he was overly fearful of falling. But he's older now. Paul is guided to assess his experience at the riding stables in a way that "includes its relevance to the present and the future" (1990b, 39).

The socialization of our memory abilities shows that developing a sense of self involves coming to take responsibility through retrospection. These developmental considerations both enrich Locke's series of connections among person, self, and moral agent and highlight a problem for his "same consciousness" condition for experiential memory. I conclude this section by making two broad points about the relation and importance of experiential memory to moral agency; I do so by using the example of Paul to motivate our reflection on what it means in practical terms to respect rememberers. Both points receive further discussion in subsequent chapters.

First, I have used the example of Paul to show that Locke has an inadequate moral psychology. It cannot, in general, be the case that I remember by repeating an action with the same consciousness I had of it at the time I acted. Agents are sometimes held responsible for an action or they sometimes take responsibility for an action that they would have experienced and described differently at the time of acting than they do at the time of retrospective evaluation. Paul's training as a rememberer illustrates the role of a changed consciousness to responsibility. Paul is learning to remember or repeat a past action with an updated consciousness. He perhaps now remembers himself as *young* and scared. He perhaps now remembers a feeling of being safe that he did not have at the time, but he has been prompted into it as he is reminded of his father's protection. He perhaps now feels a bit embarrassed or ashamed at having been so nervous. The example of Borland and Hanson also shows the importance of a changed consciousness to our developing sense of agency. Hanson narrates her betting as a moment of triumph that plays an important role in her sense of self as an independent woman who is no feminist. She likely did not have this sense of herself in her horse-betting days, but it is part of the consciousness through which she is now coming to view her past. This changed consciousness contributes to the ongoing development of her moral selfhood as indicated by her calling Borland to account. Moreover, her success at developing this sense of herself is at least partly dependent on how her memory narrations are received and interpreted by others.

In summary, this emendation to Locke's view—one that allows a changed consciousness of our pasts as part of normal experiential memory—is important in understanding the relation of memory to moral agency. Its importance recurs often in the discussions that follow. As I will show in chapter 5, the implausible thought that remembering requires an unchanged consciousness can be used to unfairly discredit others' memories and call into question the stability of their identities. I will argue in chapter 8 that this assumption also interferes with our communal ability to grasp the harms of political subordination. However, my presentation of this first point as both important and somewhat obvious gives me the task of explaining briefly why philosophers have often not recognized it. I believe its nonrecognition is due to two assumptions.

First, we may assume that a condition of the accuracy of memory is that it does not change over time. One obvious account of why philosophers have neglected the importance of retrospection with a changed consciousness is that they think this sort of retrospection simply distorts the past. Locke certainly seemed to assume that faithful memory is unchanged memory. However, few theorists would now explicitly follow him. They would instead claim that how we remember a past experience is partly conditioned by our present. Nevertheless, Locke's assumption is aligned with a venerable approach to memory as a kind of archive of our past experiences, and I believe that the assumption of accurate memory as unchanged memory is still more common than theorists will admit.

Second, we may also want to deny that we need to allow for changed consciousness in order to discuss responsibility. Dennett, for example, gives the following gloss on the importance of being aware of one's past actions to moral responsibility:

> *If I am to be held responsible for an action* (a bit of behaviour of mine under a particular description), I must have been *aware* of the action under that description. Why? Because only if I was aware of the action can I *say* what I was about, and participate from a privileged position in the question-and-answer game of giving reasons for my actions. (Dennett 1978, 191, his emphasis)

Dennett suggests that our moral practices of accountability, of explaining and justifying our actions, require a correspondence between the description under which the actions were intended and that under which they are now questioned or criticized. If this were true, our practices of responsibility would not require that I come to remember my past in new or different ways. I deny, however, that our practices of accountability require or reflect the correspondence Dennett describes. They seem rather to require and reflect the condition that to be held responsible for an action, I must be able to at least now *come to recognize* that that action fits a certain description. Children become responsible by learning how others interpret their actions and by being held somewhat responsible for their actions under adult interpretations. As adults, we continue to learn that our actions have been regarded and categorized by others as sexist, racist, unfair, unkind, and so on. How much responsibility we have for past actions under new descriptions is a complex issue. However, we often have some.

I stated at the beginning of this section that investigating the link between memory and moral agency would return us to the discussion of narrative that was initiated at the beginning of the chapter. I propose that to be able to accept responsibility for my behavior under a description that you offer is to be able to renarrate my action using that description. To be unable to do so (as opposed to being unwilling to do so) is not to be able to accept responsibility. The second general point about memory and moral agency is this: with my emendation to Locke—one that allows for changed consciousness of the past—Dennett's description of reason-giving does indicate how being and becoming responsible require that I can give articulate descriptions of past actions of which I recognize myself to be the agent. Therefore, to be responsible for my actions requires that I have the resources I need to develop articulate self-representational abilities. Memory enters as a core cognitive ability, one of the abilities through which a human is configured into a person; and the kinds of activities that can be seen to be important to developing and maintaining this core cognitive ability are activities involving self-narratives. It is, I think, only in this notion of self-narrative that we begin to have a model for the idea of a consciousness repeating an action. Hanson remembers her act of intending by repeating this act in her narrative to Borland: "I am *betting on my horse* and I am betting *ten bucks* on that horse" (67).

Communal practices of encouraging and responding to others' self-narratives form the grounds for our being able to engage in some of the memory activities we most value in persons. When we encourage a child to tell us about a day at school, what she did, what the response was from others, what that will mean for her tomorrow, we are engaged in a practice that is helping to constitute her as a rememberer, a practice vital to her abilities to make sense of her own life and vital to her ultimately being treated as responsible. Recent studies of children's memory indicate, unsurprisingly, that children who are supported in the kind of conversational remembering that Paul's mother encourages are more easily able to remember their pasts than children who are not given these social resources (Fivish et al. 1997).

Exactly how our respect toward rememberers is expressed takes many different forms: it depends on the person, the context, our relation to them, and the kinds of self-narrative—informal or formal—that might be appropriate to the context. It may even depend on the types of new memory skills that a person needs to develop. William James, for example, relates the account "given by the late Thurlow Weed, journalist and politician, of his method of strengthening his memory:"

> My memory was a sieve. I could remember nothing. Dates, names, appointments, faces–everything escaped me. I said to my wife, "Catherine, I shall never make a successful politician, for I cannot remember, and that is a prime necessity of politicians." My wife told me I must train my memory.

> So when I came home that night, I sat down alone, and spent fifteen minutes trying silently to recall with accuracy the principal events of the day. I could remember but little at first; now I remember that I could not then recall what I had for breakfast. After a few days' practice, I found I could recall more. . . . After a fortnight or so of this, Catherine said, "Why don't you relate to me the events of the day, instead of recalling them to yourself? It would be interesting, and my interest in it would be a stimulus to you." Having great respect for my wife's opinion, I began a habit of oral confession, as it were, which has continued for almost fifty years. . . . I am indebted to this discipline for a memory of somewhat unusual tenacity, and I recommend the practice to all who wish to store up facts, or expect to have much to do with influencing men. (1890/1950, 665–66)

Telling someone about your day, reminiscing about the past, providing life-history researchers with material, engaging in autobiographical or testimonial literary projects, and testifying to your past in court are all forms of self-narrative. We may consider Catherine as being unusually forbearing; but, in general, our allowing these self-narrative positions to others and our acting as listeners, readers, witnesses, or interpreters to these self-narratives are activities expressive of our respect for persons as rememberers.

The example from James shows that, as with intending, the constituting of memory abilities is ongoing, and I would argue that the very abilities that we have developed can be undermined. This dynamic is not difficult to dramatize. As Laing notes, people are doing such things to each other all the time. Consider the following sort of relationship between a woman and her partner. Fights frequently escalate into some form of abusive behavior, and these fights frequently start as discussions about what happened on a past occasion. You, as the abused partner, are challenged to give an account of yourself in the past, and this account is then challenged with hostility. What are the probable effects of repetitions of this kind of situation?

You are not being allowed to give your own account of the past when it is important that you should succeed at doing so. You may be put into doubt about the reliability of your evidence for your beliefs about yourself in the past and your beliefs about yourself in the present; and there may be consequences for how you regard your memory evidence for other important beliefs about yourself. You may be put into doubt as to whether your desires were reasonable or self-deceived, whether your actions were warranted, and whether what is of significance to you, as evidenced by what you remember, really is of significance. In sum, you may be put into doubt about the reliability of your memory as a source of warrant for your beliefs, desires, actions, and values in serious repeated situations. In becoming unsure of your descriptions of the past, you will be unsure as to who bears responsibility for past acts. Your abilities to assign responsibility, take responsibility, and be seen as responsible may all be threatened by the progressive distrust of your own recollections.

Borland's response to Hanson displays an understanding of how someone can be undermined through a challenge to their memory, and it displays an attempt to avoid this undermining. Although it is not always possible to avoid undermining others, we can be on the lookout for strategies that deliberately weaken someone's ability to make sense of her or his past and his or her ability to negotiate responsibility for past acts. I believe that a view of personhood that is sensitive to the ways in which core cognitive abilities can be undermined can and must be used to locate the ways in which downward psychological constituting is implicated in abusive situations.

CONCLUSION

In subsequent chapters, I will return to the problem, inherited from Locke, of linking identity to sameness of memory over time. Attending to the social nature of memory activity and the social nature of self and personhood should encourage us to theorize new links between memory and identity. Locke's dependence on sameness of consciousness is neither clear in meaning nor a plausible view of how memory contributes to a sense of self or a sense of responsibility. I want to end this chapter, however, by stressing the importance of memory to our development as selves and our status as persons in those cases when selfhood is undermined and when personhood is violated through deliberate harm. Our abilities and opportunities to engage in memory narratives are fundamental not only to developing and maintaining a sense of self but to repairing a sense of self rendered vulnerable through harm or abuse. This latter point becomes especially evident when we take seriously the social nature of the self.

In her essay entitled "Outliving Oneself: Trauma, Memory and Personal Identity," Susan Brison uses the context of traumatic harm to defend a feminist relational view of the self, a self that is "both autonomous and socially dependent, vulnerable enough to be undone by violence and yet resilient enough to be reconstructed with the help of empathetic others" (1997, 12). Using both her own experience of trauma and the narratives of others, Brison discusses the importance of listeners to trauma narratives. She argues that encouragement and support for relating the trauma enable the survivor to remember in ways that can contribute to mastery of traumatic events, and restored autonomy:

> Whereas traumatic memories . . . feel as though they are passively endured, narratives are the result of certain obvious choices (how much to tell to

> whom, in what order, etc.). This is not to say that the narrator is not subject to the constraints of memory or that the story will ring true however it is told. And the telling may be out of control, compulsively repeated. But one *can* control certain aspects of the narrative, and that control, repeatedly exercised, leads to greater control over the memories themselves, making them less intrusive and giving them the kind of meaning that permits them to be integrated into the rest of life. (24, her emphasis)

Brison states, "in order to construct self-narratives . . . we need not only the words with which to tell our stories but also an audience able and willing to hear us and to understand our words as we intend them" (21).

Roberta Culbertson, in "Embodied Memory, Transcendence, and Telling: Recounting Trauma, Re-establishing the Self" (1995), points out that "the destruction of the self" through traumatic violation is itself a social act "fundamentally pushing the self back into its . . . non-social surviving self, and at the same time fusing the self with that of a demanding and destroying other" (179). Drawing on her own experience of childhood sexual abuse and on others' narratives of traumatic harm, she writes:

> To return fully to the self as socially defined, to establish a relation again with the world, the survivor must tell what happened. . . . In doing so it becomes possible to return the self to its legitimate social status as something separate, something that tells, that recounts its own biography, undoing the grasp of the perpetrator and reestablishing the social dimension of the self lost in the midst of violation. (179)

According to trauma survivors and those who work with trauma survivors, the narration of traumatic harm is often a necessary part of recovering from it. Narrating the harm can help the trauma victim to restore a sense of continuity with her past, to gain control over intrusive memories, and to regain a sense of subjectivity and some sense of self-integrity.[6] To allow a testimonial position to survivors of sexual violence is to help individual survivors recover from the harms of such violence. It is to acknowledge as well that women are subject to such violence in our society and that it is a serious harm to them. Respect for those who have been harmed is partly expressed through how we respond to them as rememberers.

In this chapter, I have concentrated on one very small aspect of an account of the normativity of memory, the role of memory as a key person-ability. I have accepted the importance of our being able to engage in socially supported practices of self-narrative in order to establish and maintain a sense of self, and in order to develop as responsible agents. If this sketch of a social, activity-based view of person-abilities is plausible, it indicates that much more work needs to be done on the normativity of memory: on the value of memory experience and memory narratives, and on the consequences of failing to value others as rememberers. In the next two chapters, I continue to discuss the relation among memory, respect, and self-narrative. I call attention to FMSF strategies that undermine women as rememberers by controlling their narrative positions. In chapter 5 and again in chapter 8, I explicitly consider the representation of women as rememberers in false memory discourse to show that it does indeed devalue their status as persons and moral agents.

NOTES

1. The Freudian legacy to repression has made it a particularly good skeptical target even though clinical psychologists regard trauma-related memory problems as a more likely consequence of dissociative responses common to trauma. Many theorists dislike using "repression" to talk about traumatic memory. Judith Herman, for instance, uses "amnesia and delayed recall" (quoted in Horn 1993, 54). Elizabeth Waites uses "the delayed emergence of memory in adults" (1997, 208). Foundation members have often been unwilling to make a distinction between repression and dissociation. Daniel Schacter's everyday explanation of the difference is that "dissociation . . . creates a kind of 'horizontal' split in mental life . . . [while] [r]epression involves a 'vertical' pushing down of affectively charged and unwanted mental contents" (1996, 234). Janice Haaken (1998) contends that trauma theorists have a somewhat suspect stake in the idea of dissociation, as it is compatible with memory as an accurate mirroring of events; repression, however, may involve distortions. See chapter 4 for a discussion of Haaken's view.

2. If memory and memory processes were more appropriately regarded as social, I would not argue with this way of putting it.

3. See Diana Russell (1986/1999, xxxix), for example, for an account of Elizabeth Loftus's expert testimony at the International Criminal Tribunal for former Yugoslavia. Loftus apparently argued that a witness's continuous memory for an incident of rape/torture might be the effect of postevent suggestion.

4. For very different approaches to the idea of the reflexive self, see Richard Wollheim (1980) and Charles Taylor (1991). In her essay "Shame and Gender," Sandra Bartky has powerfully described the split consciousness that can attend certain forms of shame (1990); but certain forms of shame, as well as certain forms of pride, also seem to contribute to a sense of self. Some philosophers have held that reflexivity is a sign of all mental activity. I am using the idea in a more limited sense.

5. According to Amelie Rorty, the most important social practices relating to personhood are those involving the distribution "of liability and responsibility, of praise, blame, and punishment" (Rorty 1988, 29). Similarly, Daniel Dennett's conditions of personhood are precisely meant to ground the idea of responsibility (1978).

6. For the perspective of a therapist, see Judith Herman (1992, ch. 9) and Shoshana Felman and Dori Laub (1992, ch. 2).

3

FRAMING WOMEN'S TESTIMONY: NARRATIVE POSITION AND MEMORY AUTHORITY

> Recovery from trauma requires creating and telling another story about the experience of violence and the nature of the participants.
>
> Aurora Levins Morales,
> "False Memories: Trauma and Liberation"

Feminist epistemologist Lorraine Code writes: "most epistemic negotiations and many justificatory strategies take testimony as their starting point, as they engage different questions about who knows and how" (Code 2000, 187). Questions of credible testimony are linked to the nature of specific communicative occasions. When we challenge credibility, we represent those we challenge as narrating within the demands of certain contexts. In chapter 2, I argued that our respect or disrespect for rememberers can be expressed through allowing or denying them self-narrative positions. In this chapter, I give more texture to this claim by examining FMSF strategies to control the narrative positions of women who speak about incest. I argue that the foundation rhetorically positions women so as to limit their potential as testifiers to the past.

A woman may have a very difficult time articulating an abusive past. The FMSF tends to represent women who try to do so as either in court or in therapy. The first representation allows for women to testify, but it requires a distrustful response to their narratives. The second representation denies that women are involved in *testimonial* self-narrative: that is, narrative concerned with the *truth* of the past. In this chapter, I concentrate on the quasi-legal framing of women's abuse narratives. But I also begin an investigation into therapy as a potential testimonial site—a topic that I continue in chapter 4.

I use the discussion of FMSF strategies to reflect on some of the complex relations between narrative position and memory authority. Memory has long been regarded as a source of authoritative knowledge about one's own past. It is now regarded as more suspect. Neither the wholesale endorsement nor the suspicion of memory as a source of knowledge adequately attends to the contexts in which memory is narrated. When a woman acts as a rememberer, she is often in the vulnerable position of narrating a view about the significance of the past to the present that is not shared by the dominant members of her culture. The success of her narrative depends on her social authority as a rememberer, and this authority can be compromised through her discursive positioning.

In the first part of this chapter, I continue the project begun in chapter 2. I elaborate a view of memory as a complex of cognitive abilities and social–narrative activities while paying particular attention to the nature of memory testimony: its demands on us as rememberers and as interpreters. I use the work of C. A. J. Coady (1992) to distinguish different sorts of memory testimony—not all testimony should be thought of as formal legal testimony or as quasi-legal testimony modeled on a courtroom context. I then discuss both the general vulnerability of women as rememberers and the specific contemporary strategies that undermine them as testifiers. Finally, I describe a more political model of memory testimony—*testimonio*—as an alternative frame for survivor narrative, and I argue that FMSF writings specifically deny this position to women. At various points in the arguments that follow, I draw on the helpful and insightful reflections of E. B. Brownlie on her own substantiated memories of childhood sexual abuse: "Substantiation did not result in an easy relationship with the truth" (Brownlie 1999, 40).

SOCIALIZING MEMORY; SITUATING TESTIMONY

"Memory" is the sign for the system of cognitive capacities and abilities that make it possible for us to learn by experience. Because human memory is often self-representational, it is also a basis of self-reflection, self-knowledge, and identity formation. It is a source and story of the self that we share with others and of the past that we share with them. Theorists have described human memory as a kind of time travel (Waites 1997, 19) or as a telescope pointed at time (Schacter 1996, 15). These descriptions capture both the doubled self of autobiographical recall described in chapter 2 and the adaptively critical selectivity of memory. We recall the past from the perspective and demands of a present that reflects how our self-concepts are formed through individual and group histories, and we recall the past from a present that includes our expectations and anticipations about the future.[1]

To capture the feature of memory selectivity, I describe the meaning of memory experience very broadly as the significance of the past to the present. This formulation will move us away from our conceptualizing memory as an individual cognitive achievement: as an individual's access to her past experience as information processed, preserved, and accessible whether as episodic recall, skill, habit, or general knowledge. Individualist treatments of memory are narrow and misleading; thinking more broadly about how memory has personal and social meaning will show their inadequacies while helping us focus on the situation of women who attempt to narrate an abusive past.[2]

First, mnemonic information is not always unproblematically processed and transparently accessible to the rememberer. Part of the significance of the past may be its disruption of the present in how we remember. Writers on trauma stress that traumatized memory is often fragmentary, intrusive, sensory, and embodied: "bits of memory, flashing like clipped pieces of film held to the light, appear unbidden and in surprising ways, as if possessed of a life independent of will or consciousness" (Culbertson 1995, 169). For survivors of childhood and adult traumas, memory may take the form of "vivid and terrifying flashbacks" (Brison 1997, 23), of "images, sounds, sensations, terrors, fragmented and out of context" (Brownlie 1999, 42). These descriptions express a loss of the experience of a doubled self, of one's past and present held together, which normally grounds one's sense of security and competence as a rememberer. For a child, "the lines between life and death, ordinary and non-ordinary reality or states of consciousness, and the inner and outer dimensions of existence are all more fluid than they become in later life" (Culbertson 1995, 181). Memories of childhood trauma may thus be a complex and confusing blend of the sensory and the symbolic.

Second, narrow conceptions of memory may treat forgetting of any kind as a memory lapse or failure, but the value of our memory depends not only on forgetting much inessential detail but on strategies of motivated forgetting that protect us against unendurable pain and loss.[3] What we do not or cannot remember is often as significant to our present as what we do remember. Brownlie writes: "I find it hard to remember myself as a young girl, what it was like for me then and how I felt. Even with all the work I have done in therapy focusing on the years of my childhood, it is a rare and painful thing when I do connect to that time in my life" (43). Despite the importance of inhibitory mechanisms to functional memory, Daniel Schacter points out that they are rarely studied and poorly understood (1996, 234).

Third, until recently, theorists have tended to separate modes of memory retrieval and to distinguish, in particular, personal (or experiential) memory from general knowledge. This tendency misleads us about the nature and complexity of autobiographical memory. Useful memory requires the integration of the past, not its repetition. Almost all experiential memory contains general information; unique, singular memories may function as allegories, symbols, or lessons (Pillemer 1998); and a great deal of experiential memory is processed to signify repeated rather than singular episodes. In "The Truth about Memory," Marya Schechtman challenges philosophers to acknowledge the complications of ordinary personal memory: "How much similarity must there be between the two moments in order for the one to count as a memory of the other? How much of the content of the experience must be reproduced and how accurately?" (1994, 10) Schechtman uses research on autobiographical memory to point out that we often condense autobiographical memory: one memory comprises the details of many episodes and thus represents them (10). We also frequently summarize episodes: we remember clearly *that* we had certain experiences while sometimes remembering particular instances only vaguely or not at all (8).

Brownlie, in "trying to unravel what it means to remember childhood abuse" (1999, 42), distinguishes her own memories as:

1. memories *of* the abuse that vary in amount of detail, in conviction, and in when they were recalled (she is sure, as well, that some are composite or condensed) (42);
2. the memory *that* she was abused, "which stayed relatively constant over time"(42); and
3. day-to-day memories of living under the stress of anticipating abuse.

Schechtman argues that such processing of autobiographical memory is necessary to "usable self-knowledge" (11). For example, Brownlie's calmer, continuous memory that she was abused enabled her to distance herself from more vivid iconic memories; it provided a "continuous thread of memory" (44); and it helped her to strategize about how to protect herself as an adolescent. It was also a reason that she gave to agencies when she sought support and counseling; it helped her recount her abuse with a conviction and control that made her believable.

Thus, finally, much of the significance of the past to the present is social in nature. One compelling reason for understanding memory through attention to significance is that such an understanding can direct attention to how much of our memory experience is social and public. In encouraging the study of "remembering and forgetting as kinds of social action, rather than as properties of individual mentality," David Middleton and Derek Edwards do not deny that there is "coherence to the notion of individual memory":

> [O]f course there is. Rather, it is that the very heart of the topic, the sheer meaningfulness of memories, their content and organization (their personal and social significance), their contexts and occasionings in the flow of ordinary experience, cannot be accounted for by reference to mental processes alone. Those contents, processes and experiences are sensible only in the context of ideology and social action, collectivity and culture, and the everyday pragmatics of communication. (1990a, 19)

We do not only recognize, remember, forget, recall, memorize, and relive, but we also recount, commemorate, reminisce, remind, and testify.[4] The success with which we perform these activities depends not just or primarily on the reliability of memory mechanisms but also on the social positions we can or cannot occupy. Reciprocally, how we are positioned as rememberers creates and informs relations of power because control over the significance of the past helps determine the success of particular social agendas and the lineage of social authority. It is a mistake to try to understand the importance and structure of memory by attending solely to cognitive mechanisms or to the content of memory experiences without attending to the occasions of memory activities, including the occasions of narrative activities.

Memory narratives are extraordinarily various as to type and function. The significance of the past is not always expressed in discursive productions that make claims to truth or historical accuracy. Significance may, for example, be expressed through culturally shared stories where factual detail is of less concern than characters, themes, and values. At other times, the social context is one in which the values of truth and believability are dominant. When truth is one of the primary contextual values of a memory narrative—however contestable, difficult to arrive at, or social this truth may be—the narrator occupies a position that is testimonial. C. A. J. Coady characterizes the occasion of testimony as any occasion on which "we are . . . invited to accept something or other as true because someone says it is, where the someone in question is supposed to be in a position to speak authoritatively on the matter" (1992, 27). This description characterizes both formal, legal testimony and what Coady refers to as the natural testimony that contributes a significant part of our knowledge.

We are tremendously reliant on the natural testimony of others just as they are equally reliant on our own testimony. "Testimony . . . stands as a constant reminder of how little of anyone's knowledge . . . *could be* acquired independently" (Code 2000, 186, emphasis hers). Our reliance on testimony and the degree of social responsibility this entails has been articulated by many philosophers. Thomas Aquinas is eloquent on this subject, and Coady's study of testimony quotes him at length:

> And since among men dwelling together one man should deal with another as with himself in what he is not self-sufficient, therefore it is needful that he be able to stand with as much certainty on what another knows but of which he himself is ignorant, as upon the truths which he himself knows. Hence it is that in human society faith is necessary in order that one man give credence to the words of another, and this is the foundation of justice. . . . Hence it is also that no lie is without sin, since every lie derogates from that faith which is so necessary. (*Commentary on Boethius's De Trinitate*, qu. 3, art. 1.3. Quoted in Coady, 17)[5]

Not all of our natural testimony concerns the past, but much does. We recognize the importance of memory as a source of testimonial claims about the past by according explicit memory claims a certain authority. When someone says, "I remember," they are held to be making a knowledge claim and are regarded as having the responsibilities of one who makes a claim from a position of knower.[6] Thus, one of the most interesting and important features of articulated autobiographical memory is its status as natural testimony. Even crediting the obvious fallibility of memory, we typically have the best sense of which of our own memories are trustworthy, and of how others may be inaccurate; therefore, we are typically in the best position to speak authoritatively about our own pasts. Many contemporary writers on memory pay no attention to the fact that we are self-critical as rememberers. We all face challenges to our memories, and we all are obliged to reflect on their accuracy. Moreover, the conscious self-reflexivity of autobiographical speech-acts puts the self forward as a socially accountable epistemic agent: the person who now speaks of the past is the one who was there. In Elizabeth Waites's words, "it is the self as actor or observer who usually stands as the authoritative source of episodic memory and the guarantor of its accuracy" (1997, 88).

Many researchers have reduced the normative dimension of memory to its veridicality; or they have assumed its veridicality and have thus focused on lasting comprehensive recall, thereby conflating comprehensiveness with usefulness. For example, in his discussion "The Conditions of Goodness in Memory," William James writes that *"memory being thus altogether conditioned on brain-paths, its excellence in a given individual will depend partly on the number and partly on the persistence of such paths"* (1890/1950, 659, his emphasis). But the status of autobiographical memory as natural testimony indicates that there is a *complex* normativity to such memory. Its value resides not only in its veridicality and usefulness; it also reflects and constitutes the self as someone who can speak to others authoritatively about the past. Moreover, because we put ourselves forward as people who can be counted on, our integrity is at stake when we speak autobiographically.[7]

My characterization of memory, however, as the significance of the past in the present is meant to capture two further facts about memory as a cultural sign—both of which are political in import and troubling to the ideas of faith, mutual reliance, and justice that so move Aquinas.

First, political struggles over memory are extraordinarily intense. We do not share a communal understanding of the significance of the past to the present. Many of us have been excluded from contributing to the dominant culture's social memory; yet we also struggle at the site of memory precisely because what has been forgotten forms, for us, the significance of the past to the present. Caribbean–Canadian M. Nourbese Philip consciously remembers the history of the slave trade to "defy a culture that wishes to forget; to rewrite a history that at best forgot and omitted, at worst lied" (1992, 56).

Second, we treat others and ourselves as rememberers on some occasions but not on others. In reminding Canadians of the slave trade, Nourbese Philip claims a certain complex narrative position of memory authority—a storyteller, testifier, and historian. She designates herself a "long-memoried woman," evoking a figure of the wise-woman storyteller, a woman who can remember so far back that she witnessed and can tell "of what did not happen to me personally, but which accounts for my being here today," a story of origins (1992, 56). When she prefaces many of her subsequent statements with "I remember," she claims both the position and responsibility of a knower about the past. What I wish to point out here is that her position as a rememberer is explicitly claimed. While nearly all of what we do or say is memory reliant, we do not always take ourselves to be speaking with memory authority, nor are we always regarded as doing so by others.

In a testimonial context, I may be increasingly likely to make a claim that explicitly depends on memory when no witnesses or public records can verify what I say; when the past is contested and I want to stand as a witness to what really happened; or when I want to emphasize the significance of my own past. The circumstances in which individuals rely on memory as a source of warrant for their claims are sometimes circumstances in which there is no independent support for what they say or in which they must support people whose view of the past is under attack. Individuals who make memory claims are thus often in an inherently vulnerable social position. On those very occasions, the rememberer, while claiming memory authority with its attendant responsibilities and implications for integrity, is in a position of epistemic vulnerability; and the stance of the interpreters to the narrative—whether these interpreters operate with Aquinas's trust or with skepticism—becomes important to the success of the narrative. Finally, because what we say may have significant consequences for others, we may sometimes be put in a position that carries testimonial responsibilities and epistemic vulnerability, regardless of whether or not we choose to be in that position.

CONSTRUCTING WOMEN'S TESTIMONIAL POSITIONS

Coady identifies the ordinary testifier as one "who is supposed to be in a position to speak authoritatively." Aquinas's addendum—that "faith is necessary . . . and this is the foundation of justice"—is a warning that real epistemic authority does not come simply with occupying a testimonial position, whether chosen or determined by circumstance; rather, it depends on the attitude of those who witness the testimony. One political strategy, then, for undermining women's memory narratives is to attempt to control testimonial positions, organizing them so that women are positioned with the responsibilities of testifiers but in a context of maximal interpreter distrust. This attempted control of testimonial positions is in fact an important part of FMSF strategy.

Janice Haaken characterizes memory as a gendered activity, as "a product both of gendered social locations and of those collectively organized fantasies and beliefs about gender that dynamically shape what aspects of the past are likely to be preserved" (1998, 12). To set the context for examining how the FMSF represents women who claim they have been abused, I think it is first worth noting that women have special and long-standing social vulnerabilities and responsibilities as rememberers that undermine possibilities of their testifying to abuse. At a very general level of concern, women in most cultures seem to have less mnemonic authority than men. According to James Fentress and Chris Wickham, the authors of a historical cross-cultural study of social memory, the sense of women's view of the past varies with a culture's tolerance toward female points of view and articulacy; but, in general, their view has been prevented both by dominant ideology and, significantly, dominance over narration: "Most men interrupt, devalue their wives' memories, take over the interview, tell their own stories instead, or even, most bizarrely, themselves recount their wives' life stories" (1992, 140).

In addition to this general narrative disadvantage, women's abuse narratives in the West conflict with dominant social memory, which is the culture's authoritative articulated story of its past and its identity as formed by this past. Elizabeth Loftus speaks for dominant social memory of the family when she introduces skepticism about women's narratives of abuse with these words:

> No parent-child relationship is perfect. When we reflect back on the past, we often find ourselves wishing that our parents had given us more attention, more respect, more love. These are universal yearnings, and even people who grew up in the happiest of homes experience regret and disappointment. . . . (Loftus and Ketcham 1994, 102)

The memory of the family as a fundamentally secure place for children is what women who allege abuse are directly calling into question.

Further exacerbating the difficulty for women's narrating abuse into our social memory are their mnemonic responsibilities for commemorating the very sphere they are now seen as attacking. According to Haaken, "women's role as 'emotion managers' centers on the cultural task of holding and maintaining social knowledge" (1998, 101). In particular, women have been responsible for commemoration of the home, for "encapsulating (sanitizing and moralizing) accounts of the experienced past for young children, as part of the process of socialization" (Fentress and Wickham 1992, 142). Finally, abuse is often grounds for breaking with the past, and Fentress and Wickham describe women's mnemonic narratives as identifiable by "an absence of specific events, of life cruxes, resoluble by choices and discontinuities with the past" (1992, 142).[8] Studies of social memory indicate the highly constrained narrative positions allowed to women as rememberers and intimate the special difficulties they might have in testifying to abuse. Within this historical context, the FMSF has had little difficulty in constructing discursive arrangements that maximize interpreter distrust of women's narratives.

The FMSF was formed by Pamela Freyd and Peter Freyd (with others) some time after a visit to Jennifer Freyd and her husband. Pamela Freyd and Peter Freyd are Jennifer Freyd's parents. Jennifer Freyd's husband, in an unplanned confrontation, related that Jennifer Freyd had remembered Peter Freyd's abusing her. The Freyds' response was to make Jennifer Freyd a public accuser through publicizing her experience and theirs as her accusation.[9] Although well-known, this account of the foundation's genesis is rarely analyzed: to do so seems like prying, in bad taste, ad hominem; or it may even seem like an attempt to evade serious issues about memory. For example, in a comprehensive overview of memory science and the law—one that is quite critical of false memory syndrome—the authors are very careful when they describe the origin of the FMSF to not explicitly attribute Jennifer Freyd's loss of privacy to the actions of her parents (Brown, Scheflin, and Hammond 1998, ch. 1). In my view, however, the foundation's origins are key to understanding its strategy and force, and we should not try to avoid this discussion.[10] In FMSF newsletters and in solicited media coverage of FMSF gatherings and parents' stories, claims about abuse are made as public accusations—not by women who have been abused, but by publicizing parents' reports. In this way, a narrative position is constructed for women: abuse narratives are presented as if they issue from public testimonial positions, which then raise immediate fears about ruined reputations and the possible legal action against purported abusers.[11]

The quasi-legal framing of abuse narratives has been promoted by the FMSF's intensive involvement in legal strategizing and by the press, with headlines like "False Memories Victims Languish in Jail" (Makin 1998a). This framing has been accepted by the public and by many scholars and researchers as justified, given the legal penalties for abuse. Any attempt to reframe issues is often explicitly or implicitly criticized as either irresponsible—for example, the charge leveled at John Read by Elizabeth Loftus—or irrelevant (see chapter 1). In response to Haaken's work on the social function of incest narratives, Martin Guha writes: "In my crude masculine way I had always assumed that, in cases of alleged recovered memories of child abuse, the crucial point in question was whether abuse had actually taken place or not." He doubts whether Haaken's account will be of much use to "people who have been put in jail, driven from their homes and generally had their lives broken up on the strength of unprovable allegations" (Guha 2000, 316). Barry Allen, reviewing Ian Hacking's constructivist account of memory, reflects that "it is a nice question whether remembering is more like telling a story or playing a videotape. But when a woman claims that some decades ago her staid father led a satanic cult breeding incestuous babies for sacrifice—and it is believed by police and courts—the truth of memory is no longer a nice question" (1997, 64). My intent is not to deny that women sometimes make public accusations of abuse or instigate legal proceedings for abuse. The FMSF achieved prominence partly as a response to increased possibilities for women to institute criminal or civil proceedings that relate to historic abuse. But, in fact, many women never tell anyone about abuse, and women do not often take their abusers to court. The foundation's framing of abuse serves an ulterior strategic purpose of constructing a narrative position that isolates the incest survivor in an adversarial setting of interpreter distrust and challenge.

The FMSF's deployment of the courtroom as a cultural frame for regarding incest is, first, a way of compelling all women who need to speak of their abuse to assume the responsibilities and vulnerabilities of legal testifiers who may have a vengeful stake in the jailing of their own parents. "Parents have to witness their adult children turning into monsters trying to destroy their reputations and lives" (Ofshe and Watters 1993, 4). The appropriate interpreter response is evidently meant to be one of a watchful and alarmed skepticism.[12] I wish to stress that this position is not and could not be our general response to natural testimony. It is a response appropriate only in very particular contexts.

Second, the skepticism is given gendered historical weight by a tradition of legal writing and practice that challenges women's actual *legal* testimony, especially in cases of sexual offenses. As has been particularly apparent to feminist legal critics, "false memory syndrome" (FMS) arises in a place already prepared for it in law. In their study of syndrome evidence and the law, Fiona Raitt and M. Suzanne Zeedyk point out that "the discourses surrounding FMS . . . are embedded within a historical context which has traditionally regarded women and children as unreliable, incredible . . . witnesses" and that "special rules of evidence and legal procedure have been constructed on the basis of this belief" (2000, 151). For example, as recently as 1994, in England and Wales, "judges were *obliged* to give a detailed warning to juries of the dangers of convicting a man accused of rape on the strength of the woman complainant's testimony alone and in the absence of other material corroborative evidence" (103). The demand for corroboration of abuse narratives has become revitalized over the last decade by the conjunction of their quasi-legal framing with a scientific framing of questions about memory. Scientists freely mention the necessity of corroboration to assessing memory as reliable. A quasi-legal framing of abuse narratives can be used to provoke the need for corroboration of abuse narratives using the authority of science to do so. Brownlie points out, however, that the "intense relational environment of secretive abuse" (1999, 47) is bound to render any substantiation only partial and often subject to conflicting interpretation:

> Meanings can be communicated in ways that the perpetrator and victim fully understand, but that others would miss. An example is the tug of a phone cord that my abuser would wrap around my neck as I talked on the phone as a teenager. This subtle gesture that might look like an accident or even a joke would send a chill through me, and I would receive a message loud and clear. What exactly could be substantiated in what I just described . . . ? (47–48)

Brownlie's text makes two important points: corroboration for child sexual abuse is unlikely, and the demand for or presence of corroboration may mislead us about what actually occurred. It may focus attention, for example, only on legally salient acts, while ignoring much of the nature and harm of secretive abuse.

Third, the FMSF's insistence on a quasi-legal interpretation of abuse narratives safely places the perpetrators of abuse in a cultural position of not having to act as testifiers; they are instead deniers of the "charges." Although we might believe or disbelieve them, they do not speak with the interesting combination of epistemic vulnerability and responsibility that characterizes memory discourse.[13] Critics of the FMSF have sometimes tried to shift attention to the memories of those who deny abuse, but they have done so with little success. Jennifer Freyd has stated that she is at times "flabbergasted that [her] memory is considered 'false' and [her] alcoholic father's memory is considered rational and sane" (Freyd 1993, 28). But because of the configuration of narrative positions, his speech is not at issue as memory testimony in the way that her own is.

Fourth, narrative position can also significantly determine what counts as forgetting and whether forgetting is regarded as serious memory failure. Obviously, not everything that I once experienced but do not, at present, recall is a case of forgetting. What counts as forgetting is determined by context. Because memory narratives involve the significance of the past to the present, this context may have to do with what is important to the interpreter rather than what is important to the narrator of a memory experience. It is striking how much detail we can, as interpreters, require of someone's memory. For instance, if I say that I remember our dinner but cannot remember, on your challenge, whether it took place on a Tuesday or Wednesday or what you ordered to eat, I may have to withdraw my memory claim. The attempt to undermine memory authority by shifting significance to what is forgotten tacitly recognizes the significance that a memory claim has to the person who contests it. In certain contexts, I can maintain a memory claim only when I remember the surroundings of the past event that are specifically called into question; that is, what I am responsible for is often determined by challenge. The framing of women's abuse narratives as quasi-legal testimony encourages the public, as interpreters, to take the stance of cross-examiners who categorize forgetting as memory failure and insist on completeness and consistency of memory detail through all repeated tellings. The condensed, summarized, or fragmentary nature of abuse memories will rarely withstand this aggressive testing. Few people's memories can.

Waites's description of the plagiarism charge against an eleven-year-old Helen Keller makes vivid the contextual dimension of forgetting and returns me to the question of what is involved in respecting rememberers. Waites uses Keller's case to introduce her own theory of memory as a partly social competence where the judgment of that competence depends on contextual demands that can neglect and override the history and expertise of individual rememberers. Keller's story, "The Frost King," published while she was a student at the Perkins Institute for the Blind closely resembles a published story by Margaret Canby. Keller was challenged and publicly humiliated. Moreover, Michael Anagnos, the director of the institute, took it "as a personal affront and continued to discredit her for years" (1997, 2), causing Waites to remark that Keller learned a lesson in politics as well as psychology.[14]

Keller did not explicitly claim the position of rememberer. She believed she was creating a story that she was, in fact, probably recalling with accuracy. Waites describes her error as cryptomnesia: "a . . . high fidelity accuracy for factual details combined with amnesia for the source of the information" (2). But on Waites's analysis, what made Keller's nonretrieval of the source a case of forgetting was contextually determined. In a culture that privileges the ownership of texts, storytelling requires attending to the source of information; failing to do so is often a serious memory failure.[15] In a literate culture, "learning to pay attention to textual sources . . . is an important and carefully practiced aspect of formal education" (9).

Waites uses Keller's story to illustrate that "people possessing different capacities, guided by different habits, motivated by different needs, and confronting different tasks develop different ways of using memory to help them cope" (7–8). Keller, whose memory was remarkable, had to take in as much information as possible in a short time to compensate for the six years in which she did not have language. She was not taught to interrogate her memory in the critical way that most of us are (8) or in the more demanding way as eloquently performed in Brownlie's text. Moreover, Keller's education by Anne Sullivan consisted in the constant and casual tapping of information into her hand, which likely included the details of Canby's story. To be read to or talked to were indistinguishable. Thus Keller might not have even attended to the fact that the words came from a text—she couldn't see it. Perhaps Anne Sullivan had never even tapped this crucial information about source into her hand (8–9). But even though Waites is unsure whether Keller had at some point experienced the words as deriving from a text, Waites herself describes the error as one of forgetting, of amnesia for source, inadvertently reinforcing her own emphasis on how context structures the forgotten.

Keller's memory surely met James's criterion for an excellent memory. That it did was, as Waites points out, a part of the problem. Those of us who have poor memories for what we read rephrase out of necessity. Keller's failure to be a good rememberer was a matter of how her memory abilities reacted with the demands of a certain social context and the power relations within it. When we assess how women's narrative positions are being constructed and whether we are respecting them as rememberers, we need to keep in mind not only the individuality of memory experience and expertise but also the demands of the different contexts. Margaret Canby herself expressed not censure but admiration for Keller's memory. Those accused of abuse, whether fairly or falsely, can be expected to react strongly. My concern is how those of us who want to respect and aid women with abusive pasts allow them to be positioned as rememberers in our imaginations and the effect of this positioning.

Brownlie's attempt to understand her past and her reflections on her memory experience show an enormously sophisticated grasp of the nature of autobiographical processing, the effects of trauma on memory, and the problematic relation of substantiation to truth. But she is well aware that her contextual position as a rememberer is now formed by the demand for persuasive legal testimony under intense social cross-examination. She neither has pressed nor intends to press charges against her abusers. Largely because of the FMS lobby, however, "legal issues have become central to understanding and dealing with adults' memories of abuse" (1999, 48). "The trial [as] an unspoken metaphor" (49) for adult recollection has made it more difficult for her to speak about her experience, and it has discouraged her attempts to understand a complicated history:

> naming my experiences of abuse can quickly elicit responses of interrogation and cross-examination in others. I think this happens because many people feel at some level that not to do so would be fundamentally unjust. . . . Although the topic of abuse is frequently raised, I often feel hesitant to express my thoughts, based on what I know from my own life, because I expect that at some level the veracity of what I say may be challenged. (48–49)

Insisting that all abuse narratives issue from a particular aggressively assumed testimonial position decreases the possibility of a sympathetic hearing for women who speak about their abuse or seek legal redress; in addition, it compels women whose memories are traumatic—embodied, fragmentary, tentative, confusing, and difficult to interpret—to be silent about their experience. This silence is enforced by denying them alternative testimonial positions.

DENYING WOMEN'S TESTIMONIAL POSITIONS

In his defense of testimony as a source of knowledge, C. A. J. Coady distinguishes legal, or formal, testimony from nonlegal, or natural, testimony. The ubiquity of the latter interests Coady, and it suits his argumentative purpose to mass together a range of nonlegal contexts in which we believe what others tell us because we trust them on these matters. When doing so, Coady does not attend closely to the structures of different speech situations in which people attempt to testify. To avoid always importing a legal model, we need to recognize different kinds of testimonial positions. Moreover, as abuse narratives have lost credibility in the last several years, we also need to understand the structure of the nonlegal testimonial positions that women have claimed. What narrative positions have allowed women to testify to sexual violence, and how have these positions been damaged, particularly for incest survivors?

In this final section, I shall argue that the genre of *testimonio*—a type of political, nonlegal testimony—is a valuable perspective from which to analyze the current fate of women's abuse narratives. Testimonio illuminates both the power and fragility of women's speech. Since the 1970s, women have spoken out or written about the pervasiveness of sexual violence in their lives. Testimonio focuses attention on the collective political dimension of women's speech. At the same time, discussing this narrative form allows us to look at a number of specific ways in which testimony can be mediated by and dependent on others. We need models of testimonial speech that recognize our dependencies. People's dependencies, however, can be used to disqualify their speech and deauthorize their attempted testimony, which is why testimonio contexts are so fragile. I want to make clear the importance of this form of testimony, and I want to show how the memory debates have rendered it less accessible to women who have been abused.

Testimonio is a form of self-narrative concerned with harms done to those who belong to diminished social categories, concerned with oppression, poverty, abuse, subalternity, and so on. John Beverley writes that "*testimonio*-like texts have existed for a long time at the margin of literature, representing in particular those subjects—the child, the 'native,' the woman, the insane, the criminal, the proletarian—excluded from authorized representation when it was a question of speaking and writing for themselves rather than being spoken for" (1992, 93, his emphasis). Beverley's account, which focuses on the legitimation of written testimonios in South and Central America, is a subtle and explicit reflection not only on the relational context of testifying but also on how a dependent voice can nevertheless become authorized. I draw on it freely to describe a testimonio-like position that North American incest survivors have claimed for themselves.

The testimonial situation involves a "struggle for survival . . . implicated in the act of narration" (94). Testimonio is not only concerned with the problematic social situations but also with the difficulties of making these situations understood and urgent for others who are meant to witness or sometimes intervene. Its possibility depends on the actions and attitudes of others. As I read Beverley, the testimonio voice is triply dependent for its existence, exhibiting a complex relationality involving dimensions of address, facilitation, and uptake. First, the narrative voice, the voice of the protagonist or witness and testifier, is metonymic: she/he "speaks for, or in the name of" the community or group whose plight is described in the testimony (95). The opening lines of *I, Rigoberta Menchú* are often offered to illustrate the testimonio address: "My name is Rigoberta Menchú. I'm 23 years old. This is my testimony. I didn't learn it from a book and I didn't learn it alone. I'd like to stress that it's not only my life, it's also the testimony of my people" (Menchú 1984, 1; quoted in Beverley, 95–96). That the testimony is narrated by an individual voice in its collective mode shows "that any life so narrated can have . . . representational value" (96), drawing attention not only to the existence of a collective predicament but to the many real individuals who are affected by it. At the same time, the presence of a strong first-personal voice "is the mark of a desire not to be silenced or defeated" (96). "The dominant formal aspect of the *testimonio* is the voice that speaks to the reader in the form of an 'I' that demands to be recognized" (96, his emphasis).

Second, the testifier is dependent on those who facilitate testimonial speech through witnessing, interpreting, translating, recording, reporting, and disseminating testimonial narrative. Interestingly, the facilitation necessary to testimonio enhances rather than diminishes the presence of an authoritative speaking subject. The situation the testifier describes is sufficiently urgent to morally compel others to both witness the speech and make sure the speaker can reach a wider public. Beverley contrasts testimonio to oral history: "in oral history it is the intentionality of the recorder—usually a social scientist—that is dominant, and the resulting text is in some sense 'data.' In *testimonio*, by contrast, it is the intentionality of the narrator that is paramount" (94, his emphasis). Moreover, and I will return to this point in the next chapter, the recorder and author is also an interlocutor and witness to the testimony. He or she stands as a counterpart to the reader, allowing for a "complicity . . . between narrator and reader" absent in, for example, the interpretive context of novel reading (97).

Finally, the very existence of a testimonio voice is dependent on a particular interpretive stance. The narrator to testimonio pledges her honesty. But those who hear testimonio also understand that the narrator is vulnerable to silencing and to further harm. Because memory as evidence for claims often comes without collaboration, Aquinas recognized the vulnerability of the everyday testifier by promoting faith as the appropriate interpretative response. Those who engage in testimonio face the additional vulnerability of narrating claims that conflict with dominant social memory. Testimonio is a narrative of self and memory made possible only by interpreter trust in the credibility of the narrator, and it differs from legal and quasi-legal testimony as a narrative position. The existence of a testimonial pledge does not, of course, guarantee the truth of the testimonial claims. Rather, our assuming the presence of this pledge is indicative of the respect that we accord rememberers in certain circumstances. In our granting to others the position of testimonio, we are respecting, as rememberers, those who narrate accounts of their own harm and oppression. We are acknowledging, minimally, that the testifier is a person of integrity, that she can represent others who have been silenced by harm, that these harms take place and are serious, and that we may be called upon to act.

Within the last thirty years, women have begun to testify widely about sexual abuse and incest. Since the 1970s and the rise of second-wave feminism, many survivors have participated in oral and written testmonios, and books about sexual violence and child sexual abuse frequently contain a significant amount of testimonial narrative. Linda Alcoff and Laura Gray remark that

> [a] principal tactic adopted by the survivor's movement has been to encourage and make public survivors' disclosures of our traumas whether in relatively private or in public contexts. Speaking out serves to educate the society at large about the dimensions of sexual violence and misogyny, to reposition the problem from the individual psyche to the social sphere where it rightfully belongs, and to empower victims to act constructively on our own behalf and thus make the transition from passive victim to active survivor. (1994, 261–62)

Women's accounts of sexual harm and violation share many of the relational features of the narrative position that Beverley describes. Their survivor testimony is often an explicit political act, intended to make public a collective rather than individual predicament. The struggle for narration is evident in titles like *I Never Told Anyone*, *Voices in the Night*, and *Don't: A Woman's Word* (Brister, Bass, and Thorton 1983; McNaron and Morgan 1982; Danika 1988). For women, this struggle has involved the specific recognition that gendered violence has often been hidden and secretive; and that on those occasions when women have been able to voice their resistance, they have often not been able to do so successfully. Survivor testimonio has often been facilitated through the organization of public or semipublic forums and speak-outs. Finally, as interpreters, we have been called on to both witness survivor testimonies and intervene in the harms that they describe. As we can no longer intervene for the testifier, we are meant to prevent harm to other children and women; to make possible redress and healing for those who have been abused; and to challenge, resist, and change the structures that accommodate sexual exploitation. The false memory debate has continued to inspire women's testimonio. Jennifer Freyd writes: "I also speak about these matters today because I hope what I have to share will help, directly or indirectly, other abused children and adult survivors of abuse" (1993, 23). Brownlie writes: "FMS uses the ideal of a 'true' complainant with substantiated memories as a foil to dismiss and deny unsubstantiated memories of abuse. I want to interrupt that process, and that's why I decided to write this article" (40).

Women's survivor narratives may seem to have a more autonomous speaking voice than the testimonios described by Beverley; they have not typically been narrated to a witness who disseminates the testimony. Nevertheless, I shall argue that an understanding of incest survivors as engaged in politically powerful testimonio has not been difficult to undermine. Moreover, there is one very significant context in which a survivor of childhood sexual abuse may relate her account to a witness who then conveys the story to a wider public. Many survivors have had therapy, and their participation in therapy has had serious ramifications for whether they are perceived as testifying. I remind readers that I am here interested not in memory content but in how narrative positioning can itself have an impact on the possibility of narrative authority.

Undermining survivor testimonio has been made easier by the vulnerable position of such narrative in the first place. Testimonio is a particularly difficult narrative stance for Anglo-European women for whom the status of victim is seen as a kind of self-indulgence on the part of those who have little moral sense of what constitutes real suffering. In addition, the group held most prone to false memories are white, middle-class, and fairly young—in many ways privileged. This group of women has frequently been criticized by other groups of women for their too-easy use of the language of victimization, as well as for their naive and problematic sense of who they can represent through their own narratives. And finally, the kinds of hostile misfortunes to which women are prone are often harms done to them one by one and in private. These considerations make the collective voice that gives power to testimonio much more difficult to achieve.[16]

The presentations of the FMSF include no narrative category of incest survivor testimony. Women are often represented as "charging" their parents with abuse, and I have argued that we are meant to picture women individually as vengeful legal claimants. Nevertheless, the idea of "survivor testimony" as a collective political endeavor to force public recognition of the harm of childhood sexual abuse is very explicitly avoided. The denial of testimonio to incest survivors is also performed and displayed in many FMSF writings by suggesting that it is others who occupy this political position. Loftus, Mark Pendergast, Eleanor Goldstein, and Kevin Farmer have used a testimonial style of presentation in their books. Their work includes first-person accounts and many excerpts of such accounts that are meant to make clear to us that there is a serious collective predicament that requires our urgent political response. But all of these tellings are those of accused parents, disbelieving siblings, recanters, or women whom the authors discredit. Goldstein and Farmer dismiss all testimonial writing on incest itself as the "hundreds of books [that] have been written validating anecdotal stories" (1993, 8). This same body of testimonial writing is referred to by Loftus as "the recent incest book industry" (1993, 525).

Finally and crucially, many survivors of child sexual abuse, though by no means all, have participated in therapy. Many credit therapy with helping them find their voice as survivors. Morales, for example, writes:

> My own relief at the discovery, in therapy, that my inability to sleep, or the persistent intrusive violent images that thrust their way into my mind were a common, known and documented response to severe abuse was identical with what I felt in my first women's consciousness-raising group. As each woman in turn spoke about her life and we realized how much we had in common, we became able to identify the sources of our anger, frustration and self-doubt in the treatment we has recieved [sic] at the hands of men. Our exhilaration came from the realization that our pain was not after all a character flaw. (1998b, 17)

Nevertheless, women's participation in therapy has been offered by the FMSF as the reason why their accounts of harm should not be regarded as any kind of testimony. The FMSF has charged that while some claims of abuse are true, too many "are caused by a disastrous 'therapeutic' program" (False Memory Syndrome Foundation 1994); most cases of so-called false memory have been attributed to women's involvement in therapy. FMS advocates have thus encouraged us to position women who talk about child sexual abuse as therapeutic subjects and to interpret their speech, not as collective political testimony, but as the suspect effect of therapeutic influence.[17] I conclude this section with a particular example of an FMSF recharacterization of women's narrative that contrasts strikingly with testimonio. In assessing this example, it is important to recall that FMSF describes the issue of delayed recall as one of whether repression exists as a memory mechanism.

Many survivors have spoken and written of the effects of trauma on their memory and of their difficulties in understanding an abusive past. In false memory writings, all evidence that women may have difficulty in remembering parts of an abusive past is dismissively categorized as anecdotal, the same term used to describe first-person written accounts of incest. Loftus, in denying that evidence for repression exists, speaks of "clinical anecdotes and loose theory" (1993, 519). Richard Ofshe and Ethan Watters say that "the only support repression has ever had is anecdotal" (1993, 5). Pendergast speaks of cases of alleged recovered memory as "anecdotal evidence of . . . repression" (1995, 101).

The persistent use of "anecdote" to describe women's speech in therapy is multiply discrediting of the idea of testimony. It embeds women's experience within the claims of clinical psychologists and feminist therapists who ground their understanding in their clients' reports of experience. First, the use of "anecdote" positions experts as speaking for women, rather than women as speaking for themselves (see chapter 4). Second, it treats women who seek therapy as scientific subjects and their speech as data. Such women could not be thought of as engaged in testimonio as their intentionality is not paramount.[18] Third, when therapy narratives are regarded as data, they are charged with being merely anecdotal to mark their particularity, hence their insufficiency as data. "Anecdote" thus contrasts with the more privileged data status of studies that seek general results over research populations. Waites writes, "those who work in the laboratory usually consider their methods of inquiry superior and privileged, more scientific than case histories or anecdoctal reports" (1997, 4). Rather than taking women's participation in therapy as evidence that they are not research subjects, the FMSF instead takes it as evidence that therapists are not good scientists. In this regard, recall Loftus's claim that the problem with therapists is that they have only one hypothesis (chapter 1). Fourth, because feminist therapists and frontline clinicians are often charged with a bias toward too easily believing their clients, categorizing their evidence as anecdoctal also supports the idea that their reports, even as particular cases, should not really be trusted.

Fifth and finally, because of the use of testimonial narrative in false memory writing to represent the collective predicament of parents, "anecdote" is implicitly opposed not only to laboratory generalization but also to what is offered as genuine testimonio in foundation writings. As guided by this contrast, an anecdote is a brief, interesting story, passed along orally—that is, unrecorded. It is typically biographical, rather than autobiographical. Relating an anecdote requires no pledge of honesty on the part of the narrator, and listening to one requires no trust and no action on the part of the interpreter. "Anecdote" is at as far a remove as we can imagine from the self-narration of serious collective harm that characterizes testimonio.

CONCLUSION

The ideal of testimonio is that one testifies on behalf of those silenced. When an incest survivor is positioned in the public's imagination in the isolation of adversarial legal settings, she is denied a community of experience with other women and the recognition of group harm. The incest victim in FMSF presentation represents no group and speaks for no harm but her own. She must bear the vulnerabilities of memory narrative alone, in an atmosphere of social distrust and public cross-examination, and without the possibility of a reciprocal challenge; those she accuses are not figured as rememberers. She may be nominally positioned as a testifier, but without the possibility of success. When, in addition, she is positioned in the public imagination as a subject of therapy, we do not hear her account of the past as testimony. As Brownlie's text makes clear, women who have been abused, whether or not they have had delayed recall, feel the effects of these repositionings. More general, the ways in which we control narrative opportunities and structure the demands of various testimonial contexts are an important part of how we position others as rememberers.

The difficulties for women who engage in sexual harm narratives have been eloquently articulated by Martha McClusky, who spoke and wrote about her sexual victimization by fraternity students at Colby College in Maine. She concludes that "it is not the subject matter of one's story—victimization—but rather one's position as authoritative subject that determines whether or not narratives of harm bolster or undermine one's power and authority" (1994, 54). I have analyzed and complicated this requirement to implicate the role of the audience to testimony in its possible success, stressing the relationality of our engagements over memory narrative. Both Coady's account of natural testimony and Beverley's description of testimonio urge us to consider that our abilities to relate the past rely on our interpreters. In the next chapter, I consider the difficult question of whether women can be authoritative subjects if they are situated in the public imagination within a therapeutic project of remembering and revising their accounts of the past.

NOTES

1. Scientists express this aspect of recall by pointing out that the context of retrieval contributes to the meaning of any particular memory.

2. This is not an unusual way to describe memory. Aurora Levins Morales writes that "history is the story we tell ourselves about how the past explains the present" (1998c, 24).

3. See Jennifer Freyd, *Betrayal Trauma: The Logic of Forgetting Childhood Abuse* (Cambridge, MA: Harvard University Press, 1996), for an extended and persuasive argument

that much repression as a result of childhood abuse is a survival strategy to protect necessary attachments.

4. The editors and contributors to *Collective Remembering* (Middleton and Edwards 1990) discuss oral history and folklore; our artifactual legacy; the changes in our environment and our attempts at preservation; celebrations, commemorations, and rituals; language preservation; the media's creation of social memory; conversational remembering; structurally instigated amnesia; and the control of archives and official documents as some of the areas that engage theorists who focus in particular on what's now called social memory. "The world we live in embodies in its very design a relation to the past" (1990a, 10).

5. For a recent epistemological discussion of the importance of trust, see Naomi Scheman (2001).

6. For a description of the parallel between remembering and knowing, see Bernard Williams (1973).

7. I am indebted here to Elizabeth Waites who writes: "The integrity of the self is at stake in the process of telling" (33).

8. The possibilities of incest narratives as providing grounds for a decisive break with the past partially lead Janice Haaken to stress their powerful use as social memory for contemporary women—although again, such a break is not one that needs to be self-conceptualized in terms of choice. See chapter 4.

9. I have used full names throughout this passage to avoid subsuming Jennifer Freyd's identity to that of her parents. For a discussion of the role of subsumed identities, including the identity of "daughter," in the false memory debates, see chapter 5. In the afterword to her book, *Betrayal Trauma: The Logic of Forgetting Childhood Abuse* (1996), Jennifer Freyd, a cognitive psychologist, describes the complex professional and personal interests that led to her development of betrayal trauma theory. I refer to Freyd's theory in chapters 6 and 8. It is worth noting that Jennifer Freyd presented work on betrayal trauma, without disclosing information about her family life, before the Freyds formed the FMFS. During this period, and at a time when Jennifer Freyd was being considered for promotion, Pamela Freyd circulated her own version of family history to Jennifer Freyd's colleagues (Haaken 1998). In my view, this activity, and the formation and publicizing of the FMSF, need to be evaluated as an attempt to undermine Jennifer Freyd's professionalism, re-placing her in the public mind as a "troubled daughter." In 1993, Jennifer Freyd broke her silence and "presented [her] perspective on [her] family of origin and the formation of the FMSF" (Freyd 1996, 198). See Freyd (1993) for this initial public response.

10. According to journalist Mike Stanton, "From the beginning, [Pamela Freyd] encouraged accused parents to tell their stories to reporters and to appear on talk shows to put a human face on this 'serious health crisis' and satisfy the media's 'craving for human drama'" (1997, 45).

11. In her initial public response, Jennifer Freyd felt obliged to make clear that she had neither made a public accusation against her parents nor taken any legal action. She also stated: "I have avoided discussing memories that only came back to me within the last three years because I am aware that I probably cannot prove those events took place, and because I don't think I should be forced into putting my memories on trial

when I am not demanding to be believed about those things, when I never chose to make them public in the first place" (1993, 36).

12. When Jennifer Freyd and E. B. Brownlie make clear that they have never taken and do not intend to take legal action, they explicitly attempt to disrupt their narrative positioning. Unfortunately, insofar as they succeed at this disruption, their success is discursively at the expense of women who do press charges.

13. Even so, Mike Stanton finds it "surprising how few stories explore the question whether accused parents are guilty or innocent" (1997, 48).

14. Helen Keller herself relates that she "never played with words again for the pleasure of the game" (Keller, 1902/1988, 50; quoted in Waites, 2).

15. This is not always the case. Elizabeth Waites points out that had Keller been writing an exam, knowing the source of information would likely be irrelevant to a display of memory mastery.

16. "How can we reveal and heal previously hidden injustices, such as domestic violence, acquaintance rape, and sexual harassment, without contributing to the dominant story, which casts women as inevitably damaged and vulnerable to male control . . . [or dismisses] victim stories as individual whining that breeds division and cynicism at worst or paternalistic protection at best?" (McCluskey 1994, 54).

17. At one level, I would argue that the FMSF has recognized therapy as an opportunity for political speech. A movement spawned by the foundation has worked for several years, unsuccessfully, to introduce state legislation that limits access to feminist therapists who attempt to embody their commitments in their practice. For example, a 1994 fund-raising proposal for developing model legislation in New Hampshire, entitled Mental Health Consumer Protection Act, includes a recommendation for eliminating "politicized 'psychology' theories . . . backing up such rules with expulsion from the relevant profession" (National Association for Consumer Protection in Mental Health Practices, 1994).

18. See chapter 6. In science, because truth or knowledge arises as a result of disciplinary procedures and authority, it may be that there is no such category as research subject testimony: the narratives of research subjects are data; and when they are particular, they are anecdotes. Although Coady uses the word "testimony" when he talks about what is said by the subjects of psychology experiments, scientists themselves use the term "self-report."

4

THE SUBJECTS OF THERAPY: REVISITING *TRAUMA AND RECOVERY*

As discussed in chapter 3, the FMSF's success at positioning women's experience as a source of suspect, unverifiable anecdotes for therapists who attempt to advocate on their clients' behalf raises complex issues about the suitability of therapy as a testimonial site for survivors. Practically, therapy seems like an indispensable site. Many survivors seek therapy. In doing so a survivor may find, for the first time, an environment where she can speak about the abuse to someone who will listen to her, believe her, and help her to understand and to gain control over her past. Susan Brison and Roberta Culbertson both stress the survivor's need to verbalize what happened (chapter 2). Feminist therapists have sometimes deliberately and explicitly identified themselves as witnesses to survivor testimony; and they have advocated for the importance and truth of survivor accounts in their professional writing. They have been committed to "the feminist politic of de-silencing" (Brown 1996b, 6), not only in their practice with clients but in their determination to increase public knowledge about the nature and prevalence of child sexual abuse. Yet women's participation in therapy, especially feminist therapy, has been targeted by a number of critics as the reason why women's accounts of harm should not be trusted, even if women are no longer in therapy when they offer their accounts.

In this chapter, I use Judith Herman's *Trauma and Recovery* (1992) to try to clarify some of the relations among testimony, truth, and therapy. Herman's work is an influential affirmation of the role of feminist political advocacy in support of client testimony. Herman argues that serious harm tends to traumatize its victims and that traumatized clients often require social support in order to remember what happened. Because of the silence that shields many traumatic harms, those who work with survivors must also publicly witness their lives. Trauma-oriented accounts like Herman's have been central to false memory controversies; fully assessing these controversies requires coming to grips with Herman's account. I approach Herman through three challenges to her claim to publicly witness survivor testimony, that is, through three challenges to therapy as an appropriate testimonial site.

The first challenge highlights the complex, problematic position of feminist advocates.[1] Linda Alcoff and Laura Gray (1993) have argued that the position of therapists and other professionals as expert interpreters of women's experience displaces women's authority over their own accounts. I read this criticism as the claim that while women may testify privately in therapy, expert advocacy harms women's public positions as testifiers. *Trauma and Recovery* advocates for clients and is a defense of this advocacy. I argue that Alcoff and Gray's arguments should challenge feminist therapists to see tensions and limits inherent in feminist advocacy, but they should not be taken by Herman as a reason to give up her position. We need models of testimony that do not deny our dependencies, and Herman's work struggles for such a model.

I then take up a second way in which therapy may be thought to compromise narrative autonomy. Herman's determination to witness survivor testimony is at the same time a commitment to the general truth of her clients' accounts of the past. Yet she acknowledges that therapists provide concepts for clients to use in framing experiences and narratives. *Trauma* is one such concept. That therapists contribute to the meaning of client memory has been at the heart of false memory controversies, and feminist psychotherapist Janice Haaken (1996; 1998) has offered a critique of Herman's account that parallels the concerns of the FMSF.

The FMSF has claimed that (1) a substantial number of therapists naively believe and reinforce client confabulations, especially if these confirm the therapists' own tendencies to see abuse everywhere, and (2) many therapists suggest abusive pasts to their clients, causing their clients to confabulate accounts. According to the FMSF, we should thus now be suspicious of what women say about abuse if they have had therapy. Indeed, we are now more suspicious.

Haaken endorses much of the recent concern about false memory. She combines reasons (1) and (2) by charging feminist trauma therapists of being literalists about memory. What Haaken means is that they accept their client's memory reports as accurate, nonsymbolic representations of past events; and in doing so, they fail to recognize their own contributions to client narratives. I argue that while some of Haaken's criticism of the particular categories used by Herman is compelling, the fact that therapists contribute to memory meaning is not incompatible with survivor testimony. Here, Herman's view is right and important.

Finally, Herman joins with many other therapists in asserting that therapists are not involved in a criminal investigation; therapists are not police, jurors, or detectives. FMSF critics have taken such statements as evidence that therapists are not interested in the truth of client memories. I shall argue that therapists who make such statements are often instead rejecting an inappropriate model of testimony.

In looking at survivors as subjects of therapy, I want to reiterate that while I accept that cases of incompetent and irresponsible therapy have contributed to women's false beliefs about the likelihood or certainty of abuse in their pasts, I have not been convinced of any past or present epidemic of pseudomemories of abuse. I focus here, as elsewhere, on what we need to learn and ask about the social nature of remembering from studying the false memory debates. In the last chapter, I defended the importance of thinking about models of testimony that allow for our dependence on others. In this chapter, I argue that therapy is an appropriate setting for natural testimony, and I address the three arguments (previously outlined) that deny this position. Moreover, while I do not ignore the complications for testimonial positions posed by survivor–therapist relationships, I am persuaded at the present time that we need to defend therapists as an important category of witness for many survivors of childhood sexual abuse.

ADVOCACY AND EXPERTISE

Trauma and Recovery is the most influential feminist account of the psychological consequences of humanly induced trauma: of combat, political imprisonment, torture, rape, domestic assault, and child abuse. It is an analysis of trauma's effects, including a discussion of its impact on memory; an argument for complex posttraumatic stress disorder as a diagnostic category; a guide for those who work with or support survivors of trauma; and an act of witnessing. Herman argues persuasively and eloquently that understanding humanly caused trauma requires broadly based political movements that resist the suppression of survivor accounts, and politically committed witnesses who encourage and acknowledge narratives of harm. Herman clearly believes that feminist therapists can be such witnesses. She opens the book by stating, "Because of my involvement in the women's movement, I began to speak out about the denial of women's real experiences in my own profession and testify to what I had witnessed" (1992, 2). "The testimony of trauma survivors is at the heart of the book" (3).

Herman is committed to the dissemination of survivor testimony through the public witnessing of her writing. Moreover, as her account of the nature and function of trauma narrative is in part inspired by the work of human rights groups with political prisoners, I would argue that the idea of testimonio (discussed in chapter 3) is an important source of inspiration for Herman's descriptions of testimony and is the implicit model for *Trauma and Recovery* as an act of witnessing. Herman describes domestic and sexual violence as politically serious harms that require an urgent response. She calls on therapists to become committed witnesses who not only credit reports of harm denied or mystified by others, but who also bring such reports to public attention, thereby standing against the active forgetting that is often our response to serious wrongs. She writes: "In the telling, the trauma story becomes a testimony . . . . Testimony has both a private dimension, which is confessional and spiritual, and a public aspect which is political and judicial. The use of the word *testimony* links both meanings, giving a new and larger meaning to the patient's individual experience" (181). A larger meaning is only possible if the testimony can be disseminated. Herman's description of the therapist's task involves, of course, not only her public witnessing of client experience but also the expertise and support that she offers directly to the client. The therapist "normalizes the patient's responses, facilitates naming and the use of language, and shares the emotional burden of the trauma" (179).

Lorraine Code writes that the challenge of advocacy is "how testimony-based knowledge can cross the threshold of acknowledgment" (2000, 191), and she believes that good advocacy can meet this challenge:

> Advocacy practices rely for their "goodness" on the expertise of the advocate(s) and their responsiveness to testifiers, who, in their isolation, often require the guidance of others to know what their experiences are. . . . At its best . . . advocacy can counterbalance the patterns of incredulity into which the testimony of marginalized knowers tends to fall. (189)

I shall refer to Code's model as one of testimonial advocacy. Trauma survivors are often isolated, and Herman, with other feminist therapists, seeks to be a good advocate for them in the way that Code's work describes. But Linda Alcoff and Laura Gray (1993) warn feminists about the effect of expert advocacy on the authority of survivor narrative. They challenge us to assess whether survivor narrative, while sometimes politically transgressive, is often mediated in ways that simply reinforce dominant structures. In particular, they argue that experts tend to "recuperate" survivor accounts for dominant understandings.

The authors position survivor speech "in the contradictory space of . . . two claims—that speech is an important object of conflict and that disclosures increase domination" (261). On the one hand, as power relations are partly constituted through control of language, survivor narrative has the power to disrupt such relations. For example, if the implicit rules of our narrative practices prohibit incest survivors from actually speaking about incest, either by requiring corroboration or by categorizing their descriptions as fantasies, a survivor who narrates her experience challenges conventional arrangements about who can speak; she also disrupts dominant meanings by presuming prohibited categories or objects in her account. If a father is socially defined as someone who cares for the welfare of his children and if an incest survivor identifies her father as someone who raped her, her description of a rapist–father challenges the definition of father, parent, child, family, and rapist. How we can articulate our experience to a large extent determines its character; therefore, part of the deep transgressive effect of survivor speech is that categories like "rapist–father" force ways of experiencing the social world radically different from those normalized.

On the other hand, we must be authoritative speakers to effect change, and Alcoff and Gray point out that "in many speaking situations some participants are accorded the authoritative status of interpreters and others are constructed as 'naive transmitters of raw experience'" (264). The authors follow Michel Foucault in arguing that this scenario is certainly the case with any speaking situation that can be structured as a confessional, where a designated spiritual or moral authority exacts our account and then typically interprets the meaning and truth of our experience as its revealing of sin or pathology. Women's attempts to speak about sexual harm have often been such an opportunity; for example, what survivors say has sometimes been used by "the psychiatric establishment to construct victim- and women-blaming explanatory theories for abuse" (262).[2]

The authors conclude that a "primary disabling factor" of subversive survivor speech is the role of the expert/mediator. Survivors must be wary "of helping to create a public discursive arena that confers an a priori advantage on the expert's analysis and credibility over the survivor's" (284); they must also be wary of experts "that position themselves as dominant over a survivor's discourse conceptualized as 'non-theoretical'"(285). Their point is not that survivors should avoid private therapy but that survivors should strategize together to avoid involvement in public discursive events that position others as experts; instead, they should position *themselves* as public experts and theorists about sexual violence. Presumably, feminist therapists who want to avoid complicity in disabling subversive speech should then avoid offering public interpretations of survivor experience, as such acts will position their clients as data. When we apply Alcoff and Gray's imperatives to Herman, we immediately see complications arise; but in order to show that their account has prima facie force against her, we first need to disambiguate an aspect of their view.

It might be wondered whether recuperation is an issue of who does the interpreting or an issue of whether the specific interpretive categories serve dominant interests and meanings. Should Alcoff and Gray's worries apply to accounts like Herman's that, while positioning experts partly as confessors, nevertheless politicize women's experience of sexual violence? Alcoff and Gray are naturally concerned about interpretations that blame or pathologize women, and many of their examples and remarks reflect this concern. I will consider in the next section whether Herman's categories of analysis are recuperative. For now, however, I want to be clear that the deep issue Alcoff and Gray raise is one of the locus of expertise, not one of which particular explanations experts give.

As I understand their argument, Alcoff and Gray contend that the idea of expert analysis, as we discursively structure and interpret it, itself recuperates the experience of survivors of sexual violence to serve dominant understandings. We exercise and respond to expertise through an actual history of how the confessional—"a discourse of truth based on its decipherment"—has shaped discourses of sexuality (Foucault 1978, 67, quoted in Alcoff and Gray, 271). This history, which conditions practices of psychotherapy, social science, and media representation, demands that those who already lack social authority provide their experiences and feelings as raw data for others' theories. As the authors note, the "subjective entities," the experiences and feelings, are regarded as obstacles to theory production unless "they are made sharply subordinate to and contained and controlled by the theory" (280). The consequence of this discursive structure is that those who have the experiences and feelings are regarded as the ones least capable of testifying to their meaning. That feminist therapists like Herman do not blame and try not to pathologize women will presumably not mitigate the survivor–expert dynamic that concerns Alcoff and Gray. The issue is not one of how Herman interprets survivor experience but one of whether her expert voice deauthorizes survivors' own accounts. Moreover, as Alcoff has elsewhere explicitly argued, individual good intentions cannot defeat the power of current discursive arrangements (1991–1992). While Herman may regard herself as an ally to survivor testimony, her expert speaking may lead us to categorize the survivors that she speaks about as nonauthoritative about their experience and as nontestifiers. Alcoff and Gray are not concerned about intentions but about the real effects of speech, and their account gestures to a more general problem with advocacy.

Code positions testimony as the epistemic core of advocacy (2000, 188). But can this epistemic core stay intact in the face of advocacy? When we accept testimony, we believe what is said because we believe in the person speaking. We take them to have authority to speak about the matter in question. But advocacy is characterized precisely by a relation of speaking for those who, in a particular context, cannot speak for themselves. Sometimes, as with legal advocacy, we understand that the need for representation is simply determined by context, that it indicates nothing about the nature of the people advocated for. But as Code herself argues, and as Alcoff and Gray certainly illustrate, advocacy also takes place within and reinforces a political structure where some people, survivors of sexual violence, for example, are discredited as knowers and testifiers. They are understood as dependent on others to have their experiences, perspectives, and concerns represented and interpreted (Code 2000, 185). The structure of advocacy may simply repeat to its audience the very failure of these people to merit positions that are testimonial.

Moreover, particular problems are embedded in advocacy that reports memory testimony. As I argued in chapter 3, the authority of memory testimony is that the person who speaks is the one who was there. When we look at advocacy through the lens of autobiographical memory, we encounter an additional dimension of the problem of speaking for others. Advocacy for someone's remembered experience is not self-representational in the way that gives memory its authority as testimony. Thus, advocacy may doubly deauthorize the memory testimony of survivors. Advocacy represents the survivor as unable to speak for herself, so lacking in the authority to convey information, and the advocate cannot testify as to the survivor's memory and have that memory narrative stand as natural testimony. How can Herman respond to the problems of therapist advocacy? In the next section, I argue that while Herman's use of testimonio is not a wholly adequate response, we should nevertheless follow her initiative in modeling testimony to allow for dependence.

THERAPY AND TESTIMONY

In assuming that expert advocacy can make available the testimony of marginalized knowers, Herman and Code occupy a certain general position on the transmission of testimonial speech, namely, that it can be reported or disseminated while retaining its character as testimony. This position is argued for explicitly by C. A. J. Coady (1992), who points out that the transmission of testimony does not always preserve its authority. For example, in many legal contexts, the transmission of testimony as an attempt to support the truth of its contents is characterized as hearsay. In hearsay, neither the transmitter nor the original speaker succeeds as a formal testifier. The original speaker is neither sworn nor subject to cross-examination, a usual condition of formal testimony. Thus, the original utterance is not subject to the procedures that could affirm it as testimony, and the person who reports the utterance cannot herself witness its truth by relating it to us, even if we trust her credibility.

But Coady contends that the special contextually determined restrictions governing hearsay do not typically apply to natural testimony. I will not repeat his arguments here, but I will support his position by noting that cases of testimonio are precisely cases of successful testimonial transmission. Herman characterizes herself as testifying to the testimony of trauma survivors, witnessing their testimony publicly rather than privately; and, as I have suggested, she relies on the model of testimonio to give political legitimacy and urgency to the project. The problems I've just related with advocacy, the necessary dependence on others who bear witness to the testifier's report of her past, are exactly the sorts of problem testimonio narrative seems to circumvent. I stated in chapter 3 that the recorder of testimonio stands as a counterpart to those of us at a further remove from the narrative. In the case of testimonio, we think of the advocate as herself an individual in the collective mode who as both an interlocutor and a witness represents us and makes possible, through her witnessing, our own sense of solidarity with the narrator.[3] In other words, we imagine ourselves as witnessing direct memory testimony. But many difficulties reside in using political testimonio to model therapist advocacy, even if we assume, as I continue to in this part of the discussion, that women do testify about the past to their therapists.

A therapist bears a unique relation to her client. Her overriding concern is the recovery and safety of her client rather than the urgent political dissemination of her client's testimony. She can act as no one else's representative. In fact, she protects her client from others by shielding her identity; she thus interferes with rather than promotes the intimate relationship between narrator and audience that characterizes testimonio, thereby helping it foster political solidarity. Immediately after her early remarks on testimony, Herman states: "To preserve confidentiality, I have identified all my informants by pseudonyms" (1992, 3). As well the case vignettes that appear in her book are composites "based on the experience of many different patients" (3).

Nor do we read Herman's intent as one of faithfully recording and disseminating her clients' account while protecting their identity. While there are many compelling first-person narratives in *Trauma and Recovery*, they are embedded within Herman's theory. Trauma survivors are not represented as the narrators of testimonio with its insistent "I," who demands our attention, will not be silenced, speaks in a collective voice, and chooses what to tell. It is clearly the intentionality of Herman and not her clients that guides what is said in *Trauma and Recovery*. Laurence Thomas has characterized an ability to bear witness partly as being able to render salient what was salient for the person whose experience we relate (1992–1993). Because *Trauma and Recovery* is a defense of Herman's own theory of trauma, we inevitably suspect that her reporting of clients' experience, what is made salient for us, is shaped by this theoretical agenda. Her work thus seems to repeat the experience–theory binary that concerns Alcoff and Gray.

Finally Coady points out that, in general, successful testimonial transmission depends on our trusting the person who conveys the testimony as a person who can judge well about whether others are speaking the truth. We will not accept narrative as testimonio if we have reason to distrust the recorder's motives or judgment. Over the last decade, feminist therapists' judgments about the veracity of their clients' accounts have been repeatedly called into question. And, as I have already argued, we are not there, even as imaginary interlocutors, to question or press the client about her account of the past. In sum, we have good reason to doubt whether feminist therapy can be political in exactly the way that Herman seems to envision, in a way that uses testimonio as an implicit model for witnessing the harm done to women through sexual violence. Put somewhat crudely, the experts do not stand in for us in the right way, and we no longer trust them, if we ever did, to get it right by themselves.

It is imperative that both survivors and therapists be aware of the political complexities of advocacy and of the real effects of expert speech. The harm to women's testimonial positions since the founding of the FMSF seems to give considerable weight to the imperatives of Alcoff and Gray's analysis. The FMSF has successfully exploited the fact that many survivors seek therapy to represent these survivors as dependent therapeutic subjects and to thereby disqualify them as testifiers. What they say of their pasts is not memory testimony. It yields only anecdotes. A common understanding of therapists' writings, even by feminist commentators, positions survivors as data: "With the advent of claims concerning repressed/recovered memories, alternative accounts of memory function to those offered by cognitive psychologists have emerged. These are derived in large part from the perspective of clinical psychologists, whose 'raw data' are the narratives and observations of the interview room" (Raitt and Zeedyk 2000, 146). Therapists must be aware of the dangers of speaking for clients. They must try to realistically assess the impact of so doing. Yet in conceding how easy it is to represent women's lives as data for experts and their narratives as without authority, I am still prepared to defend Herman's advocacy and her defense of that act.[4]

My response for Herman relies on the importance of her firm representation of survivors as testifiers with the insistence that their testimony is a dependent act that requires politically committed witnesses. This representation has had a force that transcends the issue of whether *Trauma and Recovery* in fact disseminates the testimony of those on whose accounts Herman relies and whether testimonio is a wholly appropriate model to capture the aims of feminist advocacy for survivors of child sexual abuse. Alcoff and Gray's concern is the relation of expert advocacy to deauthorizing women's speech. Herman's defense of advocacy is based specifically on the extent to which it can support testimony, and her account enables survivor testimony in three ways.

First, even if some survivors are not silenced by the expectation of mistrust and disbelief and even if they would and do speak out as individuals and in groups, advocates may be required to open up testimonial opportunities in particular discursive spaces. Herman first began to speak out about what she witnessed within the context of her own profession, and her work continues to speak to her professional peers. Whether you take me or my kind to be credible is often a case of your noting who else will listen to me and believe me. The advocacy of therapists and other professionals makes room for testimony in cultural discursive spaces that have implicit rules about how the speech of others is authorized or credited, rules that often involve endorsement by those who already have authority in those spaces. By relying on testimony and by crediting it as testimony, experts can authorize rather than deauthorize testimonial speech. They can convey to other professionals by their practice, and by their explicit articulation of this practice, such imperatives as "you ought generally to believe women who say they were sexually abused by a relative." Neither modeling testimonial advocacy without engaging in it, nor engaging in it without modeling it, would have this effect. Herman's explicit crediting of survivor narrative as testimony does not make survivors theoreticians in her account; but I would challenge Alcoff and Gray on whether survivors need to be theoreticians in order to avoid being understood as naive transmitters of raw data. Some experts such as Herman may go on to use survivor accounts as evidence for their theories. But to accept these accounts as testimonial evidence about the nature and impact of trauma will set constraints on possible theoretical interpretations of survivor experience. For example, such interpretations cannot falsify or dismiss what survivors say about their lives.

Second, Herman's book is also deliberately written for a wider public, a public of both trauma survivors and of those who might listen. It positions both parties in ways that increase possibilities for effective testimony. Herman's account is premised on the believability of people who say they have been harmed; her account represents survivors as testifiers, and she places them in community with one another, thereby giving individual survivors the power of a collective voice. Those familiar with Herman's account are more inclined to hear survivor testimony as representative. Herman's defense of advocacy also provides explanations for why survivors are not believed, explanations that include "ordinary social processes of silence and denial" and "the active process of forgetting" (9). She challenges the neutrality of her audience, contending that they are already actively engaged in cultural practices that disadvantage testimony. Therefore, either they must rebut Herman or they must defend or reconsider these practices.

Finally, Herman's model of testimonial advocacy offers theoretical resources that survivors can use and have used in theorizing their own experience and testimony, including the suppression and dismissal of their accounts, while testifying to their experience. Many survivors of different types of sexual violence, including Susan Brison (1996) and Aurora Levins Morales (1998b), have found acknowledgment and support for their own testimony and their own practice of survivor advocacy in Herman's analysis. They have used Herman's work to make clear that they are testifying, to find commonalities in their experiences with other survivors and thus to speak collectively, and to call on their readers to support cultural practices of witnessing rather than forgetting.

It might be said that with the exception of the point about Brison and Morales, I have related what Herman tries to do while neglecting Alcoff and Gray's point about the "real politik" of survivor speech. The involvement of many survivors in therapy has certainly been an opportunity to portray survivors of child sexual abuse as generally dependent, as lacking autonomous judgment and an autonomous voice. Moreover, feminist therapists do not have authority themselves with broad sections of the public as witnesses for survivors; they are represented as biased and unreliable, as lacking the virtues of experts. At work here are complex representations of, on the one hand, women's dependence and susceptibility to influence and, on the other, women as inappropriate authorities on the cultural meaning of others' experiences. Alcoff and Gray's concern over expertise and Code's analysis of advocacy point to patterns of speakers and hearers where some people are disadvantaged and rendered nonauthoritative from the start. My response on Herman's behalf does not, of course, dislodge this problem. I contend that we must address what deprives women of testimonial positions when they are in relation to others—in a variety of relational contexts—and we must resist their representation as nontestifiers. Herman contributes to this project through a model of testimonial advocacy that does not take our dependence on others as defeating our narrative autonomy.

Herman attempts to provide: *(a)* a model of testimony (indebted to political testimonio) that takes into account the need for relational circumstances that can support testimony in conditions where people are harmed, isolated, and culturally silenced; and *(b)* a model in which advocacy is necessary to break the conditions of cultural silencing. No such account of relationally dependent testimony will be free of the recuperative possibilities of using the fact of dependence to reinforce a long-standing cultural picture of women as nonautonomous. Though I have argued that Herman's model does not seem entirely apt, given the unique protective nature of therapist–client relations, her theory challenges the perception that our dependencies inevitably compromise our narrative autonomy. It encourages other theorists to develop much-needed accounts of the relational dimensions of testimony. Moreover, good advocacy on the model Code offers will depend on how we respond to imagined others. They are not before us. Whether or not Herman can transmit the testimony of clients, survivors of child sexual abuse are in the background of her account as testifiers who demand witnesses to their testimony. Nevertheless, this very attempt by Herman to place women in the authoritative position of speaking to the truth in their pasts has led to one of the most powerful and compelling feminist criticisms of her work.

HAAKEN'S CRITIQUE OF TRAUMA THEORY

Feminist psychoanalyst Janice Haaken has offered the most trenchant feminist critique of Herman's trauma-oriented approach to therapy and model of survivor testimony. In this section and the next, I draw on Haaken's 1996 article "The Recovery of Memory, Fantasy and Desire: Feminist Approaches to Sexual Abuse and Psychic Trauma" and on her 1998 book on the memory debates, *Pillar of Salt: Gender, Memory and the Perils of Looking Back*. Haaken's assessment of the memory debates is bold, provocative, and often brilliant. Her intent is to "concede some of the ground claimed by the other side—by skeptics and critics of recovered memory—while reclaiming it through a psychoanalytic-feminist analysis" (1996, 1071).[5] Her book answers the call of a number of feminists to look at incest narratives as social memory and to move away from a victimology that oversimplifies the complex psychic life of family and culture (Park 1999, Meyers 1997, Wilson 1999). Haaken's critique of trauma theory as an overarching approach to child sexual abuse is a clear warning to feminists about wholehearted approval of a limited model. But her tendency to oppose interpretation and truth in her account of memory, an assumption that underlies both her critique of Herman and her alternative account of women's memory, prevents her from holding the ground necessary to defend the reality and prevalence of child sexual abuse.

Psychological trauma, as understood by both Herman and Haaken, is the consequence of events experienced as self- or life-threatening, events that cannot be effectively responded to but instead overwhelm "ordinary human adaptations to life" (Herman 1992, 33), resulting in feelings of terror and helplessness. Short- and long-term responses to trauma commonly include any or all of the following: hyperarousal resulting in startle reactions or continuous vigilance; intrusive reactions, including nightmares, flashbacks, and often forms of intrusive sensory memory; and constrictive reactions, including numbing, depression, dissociation, and degrees of amnesia. Herman writes that the human response to threat involves changes in "arousal, attention, perception, and emotion" (34). Traumatic events can cause a long-term disruption in the integration of these functions. Moreover, a traumatized person is often unable to integrate the effects of a traumatic past with an ongoing sense of self, as vividly captured in the trope of "outliving oneself" that Susan Brison (1997) finds common in the writing of those who have survived trauma.

Haaken concedes that categorizing rape, incest, child abuse, and domestic assault as traumatic for women has had a number of salutary effects. Trauma theory has normalized psychiatric symptoms previously regarded as signs of individual pathology (1996, 1076); it has encouraged us to understand the commonalities in how women and men experience harm from very different sources (1081); it has expanded possibilities for recognizing women who have been abused but whose experience is neither transparent nor articulate; and because dissociative responses can preserve memory (albeit in fragmented form), "the model provides . . . a language for articulating the pain and injury of women while preserving the position of women's essential normalcy and rationality" (1078). Women can defend their memories as literal representations of the past. But these benefits come with costs that may weigh equally.

In normalizing responses, we naturally use categories that do support dominant ways of viewing the world. Haaken argues that trauma categories may render women less individually pathological at the cost of recuperating their experience to support unfortunate representations of women's sexual passivity. When the idea of being helpless and overwhelmed, which is key to the trauma model, is applied to women in the context of sexual harm, it can activate deep cultural assumptions: that all women are easily overpowered and damaged by sexual aggression culturally coded as masculine; and that they are innocent, helpless, and in need of rescue (1998, 76). Second, treating all types of trauma under an overarching model, while offering valuable insights into common responses, confutes degrees of harm and masks the variety of victim–perpetrator relationships. Haaken notes, for example, that the trauma model does not resonate with many African-American women's incest narratives, which express complex views about the culpability of black men as perpetrators (1072); nor is the model sensitive to the sense of guilt and complicity that many women feel for having taken pleasure in a special relationship with an incestuous father (1075). Different harmful relationships have their own complex moral and emotional dynamics.

Finally, the expanded possibilities for recognizing abuse come with the increased risk of misinterpreting symptoms. Specifically, and in response to the false memory controversies, Haaken accuses trauma theorists of being naively inattentive to the social symbolic function of visual imagery and memory narrative. She charges that the trauma model, which regards women's memory as literally representing the past in a fragmented form, oversimplifies women's psychic complexity and their narrative agency (1998, 11). The therapist looks for external events to explain women's incest narratives taken as literal truth; in so doing, she often ignores the constrained cultural narrative opportunities that women have for expressing a complex, conflictual, and gendered psychic life. Psychic conflicts may result in the creation of violent sexual imagery for which no external perpetrator is directly responsible through having caused a memory.

As discussed in chapter 3, women's memory narratives have been constrained by women's duty to preserve and transmit familial and cultural values. Haaken argues that, as a form of social memory, incest narratives symbolize a collective "refusal to be appeased" for the amount of harm done to women (1998, 75) while offering individual women a rare opportunity to justify a decisive break with the past in face of the cultural injunction to preserve relationships. This account concedes to the other side that many women's narratives are not literally true. Nevertheless, it reads them not merely as the passive effect of suggestion but as a more active resistance to women's limiting familial and cultural place as dutiful daughters. When reading Haaken, we can easily agree that there are other obvious symbolic functions of incest narratives, that "sexual imagery . . . can communicate a range of experiences and conflicts associated with the body and boundary violations" (1996, 1082). In addition, in order to understand the significance of an incest narrative one might encounter as a therapist, one must attend to the many symbolic functions the narrative might have in the context of that relationship, including the possibility that it is a gift to a therapist whose reputation and expertise involve trauma-oriented therapy with survivors—therapy whose use obviously depends on locating a traumatic event. Without doubt, some cases of misremembered childhood sexual abuse have been at least partly in response to the dynamics of therapy. For example, in *When Boundaries Betray Us* (1993), feminist theologian Carter Heywood describes a temporary belief that she had been abused as a child that arose in the context of a complex relationship with her therapist.

I intend to focus on Haaken's account of memory, but I want first to briefly acknowledge and respond to her other criticisms of trauma theory. Though Herman in fact cautions therapists against thinking that they can rescue patients, *Trauma and Recovery* conveys a sense of mission that allows for a reading of sexual abuse survivors as overly helpless and dependent, an interpretive possibility exacerbated by the effects of advocacy discussed in the last section.[6] Second, Alcoff and Gray's concerns about advocacy and Haaken's critique of Herman's stress on commonalities point to Herman's tendency to overlook many of the emotional and moral complexities of relationships in which individuals and groups are harmed and in which others try to help. Theorizing commonalities is bound to result in this oversight. But while none of us is clear of this particular charge, the appropriate response here is not to defend Herman, but to try to understand and correct the ways in which theories oversimplify, distort, exploit, or appropriate some people's experiences in the service of a common account. Haaken's 1996 article is full of insight about the moral oversimplications of trauma theory.

I am less comfortable, however, with the more dramatic and rhetorical presentation of Haaken's critique in parts of *Pillar of Salt* (1998), a book that concedes, in my view, too much ground to false memory advocacy. Haaken adopts the language of the "memory wars," which she presents as an ideological and theoretical conflict between feminist trauma therapy and scientific psychology. In presenting the sides, she implies that feminists are defensively committed to the "inherent truthfulness" of women's storytelling (11). She uses research premised on the idea that women's false memories are fairly common to support a theory of women's personal narratives that does not commit these narratives to a factual representation of the past.[7] Without attention to the range of feminist responses to false memory advocacy, the critical rejoinders to the research she cites, and the amount of research on amnesia for abuse, Haaken's initial presentation of the memory wars makes it look as if science has settled facts that feminists refuse. Haaken's intent is to disrupt the entrenched positions of both sides by offering a feminist–psychoanalytic perspective as a third way to read women's abuse narratives. Although there is much of value in Haaken's project, her classic hardened presentation of the memory wars leads her to oversimplify a crucial part of Herman's account and to side with the very aspect of a scientific approach to memory that she herself critiques.

Haaken's approach to the memory debates is formulated, on my reading, using Herman's work as a foil.[8] Haaken agrees about the importance of the women's movement in making public incest narratives possible: "The women's movement . . . gave political momentum to the cultural 'recovery' of memory around family violence" (Haaken 1998, 2). In addition, her description of the role of feminism in the rise of controversies over women's memories closely shadows Herman's own account of how she came to write *Trauma and Recovery*:

> Backed by the moral authority of an emerging women's movement, psychotherapists, who were increasingly likely to be women, assisted their female patients in transforming private remembrances into public testimonials. (Haaken 1998, 2)

> The late 1980s ushered in a new era of therapeutic discovery. Whereas earlier accounts of child sexual abuse were based on continuous memories of abuse, by the late 1980s women with no prior known history of abuse began to "recover" such memories in the course of psychotherapy. . . . The many problems of women that, as Betty Friedan noted in 1963, "had no name" were being named as incest. . . . The dysfunctional family was now cast as a battleground, with women and children as the traumatized survivors of domestic wars. (3)

The new authority of the women's movement, the importance of making incest public through testimony, the role of therapists, the ideas of trauma and of commonalities between combat and abuse survivors, the claim that dissociative responses and a disguised presentation are common to sexual abuse survivors; and even the mention of Friedan: all are arguably implicit references to Herman.[9] What is worth noting, however, is that Haaken's description of the application of trauma theory to child sexual abuse is without commitment to survivors as engaged in testimony; rather, they are engaged in a complex cultural "recovery" of incest.

In Haaken's work, "recovery" is a deliberately layered, ambiguous, and generative term. The term associates recovered memory as a feature of the memory wars with popular movements that focus on recovery as personal healing (the "culture of recovery") (1996, 1073) and with Herman's thesis that we must recover our previous understandings of traumatic harm. The quote marks around "recovery" serve the double function of associating these diverse uses ("recovery" is a multiple quotation) while introducing skepticism about women's incest memory. What is also worth noting is that when Haaken aligns the social "recovery" of memories around family violence, which feminism made possible, with therapeutically "recovered" memories, she places all recent incest narratives within a skeptical enclosure. The associations of "recovery," while perhaps intended to encourage a complex, critical, historical analysis, also easily imply a causal link between the suspect excesses of feminist trauma theory and the false memory debates, thus creating the need for alternative feminist approaches—namely, Haaken's own cultural recovery of the complexities of women's storytelling. This rhetorical positioning runs the risk of oversimplifying and too easily discrediting feminist trauma theory. We need to appraise Haaken carefully. There is a great deal at stake in the differences between Haaken and Herman since the notion of women's testifying to the past is absent in Haaken's work.

Haaken's rejection of the language of testimony marks her conviction that trauma theorists' commitment to the testimony of their clients, to objective truth, leads them to adopt an incorrect literalist approach to memory: "The experiential/literalist approach could also be described as a naive realism: essence and appearance are conceived as one and the same" (1998, 10). What Haaken means is that "recovered memories are considered representations of actual events"(10); what the purported memory seems to represent is taken to have actually happened as it is represented. The literalist approach neglects other important possibilities: that memories may be altered in the course of telling or retelling and that we have the capacity to generate imagery or fantasy that has the conviction of memory. To contextualize the first Haaken writes:

> the therapeutic relationship . . . provides its own complex prompts for engaging the past. The questions asked, the responsivity evoked in relation to

> particular themes, the coconstructed memories of the patient's past, all mediate the knowledge that is gained. Much like "priming," therapeutic interpretations sensitize the patient to subsequent meanings and associations in looking back on an unfolding personal history. (251)

As an example of the second, Haaken relates that, when asked by a therapist what past experiences, or "pictures," lead to the description of a parent as morally severe, "the patient is likely to recall real and imagined scenes vivifying this parental imago" (251). A therapist would be naive to assume that what a patient offers in therapy is literal memory.

In her more general description of models of memory, Haaken places trauma theorists and many experimental psychologists, that is, those whom she identifies as adversaries in the memory wars, as still to some extent uncomfortably committed to aspects of what she calls the "old," or "storehouse," model of memory. This model, referred to by John Sutton (chapter 1) as the "archival" model (the term I shall consistently use), conceives of memories as discretely stored images or recordings that correspond to our experiences, images that subsequent occasions of remembering faithfully reproduce. The archival model was, for many decades, the favored model of laboratory researchers who tested for recall of sets of items in ways compatible with the tenets of positivist science: "This tradition assumes that there is an objective reality that can be established and consensually verified, independent of the subjectivity of observers" (Haaken 1998, 43). Put very simply, as the model has been used in the laboratory, the past is rendered objective and permanent through a list of what is to be remembered; that the past is remembered, misremembered, or forgotten can be clearly seen and agreed on by different researchers. Haaken describes the model as minimizing interpretive activity. Haaken, like Middleton and Edwards (discussed in chapter 3), considers types of narrative activity in the context of actual relationships as central to the study of memory processes. But looking at memory as it is actually communicated may leave a researcher confronting multiple alternative viewpoints with no laboratory script as the single ideal object of memory (Haaken 1998, 58).

As a terminological note, I shall use the general term "reconstructivist" for models of memory that deny the viability of the archival model. Haaken's storyteller model is a particular version of a reconstructivist view, one that "places memory processes in the context of narratives and personal relationships" (43). As will be evident in the next chapter, there are different kinds of reconstructivist models, not all of which make narrative important to memory. All do stress, however, that change in memory over time and occasion is a normal feature of remembering.

Herman's *Trauma and Recovery* does highlight the importance of narrative to autobiographical memory. An important insight of trauma theorists, beginning with Pierre Janet, has been that telling a memory transforms it. As elaborated by both Herman and Brison (1997), the choices of vocabulary, of how much to tell, and of narrative ordering transform static and intrusive imagery and thus give a traumatized person a greater sense of mastery over the past. The telling allows the traumatic event to be integrated in an ongoing self-narrative (the event shifts in meaning); and, at the same time, the narrator generates or reestablishes social relationships with others. Trauma theorists not only see that memory can be transformed, they insist on it. According to Haaken, they do not, however, attend to how narratives may be factually inaccurate but symbolically meaningful. Nor do they consider how representations of the past may change in response to the relational demands of an interpretive context, "in response to emerging ideals, concepts, and social alliances" (37), including the demands of a therapeutic alliance. They believe that transformed traumatic memory accurately represents past events.

In a different kind of clinging to old ways, many scientists, including those involved with the FMSF, now explicitly identify themselves as reconstructivists; that is, they explicitly deny the viability of the archival model. Many, including Elizabeth Loftus, concede that narrating memory in relational contexts helps form memory experience, but they regard this as for ill and not good. For Loftus, for example, thinking about the past with others tends to give rise to "story-truth" as opposed to "happening-truth." As the chapter "The Truth That Never Happened" makes clear, story-truth is not real; it is often a distortion of the past, and we should not be satisfied with it (Loftus and Ketcham 1994, ch. 6). In discussing Loftus's recognition of the "vulnerability" of memory to social influence, Haaken notes that objective truth remains a deep concern of her work:

> The fidelity of memory to some original scene—which is assumed to be essentially "true" and unproblematic—is the dominant interest; emotional and social variables are introduced as factors that weaken and impair memory. There is also an implicit individualism in this model in its counterposing of the individual mind and the compromising effects of the social field. The potential for social influences to enhance or potentiate memory in positive ways and the importance of group support in the preservation of collective forms of remembering are missing in this line of research. (1998, 51)

Haaken agrees with Herman that narrative is essential to memory function but rejects the representational transparency of memory. And in contrast to Loftus, she allows the social field to effect memory in positive ways. On Haaken's reading, trauma theorists and false memory advocates remain somewhat committed to the archival model in that they do not disagree that the function of memory is to preserve and accurately represent the past. They simply disagree on how well memory does so.

Haaken thus articulates her difference from the combatants of the memory wars in terms of her unambivalent allegiance to a psychoanalytically informed, reconstructivist, storyteller model of memory that acknowledges and appreciates memory's symbolic content and the high degree of interpretive activity that goes into narrative construction. This allegiance is meant to explain her rejection of literal truth as a primary value of memory narrative. Haaken categorizes "the contemporary fixation on the question of the literal truth of memory" as "a phobic reaction to the irrational and nonrational aspects of mind and of the [false memory] debate itself" (10). She identifies her own "conceptual turn" as one of "shifting the terms of the debate from whether sexual abuse actually occurred to a 'symbolically laden terrain'" (1998, 9). Haaken often continues to talk of truth in memory but not in a way that supports the idea of testimony. She thinks, for example, that false memories can be true in the sense of symbolically revealing structures of conflict that are both cultural and intrapsychic. This use of "true," however, has little to do with the kind of testimonial truth that interests Herman: that is, whether memory narratives give an account of events as they happened.[10]

INTERPRETATION AND TRUTH IN MEMORY

Haaken is wrong to identify Herman's commitment to truth as a naive literalism about memory, where essence and appearance are conceived as one and the same, and in this section I argue that her own separation of interpretation from truth is problematic. Herman does often ignore the possibilities of memory distortion. I do not intend to defend her fully on this point. For example, she does not warn readers that the hypernesia (greater recall) associated with hypnosis may be less accurate than normal remembering (Hilgard 1965, 166), nor does she explain that apparent flashbacks may not, in fact, be flashbacks at all (Schacter 1996, 266–67; Haaken 1998, 53). But what is important to see about Herman's view is the allowance that interpretation can be in the service of representational fidelity, that interpretation and truth are compatible. When trauma survivors testify to the past, the therapist "facilitates naming and the use of language" (Herman 1992, 179). Herman, with other trauma theorists, stresses the amount of conceptualization necessary to integrate traumatic memory in one's ongoing sense of oneself. A survivor needs not only to describe the event but also to find words for her sensations and emotions; she must examine moral questions of guilt and responsibility; and she must, if she is able, "reconstruct a system of belief that makes sense of her undeserved suffering" (178). Much of this interpretation may rely on a therapist's suggestion of concepts and vocabulary that may strike the narrator as apt.

Therapists also sometimes actively encourage a change in the meaning of a memory. Herman relates the story of a rape survivor who is led to re-remember and reinterpret her compliance with her rapists' insistence that she tell them it was the best sex she had ever had "as a strategy that hastened her escape rather than simply as a form of self-abasement" (179). Because they had threatened to rape her again if she did not tell them it was great sex, her saying so did hasten her escape. It was not simply an act of self-abasement.

In Herman's account, memory does and should alter in response to emerging ideals, concepts, and social alliances. A client may in fact be remembering through categories that distort the past in ways that a therapist committed to truth must resist. Herman describes a therapist who works with survivors of the Holocaust. "When survivors speak of their relatives who died, she affirms they were, rather, murdered" (135). For Herman, good interpretation supports truth—personal–historical truth and social–historical truth. In addition, Herman's commitment to testimony does not lead her to ignore the symbolic function of memory. She recognizes, for example, that intrusive memory in flashbacks and nightmares may take on symbolic meaning—the meaning of "keeping faith with a lost person"—explaining a survivor's reluctance to transform and integrate memory (183–84).[11]

Haaken's oversimplified reading of Herman and her elaboration of her own storyteller model are premised on the assumption that to talk, as Herman does, about the (objective) truth of memory, or its accuracy or facticity, is to commit oneself to an inadequate and discredited archival model of memory processing. Her distinction between memory models suggests that if normative interpretations are a part of memory narratives, as they inevitably are, then we will often face multiple perspectives on the past; and when this is the case, we need to move away from a commitment to literal truth, a commitment that could only be secured on a noninterpretive archival model. But a commitment to multiple perspectives on the past does not rule out some accounts being true of the past and some not. In addition, there may be more than one way of truly relating what happened and more than one level of significance to the events related.

These points should be somewhat familiar from discussions in previous chapters. In contesting Borland's interpretation of her memories, Hanson finds a different significance to her past—she remembers herself as an independent woman who was no feminist. Moreover, in keeping with the way she has described memory models, Haaken seems to take a distinction between literal expression and symbolic representation to correspond to a distinction between truth (as transparent correspondence) and significance or importance (as in need of interpretation). As stated earlier, she wants to shift the discussion from whether abuse occurred "to a 'symbolically laden terrain'" (9). Haaken's sharp contrast between the literal and symbolic, with its associated implication that in investigating the symbolic, we leave behind the considerations of truth and accuracy, is misguided. The literal expression of memory may be, itself, a symbolically laden terrain. Particular autobiographical memories may symbolize a time in our lives, an important relationship or its loss, or a life-altering choice or event. For example, Diane Ackerman relates the memory of smelling eucalyptus at a flower market in New York. This scent memory symbolizes one of the happiest times of her life, a time spent marking Monarch butterflies in California, a time made happy partly because the scent of eucalyptus transported her back to the comforting medicinal smells of her Illinois childhood. Ackerman's narrative of how combined scent memories endowed eucalyptus "with an almost savage power to move [her]" (Ackerman 1996, 22) is an interlayering of symbolically rich memory that is at the same time a literal description of the events of her past. Passages in Haaken affirm that the literal expression of memory can have complex symbolic meaning, but these passages always contain what she would consider an advance and what I would consider a retreat from an interest in the objective truth of the past.

We will, I contend, simply take Ackerman's account as natural testimony. If, when pressed, we say we are not interested in whether Ackerman really was in California, we are certainly not driven to this position by the fact that her memory is symbolically rich, but rather by our assessment of the contextual significance of truth as a value in assessing her narrative. We may think that no value of Ackerman's narrative depends on how faithfully she relates her past. I make this point to show where Haaken's account goes most deeply wrong. She leaves truth with a particular model of memory.

Haaken's critique of memory psychology is excellent. She picks out and forefronts a tendency that is key to diagnosing the inadequacy of contemporary accounts of memory. Scientists have tended to move toward a reconstructivist account of memory, but in doing so, they regard the relational dimensions of remembering as an inevitable source of distortion. Why is this the case? Haaken's analysis does not forefront the cause and subject it to equal scrutiny. The reconstructivist model has been explicitly adopted by scientists because the amount of variation and error in memory rules out simplistic versions of an archival theory as an adequate model for normal memory functioning (Brewer 1998). The key interest of a reconstructivist like Loftus is in locating sources of error and distortion. But error in memory is also the justification for Haaken's adoption of the storyteller model. Storytelling is introduced as "an alternative way of approaching the seeming human tendency towards error-proneness" (1998, 54), the "mountainous evidence that remembered events may not always be factually correct" (110). Haaken's mistake is in assuming that because the move to a more narrative model of memory has been contingently motivated by the recognition of memory error, insofar as the model can be used to support a theory of good remembering, such remembering will not have truth as one of its values. Haaken's move to storytelling is tantamount to failing to reject the storehouse model via leaving the notion of objective truth governed by it. If we see the move to a narrative account as an explanation and model for memory error governed by an understanding of truth that is derived from the storehouse model, we will not recognize the ways in which a narrative view is compatible with objective truth.

On the one hand, Haaken does not consider that Herman's commitment to objective truth is one compatible with, rather than at odds with, a sensitivity to the ways interpretation shapes memory. On the other, for Haaken to claim that the social can potentiate memory in a good sense but to give up all talk of objective truth seems to me a problematic rendering of the ideal of good social influence. It is especially unfortunate given the testimonial demands of so many of the contexts in which people narrate memory, including, of course, the testimonial demands of contexts in which we talk about the harm done to us by others. Haaken clearly sees the problem with memory science, but she doesn't see her own repetition of its assumptions; she doesn't see that she, like Loftus, continues to be governed by an understanding of truth derived from a model that she repudiates. What Haaken really needs to reject is the picture of objective truth as simple correspondence that she identifies with the archival model.

The defect of contemporary approaches to memory—that is, their endorsement of a norm for memory accuracy derived from a model of remembering that they reject—is consistently missed or misdiagnosed because scientists are represented and represent themselves primarily as critics of naive approaches. Shelley Park (1997), for example, in a thoughtful epistemological assessment of the false memory controversies, calls into question the adequacy of both the archival and reconstructivist models. Park identifies the archival view of memory as committed to a naive correspondence about truth. The ease with which we think of memories as visual representations tempts some theorists to speak as though our memories literally mirror the events of our past. Because memory has not been a central topic in contemporary epistemology, it has benefited little from the more general rejection of naive correspondence. Park writes that experiments "illustrating pseudomemory creation" (15) have challenged this naive realism by showing that memory is active and reconstructive. Confronted by science, those who want to defend the "truth" of recovered memories have thus sometimes been moved to give up objective truth for values like narrative coherence, values they might refer to as subjective, narrative, or experiential truth.

Park considers both alternatives unpalatable. In the face of science, feminists cannot affirm naive realism; nor, as cultural critics, can we abandon objective truth. We need it. Park claims rightly that we must examine the starkness of our options. But she also warns that we cannot retreat to the deceptively easy allowance that *(a)* some seeming recovered memories are false and caused by therapists while *(b)* some are representationally faithful memories caused by earlier experience and merely triggered by therapy. Her reasons for this warning bear examination. She contends that the frameworks of psychology and naive clinical practice are incompatible: "the model of memory utilized by Loftus and her colleagues suggests that recovered memories as described by clinical therapists are not only unlikely, but impossible" (1997, 32); that is, their possibility would depend on the correctness of the archival model.

In Park's account, the mistaken commitments about memory are allied with recovered memory theorists, not with scientists. Her reading places therapists in the position of trying to defend the truth of a client's past by affirming naive mirroring or by abandoning historical truth. Loftus's work, from within the experimental framework, is discussed only as a corrective to the naive view, rather than as a theory of truth in memory. I would respond to Park that Loftus's sole focus on error and distortion as her understanding of reconstruction shows that the naive realist model (archival) and the experimental model (reconstructivist), as we now encounter them, do not have incompatible commitments about truth in memory. The reconstructivist view endorsed by Loftus has no resources within its acknowledgment of the interpretive dimensions of memory narrative to talk about truth; it remains wedded to an understanding of truth governed by the naive correspondence that it rejects as a possible account of how memory actually functions in the world.[12] Given the complexity of memory and memory activities, I am very doubtful that any single version of an archival or reconstructivist model will be an adequate representation of memory; and in the next chapter, I use historical work on memory to argue that we must be very cautious both of the current claims about a necessary transition in models and of the current optimism about a single adequate one.

In summary: for Haaken, the move to an interpretive view is through error; for Herman, good interpretation supports truth. I think Herman is absolutely right. I share the conviction with Park that feminists cannot move from allowing the fact of bad therapeutic influence to an account of memory narrative that is no longer concerned with objective truth. Such a move can only further discredit women's abuse narratives. Haaken states that we should avoid the temptation to oversimplify women's stories by closing ranks around a plausible version of the truth (1998, 9). One doesn't have to endorse the inherent truthfulness of all trauma narratives in order to think that women ought to be and are concerned with the truth. Haaken seems to me right about some of the other functions of abuse narratives. Women lack narrative opportunities and resources to articulate diverse and complex forms of sexual and familial harm. This lack of resources may explain why many women do review their past wondering whether it was abusive and conclude, sometimes rightly, sometimes wrongly, that it was or that it wasn't. But I think we must close ranks around the idea that the truth matters. Why think that it doesn't to those in therapy?

THERAPISTS ARE NOT DETECTIVES

In 1982, Donald Spence, later an FMSF advisory board member, published *Narrative Truth and Historical Truth: Meaning and Interpretation in Psychoanalysis.* Spence's famous work is a critique of the idea that client narratives yield historical truth. He argues that therapy is an interpretive process, one that yields a coherent and compelling narrative of the client's past that should not be mistaken by the therapist or by the client for literal, historical truth. Spence's distinction between historical truth and the "narrative truth" of a good story commits therapists to a reasonable interest only in narrative coherence, or narrative fit, on the inadequate grounds that interpretation is incompatible with truth. It also commits historians, unrealistically, to the project of discovering a clear unambiguous truth to the past, immune from either irreconcilably different perspectives or serious doubt about the adequacy of their interpretive categories. As Loftus's distinction between happening-truth and story-truth shows, many FMSF writers, as well as many other commentators on memory, have depended on Spence's work to secure a separation between interpretation and truth, a separation I have argued against.[13] What interests me here is that, as Park points out, therapists have also sometimes depended on a distinction like Spence's to explain their practice (Frawley-O'Dea 1999); or at least they have seemed to disavow an interest in objective truth as a part of therapeutic practice.

Herman writes that "the therapist has to remember that she is not a fact finder and that the reconstruction of the trauma story is not a criminal investigation" (1992, 180). Margo Rivera states that "my focus was not on accuracy or corroboration; they were not taking anyone to court" (1999, 21). Frawley-O'Dea writes that the truth of a client's past is often "not always a truth that can be proven 'beyond a reasonable doubt' in a courtroom" (1999, 85). Such statements have often been read by the FMSF as a self-damning indifference by therapists to the truth of the past. Loftus uses Herman's remark to introduce Spence. In the same breath therapists have stated that "it is the client who must be free to choose the words with which to give voice to her own internal states" (Frawley-O'Dea 1999, 86) and that "only she has the right and responsibility to decide what happened and what it meant" (Rivera 1999, 33), perhaps seeming to endorse the idea of "subjective truth" or narrative coherence as a norm for good therapy narratives. I agree with Park that therapists make a mistake when they replace truth with narrative fit, but I also think their apparent rejection of truth often misrepresents their practice. Rather than rejecting truth, I suggest they may often be struggling to articulate the inadequacy of a quasi-legal model of testimony as an appropriate way to conduct therapy.

Therapists confront questions about the truth of their clients' past because seeking clarity about the past is an important motivation for therapy; and it may be especially so for clients with an abusive past. Frawley-O'Dea writes that "chronic doubts about what did and did not happen, along with a persistent inability to trust one's perceptions of reality, are perhaps the most permanent and damaging long-term effects of childhood sexual abuse" (83). The character of sexual abuse "drags the issue of what really happened into the foreground of the therapeutic encounter" (82). For Herman, "The fundamental premise of the psychotherapeutic work is a belief in the restorative power of truth-telling" (181), and the client's commitment to tell the truth is an essential part of the therapy contract. Elizabeth Waites, one of the few therapists to examine and explicitly reject Spence's distinction, maintains that "clients who are used to the subversion of their memories by dismissive people are likely to be dismayed rather than reassured" by a therapist who thinks that truth does not matter (1997, 158). She contends that "however doubtful a memory, the distinction between memory and fantasy is so significant for most people that it continues to guide the process of the search" (14) for a personal past, and that "the difficulties in sorting out facts can be acknowledged without discouraging attempts to do so" (158).

These therapists show a respect for a client's desire to go forward with clarity about the past. Remarks that repudiate the role of a police officer or juror may just reflect their sensible conviction that the juridical model of assessing testimony is not always a good way to get at the truth; in fact, we have reason to think it is a bad way when potential testifiers struggle with a high degree of self-doubt. E. B. Brownlie writes:

> For most people, therapy is a setting that allows a number of possibilities to be freely explored, a place where contradictions are allowed to exist. I think I would have found it much more difficult to say things I was unsure about in therapy and to explore my own beliefs and doubts, if I thought that everything I said about abuse would be permanently recorded. Given the difficulties I had coming to believe myself, I probably would have avoided admitting that I no longer thought something I said some weeks ago was true, if I knew it would be on record that I had taken it back. I wonder how often I would have garnered the courage to say something that I thought was a possibility, but not a certainty, or to cast doubt on something that I had been certain about before. (Brownlie 1999, 48)

Relatedly, in stressing the importance of the client's own narrative perspective, many therapists may be emphasizing that the point of therapy with survivors of childhood sexual abuse is to help restore and foster client autonomy. Culbertson (1995) and Brison (1997) articulate the importance of telling what happened as contributing to a survivor's restored sense of self as someone who tells her own story, someone who is no longer the object of an assailant who disrupts and violates the course of her life. A survivor's renewed sense of herself as a subject cannot be achieved without our commitment to her intentionality guiding her narrative. This commitment to survivor intentionality need not deny that narratives are co-constructed. Co-construction is the norm for autobiographical speech, and it does not settle issues of narrative authority. Hanson's narrative is co-constructed with Borland, and Hanson challenges whose intentionality counts in this construction. She refuses to be made into a feminist, and she insists that her own intentionality guide the presentation, not "what pleases" Borland. But though Borland compromises on the presentation of Hanson's narrative, she also acts as a social historian who prefers her own account. In contrast, the client's own narrative perspective remains crucial in therapy in ways that it might not in other truth-seeking endeavors. In caring about client autonomy, a therapist cannot simply prefer an interpretation that a client insists is at odds with her self-understanding.

Therapists do appropriately take a great deal of what their clients say as natural testimony, even while assisting these clients in achieving greater clarity on their past. We have no reason to believe that people who seek therapy are especially deceptive or self-deceptive; a client's desire to engage another's perspective may even count as some evidence against this assumption. Moreover, expressions of reflection, doubt, and confusion about what was the case do not count against the good critical faculties that we seek in natural testifiers; in fact, they are often evidence of their exercise. We understand what it is for people to be qualified to speak on a matter while leaving room for them to express doubts and to revise their understandings, and we do not require that the ways in which they express themselves should correspond exactly to the categories through which we understand what they say. There is an interactive, interpretive dimension to all occasions of speech, including occasions of natural testimony. Finally, although we do not automatically regard natural testimony as having a public juridical dimension, therapists like Herman have no reason to avoid taking and portraying their clients' accounts of harm as representative, thereby giving their testimony a larger, collective, and more political meaning.

Although clients in therapy may not be especially deceptive, they may certainly be vulnerable to influence, and there are limits on what we regard as influence compatible with natural testimony. What I have resisted in this chapter is the general claim that the interpretive dimensions of therapy should lead us to give up the idea that women are predominantly natural testifiers in this context. Therapists can both appropriately believe much of what their clients say and accept "as inevitable the therapist's influence on the particular constructions of meaning that emerge for the client" (Frawley-O'Dea 1999, 82).[14] Herman, Frawley-O'Dea, and Waites all caution therapists against premature certainty and the risks of overinterpretation. They insist that part of a therapist's task is to sometimes encourage clients to resolve the past by learning to live with doubt and uncertainty.

Haaken's critique of literal truth as in tension with interpretation and the symbolic function of memory leads her to avoid speaking of women as testifying to harm in therapy. I want finally to reemphasize the cost of sacrificing talk of women's testimony.[15] In the section of *Pillar of Salt* entitled "Recovering Historical Memory," Haaken writes: "My main argument is that the reality of sexual abuse and incest in women's collective history gives rise to the legendary and social symbolic use of the idea of intimate invasions of the self" (1998, 108). She makes the explicit assumption that child sexual abuse is no longer incredible (3), but I find it difficult to endorse this assumption in light of the last decade's skepticism. As I have made clear and will continue to, cases of recovered memory are not the only ones implicated in current skepticism. I have pointed out, for example, that even in Haaken's text, all recent incest narratives become skeptically bracketed. Haaken's book does not detail the present reality of incest and sexual abuse, and we must now also assume that discussions of abuse take place in a less acknowledging context. My concern is not with Haaken's project of theorizing the social meaning of incest narratives, which I think is important; rather, my concern is with how well this project can be realized if we do not undertake it with an understanding that women are testifiers to child sexual abuse in many contexts, including therapy. Because Haaken does not see how to unite interpretive contexts with truth-telling ones, her work does not provide this understanding—and there is a cost. In John Sutton's very positive review of Haaken's book (2000), neither the current nor the historical reality of abuse is identified as affecting women's memories. Rather than repeating Haaken's reasonable view that the false memory debates have paid too little attention to women's psychological complexity, Sutton summarizes Haaken's positive account of female remembering as intending to help women "confront the genuine but mundane problems of everyday existence."[16] In the absence of any acknowledgment by Sutton of the present and past reality of child sexual abuse, only mundane problems, and not child sexual abuse, are genuine.

Suppressing doubts and closing ranks "around a plausible version of the truth" are not our only options. The lack of a present reality about child sexual abuse may be a consequence of the decline, as speaking subjects, of women who are abused. As we move to thematically exploring women's memory, I find it vitally important that we keep a keen critical grip on how we have been made skeptical of their narratives. In the next chapter, I continue this project by looking at how women are represented as suggestible in false memory writings.

CONCLUSION

The value of Coady's work is in pointing out that trust in what others tell us is a baseline attitude for getting around in the world. The FMSF has highlighted therapy as a context of dependency to raise concern about whether women who seek therapy can be trusted as testimonial agents about abuse and, more generally, whether the truth of the past can emerge when others are influencing our understandings. In this chapter and the last, I have been concerned with the authority of narrative positions. I have argued that feminists must continue to offer alternative models of testimony that allow for our reasonable dependence on others. I have also argued that a common kind of relational dependence—the contribution of others' meanings to our memory narratives—may aid, rather than hinder, our attempts to understand the past. Even theorists as sophisticated as Haaken have difficulty in allowing both the interpretive and testimonial dimensions of autobiographical memory without placing them in conflict. We need, however, to be able to talk about memory as both interpretive and true. In order to leave it possible for people to testify to harm, we need quite generally to rescue witnesses to testimony from the untenable position of thinking that their attention and questions inevitably corrupt or distort what they hear. In later chapters, I will continue to argue that reliance on the perspectives of others is necessary to good remembering and that the disturbing portrait of gendered suggestibility that emerges in false memory writings misleads us about exactly this point.

NOTES

1. The discussions in this chapter have benefited from working with Jennifer Epp, whose master's thesis is on feminist advocacy (Epp 2002).

2. Linda Alcoff and Laura Gray's extended illustration of a recuperative discursive structure involves a survivor's attempt to use a television talk show as an opportunity to say something useful to other women struggling with the aftermath of campus date rape. She becomes instead "an object of analysis and evaluation for experts and media-appointed representatives of the masses" (274).

3. In other words, in testimonio, both the address and the position of the facilitator are metonymic.

4. Linda Alcoff and Laura Gray's intent is to "reconfigure the practices and meaning of expertise towards legitimating survivor discourse" (263)—to get it accepted as both experiential and theoretical, as expert and authoritative. As the authors identify as survivors, their text is not just an argument for this position but the performance of their claims. We could fairly argue that Herman could reconfigure practices of expertise more radically. An example of a text more alert to Alcoff and Gray's concerns is Toni Laidlaw and Cheryl Malmo (1990), where the reflections of feminist therapists and of their clients are both represented.

5. Though I criticize an important aspect of her view, her book, like Judith Herman's, is essential reading for those interested in contemporary accounts of memory.

6. Writers like Susan Brison (1997) have managed to make use of Herman's model while stressing the resilience of many survivors.

7. In three separate footnotes (chapter 1, notes 6, 10, and 15), Janice Haaken refers to D. Stephen Lindsay (1994), Elizabeth Loftus and Katherine Ketcham (1994), D. A. Poole and others (1995), and Michael Yabko (1994b). These references support the claims that "there are compelling bases to FMSF concerns over therapeutic influences" (Haaken 1998, 23) and that most accounts of new memories "involve the use of 'memory-enhancement' techniques" (24). These authors are all also used by the FMSF in support of these same claims. The responses to this work need to be considered in order to come to a balanced view of how much grounds for concern there are about psychotherapy. See, for example, Kenneth Pope (1996, 1997); James Chu and others (1999); and Daniel Brown, Alan Scheflin, and D. Corydon Hammond (1998). I argue throughout this manuscript that we must not let grounds for reasonable concern lead to an inflated representation of either memory error or women's susceptibility to influence.

8. Judith Herman is not *explicitly* referred to in chapter 1. The text to which Janice Haaken makes explicit reference is *The Courage to Heal* (Bass and Davis 1994).

9. See Judith Herman's introduction and chapter 1, "A Forgotten History." The reference to Betty Friedan, echoed in Janice Haaken, is on page 28.

10. For example, on pages 39–41, Janice Haaken relates an encounter with her mother that has several different layers of meaning for her on the different occasions when she relates the memory. Not completely sure of the conversation, she refers to it as a "memory/fantasy" and concludes, from the range of interpretations, that "the truth of memory is intimately related to how it is deployed" (42). But there is a confusion here. Both a memory and an imagining can have multiple layers of meaning. To hold that memory has layered significance is compatible with holding that whether the event really happened is relevant to the assessment of the truth of the memory. Haaken uses the fact of different interpretations of a memory to back away from concern about its objective truth.

11. Judith Herman also allows that testimony can take place in highly figurative language that requires not just interpretation by deciphering (127).

12. The key defect may be methodological: the belief that attention to error and distortion can by itself yield an account of good remembering.

13. Richard Ofshe also makes considerable reference to Donald Spence (Ofshe and Watters 1994, ch. 2). For other commentators' use of Spence, see Janice Haaken (1998, 72) and David Pillemer (1998, 10).

14. "The questions we ask, the theories through which we filter data given to us by the client . . . our own personalities and predilections as professionals and as people cannot help but contribute to the client's eventual understanding of herself" (Frawley-O'Dea 1999, 82).

15. Although Janice Haaken endorses a view of memory that is meant to affirm women's agency, women are often reduced to therapeutic subjects in her work. She writes, "my own reading of female autobiographical memory speaks to both the blunting side of female oppression and its generative effects, particularly for those middle class women who constitute much of the subject matter of the psychology of women. As defined by class and race as by gender, women patients and psychological subjects express the contradictions and tensions of their social locations" (1998, 13). Middle-class women here quickly become therapeutic subjects as they slide from psychological subjects into women patients with their narratives as data for expert interpretation but without the narrative authority to interrupt or contest such interpretation.

16. This quote is apparently from Janice Haaken. The point here is that Haaken makes such remarks from within an acknowledgment of child sexual abuse as a serious problem. John Sutton repeats them without situating them in this context.

5

"THE FEELING OF IDENTITY IS QUITE WANTING . . . IN THE TRUE WOMAN": MODELS OF MEMORY AND MORAL CHARACTER

Diana Russell's *The Secret Trauma: Incest in the Lives of Girls and Women* (1986/1999) is perhaps the most well-regarded study of the prevalence and nature of child sexual abuse in the United States. Using data gathered in 1978 from a random sampling of 930 women in San Francisco, Russell reported that 16 percent of the respondents disclosed sexual abuse by a relative before the age of eighteen and that 38 percent disclosed at least one experience of child sexual abuse (xvii). Russell's figures have been widely accepted as an accurate statistical picture of child sexual abuse in the mid-1980s. Over the last decade, however, a sense of direct encounter with the voices and experiences of women with abuse in their pasts has been steadily annulled by the dramatic shift in attention to memory confabulations and memory processes. This effect is striking to me, and it is one of the most disturbing consequences of the false memory debates. It has taken place in a complete absence of agreement about how many women have misremembered or confabulated abuse in their pasts, and it has taken place with too little attention by theorists to how we are now thinking about women.

Women who have been abused have simply disappeared from much of the writing that now frames our attention to child sexual abuse, and there are two reasons why this is so. First, Fiona Raitt and Suzanne Zeedyk comment that because "the psychological community regards the issue as one of cognitive function," as one of the nature of memory processes, a great many articles on false and recovered memory do not even mention child sexual abuse; and they make little attempt to situate an analysis of false memory syndrome within the context of child sexual abuse (2000, 140–41). If child sexual abuse is not the issue, the testimony of women who have been abused has become oddly irrelevant to a debate that has such serious implications for their credibility. Second, women who have been abused have often been replaced in false memory writings by women who misremember or confabulate abuse. There is an obvious ethical issue regarding how our attention to child sexual abuse is currently being framed, one that John Read (chapter 1) tried unsuccessfully to raise in New Zealand. The problem is not just that our skepticism about women's claims of abuse has been quickly normalized; the problem is also the increasing absence to us of women who have been abused as moral agents to whom we owe our response. It may seem though that discussing memory processes and situating women as confabulators are quite distinct ways in which writers on the memory debates can fail to talk about women who have been abused. Moreover, we may be less concerned about the former, thinking that it is reasonable for scientists interested in general features of human cognition to concern themselves just with memory processes. I shall argue, however, that these two forms of disappearance are often very closely connected.

In this chapter, I return to the writings of people directly associated with the FMSF to explore some of the links between memory and personhood introduced in chapter 2. Specifically, I investigate how skepticism about women's memories, as expressed in false memory writings, interacts with representations of women as persons and selves. I agree with a number of commentators that dismissing the existence of the FMSF as mere backlash to activism about child sexual abuse is an oversimplified and inadequate response, one that refuses to grapple with a number of important issues about memory. I maintain that one of the issues that we must grapple with is the phenomenon of cognitive undermining. That false memory syndrome pathologizes women has been widely acknowledged; however, little recognition has been given to the representations of women as failed rememberers and failed selves that descriptions of false memory syndrome exploit.

I am particularly concerned with representations of women as lacking a cohesive identity. In April 1992, the Nova Scotia Court of Appeal set aside the sexual assault conviction of Kenneth Ross and ordered a new trial based on evidence about the complainant's past, including her psychiatric file. One week after Ross's conviction was set aside, Lyman Nickerson, convicted of sexually assaulting a woman three times and threatening to kill her, asked the Court of Appeal for access to his victim's psychiatric records, claiming they showed that the woman might have multiple personality disorder (*Halifax Chronicle Herald*, May 1, 1993). Nickerson's strategy, rejected by the Court of Appeal in this case, was to suggest that his accuser lacked a sufficiently integral self to be a reliable testifier to her past.

I shall argue that there is a systematic discrediting of women that is parasitic on the fact that a rememberer, self, person, and responsible agent mark a single cultural location. I first examine a historical example of this strategy in the work of the notorious Viennese philosopher Otto Weininger. Weininger links women's untruthfulness to their incapacities as rememberers and their resultant weakness of identity. Though I shall show that Weininger's view, while remarkably developed, is in many ways not a unique historical representation of women, I do not claim that Weininger's work has any direct line of influence to the writings of the FMSF. Weininger's work interests me because it offers a clear and detailed historical precedent for the strategy of discrediting women as rememberers by arguing they have a weak sense of self. I then show the opportunistic revival of this kind of strategy in the FMSF's writings through the creation of false memory syndrome as a new identity pathology. The discrediting is often masked through the claim that the FMSF's writings are about memory, not about child sexual abuse or women. One conclusion of my reading of this literature, however, is that it is easy to personify and symbolize memory in ways that discredit women as rememberers. Our picture of memory is also our picture of rememberers. In the final sections, using the historical distance provided by studies of early modern theories of the mind, I examine how a stereotype of women's suggestibility is helping to shape contemporary reconstructivist accounts of memory in ways that can and should be resisted.

My intent is to isolate a representation of women that I take to be at the heart of accusations of false memory syndrome and to draw attention to its cognitive and moral undermining of women. I contend that this stereotype profoundly disrespects women as persons, and concern about the accuracy of recovered memories in no way licenses it. When this stereotype begins to inform our models of memory, we must also be critical and cautious about the direction of these models. Finally, in identifying this stereotype, I introduce the themes that dominate the second half of this study. What does it really mean to say that women are suggestible? What kind of representation of women in relationships is conveyed through this alarm? How does this representation reciprocally affect the models of memory we are prepared to endorse, and on which groups will these models have their effect?

DO WOMEN HAVE A SENSE OF SELF?

Otto Weininger's *Sex and Character* (1906/1975) was first published in German in 1903 in response to the emancipation movements for women at the end of the nineteenth century. The book is misogynist, anti-Semitic, and racist; but it was influential from the time of its publication until the Second World War, going through nearly twenty-five editions in the interwar years (Harrowitz and Hymans 1995, 8). In the introductory essay to *Jews and Gender: Responses to Otto Weininger*, the authors note that "Weininger's . . . impact on his own generation and the next was widespread," citing Ludwig Wittgenstein, Karl Klaus,

Elias Canetti, Sigmund Freud, Franz Kafka, Hermann Broch, James Joyce, D. H. Lawrence, and Gertrude Stein as among those influenced (5). In *The Feminine Character: History of an Ideology* (1946/1971), Viola Klein chose Otto Weininger as one of the prominent theorists of female nature and character whose work she examined in depth. He is her representative of a philosophical approach.

I use Weininger to draw attention to an account of women and memory that explicitly makes the case that women are not competent rememberers or testifiers because they lack a sense of self. Weininger's compelling presentation illuminates the contemporary reconstruction of this same figure of woman in FMSF writing. FMSF writers present their views on women and memory as if these views were the outgrowth of important new scientific research on memory. Crucial to an analysis of the foundation's work is to see that these writings actually offer a variation of a quite specific and historically precedented strategy for discrediting women. Through a comparison of the two sets of writings, I hope to lift the strategy into clearer view. Moreover, *Sex and Character*, like false memory writings, calls on the sciences of its day—zoology, botany, evolutionary theory, and psychology—as support for distrust of women's narratives. Appeals to science dangerously bolstered the public appeal of Weininger's writing, obscuring the fact that the alarm raised depended on accepting a stereotype of women as sexualized, dependent, and suggestible. Similarly, the appeal to science in false memory writings allows the public to endorse the foundation's use of false memory syndrome without taking adequate responsibility for the stereotype that this alleged pathology embeds.

Weininger's intent in *Sex and Character* is to lay out a Kantian-inspired theory of the moral position of Aryan man in the universe while at the same time refuting the possibility of the emancipation of women. As men and women embody complementary psychological principles that explain their different destinies, each can only be fully understood in contrast to the other. Thus Weininger proceeds by a characterization of male and female as ideal types. Although actual men and women are a mix of male and female and although Weininger contemplates that whole races might consist of "intermediates," his analysis blurs the distinction between male and female as types and as people. Moreover, Weininger claims never to have "seen a single woman who was not fundamentally female" (188). I shall thus take Weininger to be referring to actual men and women in the discussion that follows on the understanding that he is restricting his analysis to Christians of Aryan descent.

The most morally significant difference between male and female psychology concerns memory, and Weininger considers his reflections on memory and ethics to be one of the most original and important aspects of his work. I believe that Weininger has a right to this claim. He recognizes that memory is not just a biological capacity but has important connections to value through our ability to form and maintain an individualized self. The development of this idea is more detailed and interesting in Weininger's work than it is in Locke's work. As well, Weininger may be articulating embedded cultural connections among women, memory, and identity that other theorists have not made explicit and that need our attention.

According to Weininger, the fundamental difference between men and women, the difference that accounts for the destiny of each, is that men's thoughts are clear and detailed while women's are not. "Clearness of consciousness is the preliminary condition for remembering" (114); and remembering for Weininger, as for Locke, is the cognitive ability key to personhood through its links with morality. Weininger goes on to elaborate the relation between being a rememberer and occupying a moral position in the universe through the figure of the genius, which he thinks represents "ideal masculinity in its highest form" (113). For Weininger, genius is the moral zenith of personhood and a position to which every man can aspire (183). It "is identical with the highest and widest consciousness" (111), one in which the impressions of experience are so detailed and bold that they cannot help but become comprehensive memory. The genius "is the mind for which everything is unforgettable" (116). Because "the extent to which a man can detect differences and resemblances must depend on his memory" (117), memory also fits men for the moral life in ways additional to Locke's interest in responsibility. The ability to detect differences and resemblances enables men to formulate principles and apply rules.

In Weininger's work, memory has multiple connections to a sense of self. Because of comprehensive memory, the genius's sense of self is characterized by a high degree of continuity and integration. He can see how every incident in his life has contributed to his development; and in understanding his present through the detail and trajectory of his past, he experiences each event as deeply significant and thus sees himself as highly individual and as having a destiny (126–27). In addition, because the holding together of past and present makes it possible for a man to free himself from time—memory is a kind of time travel—the genius can experience himself as a pure "I," a center and subject of consciousness. Finally, maximal personhood is associated with the ability to occupy a certain narrative position, which in Weininger's day would have been regarded as testimonial. In chapter 2, I linked our abilities to form a self and to be regarded as a person and moral agent to our opportunities for self-narrative activity. These links are explicit in Weininger's account. The comprehensive memory of genius leads to a reverence for the past and for the truth that often gives rise to the desire to write an autobiography, "always the sign of a superior man" (126).

The psychic life of women, by contrast, is characterized by a series of vague impressions that are too imprecise to remember; Weininger introduces the term "henid" for these impressions. There is no recollection of henids; they are too vague; thus, strikingly, women have little or no memory (114). Because women have little memory, they have only the vaguest sense of self: "The feeling of identity in all circumstances of life is quite wanting in the true woman" (146); "her experiences float past without being referred, so to speak, to a definite permanent centre; she does not feel herself, past and present, to be one and the same throughout her life" (146). The next stage of Weininger's argument contains a very interesting twist to what looks like his Lockean theory of personal identity. Weininger elaborates on the consequences of vague memory and vague identity for truth-telling, in particular, for "the profound falseness of women" (195).

According to Weininger, someone "who is not conscious of identity at different stages of her life, has no evidence of the identity of the subject matter of thought at different times" (147). If a woman cannot hold her past thought with her present one, she cannot judge whether they are the same or different. She cannot pronounce judgment on the identity that *A* equals *A*, nor on the opposite pronouncement that *A* is not equal to *A* (147). I might think "I have always remembered being abused," not realizing that a previous self associated with me qua woman had had the thought "I was a happy and well-loved child," a thought exclusive of my present thought. Invoking weak identity has serious consequences for women's veracity. For according to Weininger: "a creature that cannot grasp the mutual exclusiveness of A and not A has no difficulty in lying; more than that, such a creature has not even any consciousness of lying, being without a standard of truth" (150). Weininger's theory of the nature of women's memory is meant to explain the most salient feature of her moral nature, that she is organically untruthful, a natural liar (266). Weininger concludes that we should

> not . . . be surprised at the existence of the numerous proverbs and common sayings about the untruthfulness of women. It is evident that a being whose memory is very slight, and who can recall only in the most imperfect fashion, what it has said or done, or suffered, must lie easily if it has the gift of speech. (145–46)

Weak memory and weak identity are closely interrelated in Weininger. The primary importance of identity to ethics is one's ability to compare conceptions, aware that these conceptions are the subject matter of one's own thought. Comparison depends on good, specific memory and a continuous identity of oneself as a subject while continuous identity is itself a function of memory. For Weininger, a woman obviously cannot be a Kantian moral subject or a full person. Her inability to make the kinds of comparisons necessary to the application of principles puts the requirements of ethical behavior beyond her reach: "woman cannot grasp that one must act from principle" (149); she can have "no duty to herself" (186); she has "no possibility of reaching, or of desiring truth" (194).

Weakness of identity is also, however, related to a longer series of moral failings. Because a woman does not feel herself to be one and the same across time, "it costs [her] . . . very little to break off with her past" (127). She has no self-understanding and no interest in self-understanding or in being comprehensible to others. Weininger also connects weak identity to susceptibility to influence. Because a woman has "no definite individual limits" (198), she lacks the sense of individuality and destiny of a man. She is instead characterized by "suggestibility" (294), "astounding receptivity" (280), and the desire "to feel herself under another's will" (292). Further, because she is by nature always sexual, she will especially desire to be sexually seduced; moreover, having no interest in truth, she will often believe herself to be the victim of sexual overtures (194). Finally, one of the manifestations of her astounding receptivity is that "all women can be hypnotized and like being hypnotized" (270). For those women who tend toward hysteria, "the memory of definite events in their life can be destroyed by the mere suggestion of the hypnotizer" (270).

Weininger's account of memory is obviously flawed. No one would endorse his optimism that all the details of one's life are memorable or think that the ability to recall all the details of one's life would make for good memory rather than overwhelming noise. Nor would people now agree that consciousness of the self is a necessary condition and accompaniment of each thought. Finally, it might be thought that Weininger's discrediting of women is so blatant and implausible that we can learn little from it. I deny this; I think we can learn quite a lot from Weininger's account.

Whether or not Weininger's precise account of the relation of memory to logic and ethics is conceptually and empirically sound, he did see that memory is connected to value in detailed and intimate ways that support various character ideals. He thus saw that discrediting the members of a group as rememberers could discredit them in multiple ways as moral agents. And interestingly, he saw how this discrediting could take place through mining the relationship between memory and identity, arguing that a woman's inability to maintain a sense of self or relation to her own past would have consequences for whether we should rely on her truth-telling, her self-understanding, or her sense of responsibility.

But Weininger's influence obviously had as much to do with cultural politics as with logic, and we should also take this lesson from his account.

Weininger recognized and exploited the fact that character ideals and cultural representations of men and women as different kinds of selves offered opportunities for repicturing them as rememberers. Men are unsurprisingly represented as highly individualized, good at logic, interested in history, and Kantian rule followers. Men may also have notable lives. Clear and comprehensive memory is plausibly adduced as the undergirding of their characters. Similarly, Weininger's ability to attribute weakness of memory to women depends on extant stereotypes of women's having weak identities; these stereotypes are all the evidence Weininger offers for their weakness of memory. Women are multiple, fickle, or changeable; but also and most important, they are only given shape or completed through their relationships with others. Representing them, in contrast to men, as dependent on others for their identities allows for a connection between weak identity and susceptibility to influence not offered in the logic of Weininger's position.

Through understanding and exploring the connections between remembering, being a self, and being a person and moral agent, Weininger was able to wind reflections on memory with cultural representations into a brilliant and cohesive story about how women lie. His work was effective. Karen Horney was appalled to find his observations plausible (Klein 1946/1971, xix). Neither did Klein herself question the plausibly of Weininger's descriptions of the women of his time. She accused him of describing not the eternal feminine but the late-nineteenth-century effects of political subordination (69).

FALSE MEMORY MONSTERS

In Weininger's account, women are regarded as the negation of self, memory, responsibility, autobiography. Because of the nature of their memory, their status as selves is called into question; and Weininger uses speculation on their inability to maintain identity or self-integrity over time to argue that they are necessarily liars, organically untruthful. They cannot, therefore, occupy testimonial positions. If the narrating of personal memory is an ability central to being regarded as a self and a person, and if the respect we accord persons as persons is partly the respect we accord them as rememberers, how do women fare as persons in FMSF presentation? I shall show that certain FMSF writings similarly glide back and forth between the character of women's memories and their lack of sense of self, or subjective identity, to present a picture of the falseness of women. Although it may seem that the FMSF is merely challenging the content of specific memory claims—that is, those that arise in the suspect circumstances of therapy—I will argue that the foundation destructively calls into question the competence of women as rememberers. I restrict my evidence to the writings and theorists recommended either by the FMSF or recommended in very prominent reviews in prestigious popular publications, reviews the public might think it has excellent reason to trust. I am especially interested in the writings of Elizabeth Loftus and Richard Ofshe. Their writings have had a great deal of influence, and they are regarded by the public as intellectually trustworthy spokespersons for the FMSF. In a prominent review of the false memory controversy in *The New York Review of Books*, Frederick Crews, himself a board member, described their work as "astute, scientifically informed, and compassionate" (Crews 1994, part 2).

A major strategy of the FMSF has been a simplification of the complex normativity of assessing memory claims to a question of truth or falsity—a strategy thought justified by the penalties in the legal contexts in which claims of abuse are sometimes assessed. As well, Loftus has performed many memory experiments in which subjects are manipulated into providing false information in answer to questions about what they remember. In her recent experiments, already referred to in this book, some subjects have been led to think they remember events that never happened (being lost as children, for example), because they are persuaded that others in their family remember these fake events. Loftus describes her results as the creation and implanting of false memories (Loftus and Ketcham 1994, ch. 7). Some of the responses to the foundation's work have concentrated on whether the experimental circumstances in which "false memories" have been implanted by researchers are cause to worry about the general reliability of memory claims and the particular reliability of claims about remembered trauma (Russell 1986/1999, xxvi–xxvii). My concern here is in the implanting of "false memory" into our memory discourse; "false memory" is a new way of talking about memory, and its purpose is important to understand.

I am not saying that all apparent memory has been thought to be veridical or that claims made on the basis of memory have been thought to be true. Rather, what I am saying is that, traditionally, in accepting the description that "Jan remembers event Y," we accept that Y happened and that Jan's information has the appropriate source for it to be a case of memory. We may accept that Jan remembers an event even if her account has omissions and errors. But if we find out that Y didn't happen or that the source of Jan's information precludes its being memory, we do not accept that Jan remembers event Y. Instead, we consider it a case of seeming memory, apparent memory, or misremembering. Theorists have occasionally referred to misremembering as false memory, but most have wanted to avoid the air of oxymoron carried by this expression.

In the work of psychologists and memory scientists, "false memory" has only recently become a common term, and it has become so because of the false memory debates (Schacter 1999, 193). What are seeming memories that turn out not to be memories have previously been referred to as pseudomemories, screen memories, fantasies, or confabulations.[1] These descriptions have marked useful distinctions. Screen memories, for example, mask real and disturbing events in the past. Fantasies carry no such implication. I mentioned in chapter 1 that Daniel Schacter raised concerns in the mid-1990s about how the term "false memory" might discourage our understanding of the complexities of memory accuracy. In 1999, Schacter edited *The Cognitive Neuropsychology of False Memories*. His adoption of "false memory" as a general label for memory error and distortion is good evidence of how rapidly and thoroughly this term has achieved preeminence. The general shift in vocabulary to "false memory" is disturbing. In the false memory discourse promoted by the FMSF, information that is alleged to be completely false becomes a person's actual memory. It does not fall outside what could be counted as memory. Early assessments of Loftus's work by her colleagues in psychology criticized her assumption that misleading information becomes replacement memory.[2] But few have responded to the FMSF expressing particular concern about this replacement memory discourse. How do "memory" and "false" act together?

I offer the following as an outline of a major rhetorical strategy of the foundation:

1. "False" and "memory" act together to support the claim of a change in identity for the woman who has alleged abuse. The foundation, in fact, charges that a very large number of women who allege childhood sexual abuse are prone to identity disorders.
2. Because the memories are false, the identity is also false.
3. The intent of the charge of identity disorder is to call into question whether women have sufficiently integrated selves to occupy self-narrative positions that are testimonial.
4. Any woman who might bring a charge of incest is implicated in the discrediting because the identity of incest survivor is the false identity.

This schema is an oversimplification of the strategy I will now attempt to illustrate.

In the FMSF's literature, false memory syndrome is defined, in part, as "a condition in which a person's identity . . . [is] centered around a memory of traumatic experience which is objectively false. . . . The syndrome may be diagnosed when the memory is so deeply ingrained that it orients the individual's entire personality and lifestyle. . . . The analogy to personality disorder is intentional" (False Memory Syndrome Foundation, 1994).[3] In other words, completely false information becomes a woman's actual memory. This memory leads to a change in her identity, which then becomes centered on falsity. The emphasis on change in identity and on false identity is persistent in this writing. Loftus's account of one father's story, entitled "All I Ever Wanted," includes:

> The September letter firmly marked the line between before and after. "Before" was the time when the bad "memories" didn't exist, and Megan was still Megan; "after" was this new, strange time when Megan became someone else and her memories held the family hostage. (Loftus and Ketcham 1994, 186)

If I one day wake up and my significant memories are different and if these are the memories of the person who just woke up, am I the same person as the one who went to sleep? In a fanciful philosophical thought experiment, Bernard Williams asks us to imagine the case of Charles, who wakes up one morning with the memories of Guy Fawkes: "The uncanniness of someone's acquiring a new past is connected with our increasing reluctance to describe the situation as one in which the same man has acquired a new set of qualities" (Williams 1973, 3). In other words, we wonder whether Charles is any longer Charles. A way of reading the strategy of the foundation is that they ask us to wonder whether a new rememberer, formerly Megan but now someone else, could engage in an act of testimonial self-narrative about Megan's past.

The new rememberer's ability to engage in an act of memory testimony about the harm Megan suffered in her past can be discredited on two grounds. First, Megan's identity has changed, and the new "someone else" cannot perform Megan's self-narrative. It is no longer the case that the one who remembers is the one who was there. The new rememberer is other. Second, the new identity is a false one; it now comprises bad memories. The new other has been created through misinformation, confabulation, and fantasy; she thus cannot be trusted anyway to testify truly. The FMSF's writing suggests that many women who contend abuse fail to maintain a secure enough identity to have a standard of truth with respect to testimonial claims. That we are meant to wonder about their psychological stability seems very clear from this passage in Loftus:

> What a story, you may be thinking . . . what an amazing bizarre, fantastic story. Perhaps, like many people I know, you find yourself wondering. . . . Why did she come to accept memories that she initially insisted were false? Was there something inherently wrong with her—a mental weakness of some kind, a psychological flaw, an inability to separate fact from reality. (Loftus and Ketcham, 19)

Foundation writings seem to accept, with Weininger, a Lockean view of sameness of memory as grounding identity, or self-integrity. But the question remains of how false information, even supposing it became actual memory, could be responsible for an actual change in identity, as foundation writings charge. Loftus never claims that her experimental subjects have undergone an identity change. According to Williams, we are only inclined to postulate a change in identity on the basis of changed memory if the changed person can now be thought identical with someone. In Williams's example, we contemplate that Charles may have changed identity rather than have merely become confused, because we can say with whom he is now identical: Guy Fawkes.

At this point, we must shift to what counts as a new false identity for women. It is the incest survivor. Many of us would naturally think of an incest survivor as someone who has survived incest. In Weininger's theory, however, someone we might now think of as an incest survivor is a wholly discredited figure. To allege sexual assault is actually one of the manifestations of weakness of identity. Disturbingly, in many FMSF writings, "incest survivor" marks the identity centered on falsity. In this quite remarkable paragraph from *True Stories of False Memories*, recommended by the FMSF, Kevin Farmer and Eleanor Goldstein imply that the change to a false identity is a kind of project of the incest survivor for which a diagnosis of multiple personality disorder is an aid: "We know the anguish of incest survivors who say they repressed their memories for decades and claim new identities sometimes with a diagnosis of Multiple Personality Disorder (MPD). They often confabulated these memories in therapy" (Goldstein and Farmer 1993, 9).[4] The idea of "incest survivor" in the passage is not bracketed; that is, the authors make no suggestion that they are talking about women who are not, in fact, incest survivors but who falsely believe that they are. Instead, the authors associate "incest survivor" with someone who has a new identity as the result of confabulating abuse.

The passage just quoted and many others make clear that "incest survivor" is the new false identity. In the section entitled "Survivor," in Mark Pendergast's *Victims of Memory* (1995), I had anticipated interviews with women who were acknowledged survivors, but instead, I found that Pendergast had used the section for interviews with women he does not believe (chapter 8). Pendergast makes clear exactly what the transition in identity has been. Pendergast believes that the process of becoming an incest survivor is one in which "a system of influences . . . disrupts an individual's identity . . . and replaces it with a new identity. . . . Certainly, this is what has happened to many who have recovered 'memories.' They are no longer someone's daughters; they are Survivors" (478). In Loftus's work, when a woman who has alleged abuse has "recanted," she discovers that this false identity, incest survivor, does not belong to her: "The truth hit Erin hard, 'I wasn't withdrawn like that,' she thought. . . . In that moment of insight she knew she had adopted a false identity. She was not an incest survivor" (Loftus and Ketcham 1994, 28). Ofshe hopes that women will realize that "'survivor' is not the stuff out of which . . .

a meaningful identity can be created" (Ofshe and Watters 1994, 303–4). "Incest survivor" is a common gloss on the idea of false identity in FMSF writings. So, the incest survivor is not now someone who has survived incest; the rhetorical strategies of the foundation occlude this possibility. She is rather someone who has a changed, false identity through false memory and consequently cannot testify to her own abuse. Like "rapist father," "incest survivor" risks becoming an impossible object within a discourse.

Ofshe and Watters suggest that any therapist will be a potentially disreputable influence, that only pre-therapy memory is trustworthy. However, for me, the problem in these accounts is the presentation of women. Ofshe and Watters claim that women who enter therapy are in fact eager to be under the will of another: "Therapists prep these victims-in-training for key turning points in their therapy drama" (1993, 9). The claim that victim-in-training is an engaging role for women when combined with the description of their subsequent actions—"Parents have to witness their adult children turn into monsters trying to destroy their reputations and lives" (1993, 4)—echoes Weininger's charge that it costs women little to break with their pasts, that they do so with no regard for harm to others, that, in fact, they cannot be trusted to act on ethical principles:

> Several months passed. Lynn found an apartment, bought an old car . . . decided she was strong enough to live her life without drugs, and entered an alcoholism and drug treatment program. . . . These counsellors were telling her to stop trying to "fix" herself and start taking "responsibility" for herself. She wondered what the word "responsibility" meant. (Loftus and Ketcham 1994, 18)

These writings make clear why we cannot endorse Locke's claim that personal identity consists in one's being able to repeat a past action with the same consciousness as one had of the action at the time it was performed and with the consciousness one has of oneself at the present time. Locke's view of sameness of consciousness has been standardly criticized by pointing out that to remember myself doing something presupposes my identity and cannot form the basis of it. My diagnosis of FMSF writings offers grounds for a more politically engaged criticism of Locke, for the influence of Locke's formulation of the links among memory, identity, and responsibility leads to the possibility of the rhetorical manipulations that characterize FMSF writings. The FMSF presents an unrealistic and damaging picture of self-integrity as sameness of memory experience over time, encouraging the public to challenge credibility whenever memory experience varies over time.

All women are at risk of an identity change to the false identity of survivor with its moral evasions and failings. In one of the first prominent articles to bring the crisis of memory to public attention, Carol Tavris warns all women to "Beware the Incest Survivor Machine" (Tavris 1993). In Loftus's book, Elizabeth thinks of her so-far perfectly normal daughter: "[Her] voice catches. She takes a deep breath. 'How do I know that someday she won't accuse me?'" (30) In reading this passage, we are meant to be concerned that every woman is equally susceptible to false memory syndrome. As well as targeting therapists, the foundation targets self-help books, incest narratives, and feminist theory as destructive sources of suggestion. In the 1990s, the alarm number offered by FMSF writings—that is, the suspected number of cases of women suffering from suggested false memories—ranged from tens of thousands (Ofshe and Watters 1993, 14) to over a million cases a year. In the next chapter, I scrutinize some of the grounds offered for the more remarkable estimates. Understandably, these numbers have moved the public to considerable wariness about abuse claims, giving weight to the concern of John Read and many others: that the foundation's work makes it more difficult for victims, especially girls and women, to be able to come forward and say, credibly, that they were abused.

To return to a remark made at the start of this chapter, I would stress that the writings I have discussed do seem to me a serious attack on the credibility of women as a group. They present women as so suggestible, as so little able to maintain a sense of self, that unless any particular woman can disprove her being influenced, we are being advised to regard her claims of incest or abuse as prima facie unreliable. FMSF members have argued that their work either complements or serves the interests of real victims of child sexual abuse. However, their framework for assessing abuse claims is characterized by the suspicion that the mere discussion of child sexual abuse puts all women at risk of contagion by an epidemic of suggestibility. All claims of abuse that are not irrebuttably corroborated are pulled into this intensely skeptical framework. Moreover, because incest survivor is the false identity in FMSF writings, those who claim this identity speak from a subject position only recently allowed and now again discredited.

Why have we been so quick to accept the rhetoric of false memory and weak identity? I pointed out that Weininger's success at discrediting women as rememberers depended on his ability to take extant cultural representations and stereotypes and convert them into specific portraits of rememberers. Can we find our acceptance of easy identity shifts for women within our own cultural representations?

First, if women's identities are still thought to be very dependent on their relationships, an unremarkable claim of Weininger's, then they will be perceived as shifting identities when certain relationships become newly important—which is in fact what the material on false memory syndrome implies has happened. Women's relationships with unwittingly or intentionally deceptive therapists become central to their self-definitions. But I have argued that we all have dependent identities and that our self-concepts are relationally shaped. Margaret Walker proposes that the problem for perception of women's moral agency is not just that women's gender scripts are

> relational for men's are too. These are stories of relational and *subsumed* identities, ones which are seen in our society as functions of, or in terms of function for, someone else. . . . The women to whom they apply are pressed towards self-descriptions that serve as plot functions in someone else's tale within societies in which having one's own story . . . is emblematic of full moral agency. (1998, 127)

Walker is not writing about false memory, but her description of women's identities is a useful characterization in understanding the particular import of representations of women's dependence. Women's identities as incest survivors are seen as now distortedly shaped by overly dependent relationships with therapists; that is, they are seen as a *function of* those relationships. And this dependence, moreover, is seen to threaten and violate the women's family identities as good daughters; that is, the dependence threatens the more proper *function for* their identities. When Pendergast claims that therapy changes women from daughters into survivors, he offers only subsumed identity categories. In FMSF newsletters, women and men who have allegedly accused their parents on the basis of historic memories are exhaustively categorized through their relations to their families as recanters (those who have withdrawn their claims), returners (those who have resumed contact without recanting), and refusers (those who have neither recanted nor returned). Walker's concern is that those with subsumed identities are thought to lack full moral agency. I agree, but I also take as a lesson from both Weininger and the FMSF that those with subsumed identities are also easily pictured as prone to the identity disorder of a shifting and unstable self, which reflects on their credibility as rememberers.

Second, we have a particular contemporary representation of women's multiplicity in therapy. As the Farmer and Goldstein passage illustrates, the FMSF representation of women's unstable identities has been given a major impetus by the alleged connection between child sexual abuse and multiple personality disorder. Although the FMSF tends to deny the actual existence of the disorder, categorizing it as iatrogenic[5] (Ofshe and Watters 1998, ch. 10), it has been able to exploit this representation of women with fragmented or multiple identities as a compelling portrait of women in therapy. Raitt and Zeedyk note that in formulating the definition of false memory syndrome, Kilstrom, a professor of psychology at Yale and a foundation advisor, "draws explicit parallels between FMS and Multiple Personality Disorder" (2000, 140). Raitt and

Zeedyk believe that he does so to emphasize that false memory syndrome is a clinical condition. I am doubtful that foundation skeptics are drawing on the clinical legitimacy of MPD. Kilstrom's definition of false memory syndrome is better read as a restatement of multiple personality disorder severed from its connections with child sexual abuse and genuine dissociated memory. In other words, false memory syndrome is multiple personality disorder reformulated as a therapeutically induced condition to which all women are susceptible and to which millions have allegedly succumbed.

FEMINIZING MEMORY

I have argued that part of the use of "false memory" is to mark out a discursive location where a shift can easily be made to talk of an identity disorder, talk that can discredit someone who attempts to testify to sexual abuse or incest. Theorists can mask such discrediting, to themselves and to others, by taking the position that they are only talking about memory processes or that they are only interested in memory processes. In the author's note to *The Myth of Repressed Memory*, Loftus instructs her readers as to what would be the appropriate understanding of her work: "We hope readers will remember that this is not a debate about the reality or the horror of sexual abuse, incest, and violence against children. This is a debate about memory" (xi). I find these remarks disingenuous. Because a rememberer is a self is a person, the FMSF has had little trouble in making a description of memory bear metonymic significance for the woman. As described in the last section, false memory is her false identity. In this section, I examine a further manifestation of this metonymic shift, one that shows a disturbing tendency to feminize suggestible memory through its association with women and children, one that therefore brings representations of their characters into descriptions of memory processes. These representations influence our sense of memory as suggestible, and they have likely ramifications for how we regard women's memory in particular. They should be resisted.

In "Making Monsters," Ofshe and Watters identify memory as their subject (1993, 5). Their claim, however, that "memory is malleable," that memories can be easily influenced, especially by the circumstances in which they are recovered (6), becomes the claim that *women* are malleable, as shown in the following dramatized description of the therapeutic circumstances in which memories are recovered. Clients are "blank canvasses on which the therapist paints. . . . [They] are exceedingly vulnerable to influence" (9):

> Clients discover that playing the sexual abuse victim is both a demanding and engaging role. . . . Whatever doubts they have are subordinated to the

> therapist's judgement, the images they have fantasized, the stories they have confabulated and the identity they have developed through the course of this process. (10)

In Loftus's work, where "certain scenes and dialogue have been dramatically re-created in order to convey important ideas . . ." (Loftus and Ketcham 1994, xi), the woman is infantilized under the screen of a description of her memory. First, the memory child is offered as the locus of suggestibility: "memory surprises me again and again with its gee-whiz gullibility, its willingness to take up the crayon of suggestion and color in a dark corner of the past, giving up without any hint of an argument an old ragged section of memory in exchange for a shiny new piece" (4). Later, in describing a "typical" meeting of a survivors' group, the women themselves are made to look childish and without individual character. In this "typical" session, one woman is sitting, crying, telling her story:

> Sitting in a circle around her were three women holding hands. . . . On the other side of the room a woman was beating the wall with an "encounter bat" . . . while another sat moaning in the corner, her hands pressed against her ears, and yet another hunkered down in the middle of the floor. . . . (16)

The dramatized presentation is powerful enough to elude Loftus's infantilization narrative, but the intent of the description is to suggest that incest survivors have regressed to a sort of twisted nursery school behavior; for Loftus comments, "no one ever told you to stop, to grow up, to behave yourself, to get a grip . . ." (16).

Both Weininger and the FMSF show that it is easy to shift between talking about the character of a mental faculty and the character of a group of people. Because cognitive functions are definitive of personhood, this shift is completely unsurprising; and as I have argued, it allows theorists to discredit groups under the screen of discussing mental processes. But these fluid shifts are also bidirectional. On the one hand, false memory becomes a woman's false identity. On the other, descriptions of women's identities are used to personify memory. Sometimes this personification is subtle. For example, the falsity of the new Megan, her deceptiveness, colors how we think of the "bad" memory. In Ofshe and Watters, memory is said to be malleable; their subsequent description of women as eager and wholly suggestible confabulators reflects back on how we vivify and understand this malleability. Sometimes there is nothing subtle about the personification of memory. Loftus's description of the women in group therapy as wanton and in need of control is encouraged by the direct personification of memory as a child in need of control. In certain FMSF writings, the close metonymic association of malleable memory with suggestible women and children contributes a symbolic dimension to memory as feminine and infantile; and Loftus's explicit imagery, of course, also contributes to this dimension.

Using explicit imagery of women and children to symbolize memory is not new to Loftus's work, and I am not the only theorist interested in her writing as a cultural text. Janice Haaken is intrigued by Loftus's "feminine" metaphors and allowance of emotion into memory, which she reads as a break from and challenge to the mechanistic conventions that govern scientific work. She is particularly struck by the following passage from *Witness for the Defense* (1991), a book whose publication just predates the false memory controversies. The passage mixes messiness with the need for order: "Like curious, playful children searching through drawers for a blouse or pair of pants, our brains seem to enjoy ransacking the drawers, tossing the facts about and then stuffing everything back in, oblivious to order and importance" (1991, 20; quoted in Haaken 1998, 51). The brain can impose a certain order on memory, but Loftus's prose suggests that it's a feminine idea of order with more concern for appearance and household harmony than for truth: "We interpret the past, correcting ourselves, adding bits and pieces, deleting uncomplimentary or disturbing recollections, sweeping, dusting, tidying things up" (1991, 20; quoted in Haaken 1998, 51). Haaken does not mention an important corollary of describing memory as women and children who cannot keep appropriate order: Loftus's imagery clearly marks out a place for a rational paternal authority that comes to sort memory out, the same figure I suggest that arrives to shout at the women in the encounter group to stop, grow up, and behave themselves. What are we to make of the feminizing and infantilizing of memory in these writings?

Loftus is a forensic psychologist. She sometimes maintains that her metaphorical explanations are used to simplify to juries "the complex neurological and biochemical processes involved in memory storage and retrieval" (Loftus and Ketcham 1994, 4). She means to imply, I believe, that metaphor's place in her work is only in explaining science to nonscientists, which leaves me the task of defending the seriousness with which I regard this imagery. Genevieve Lloyd's writing on the maleness of reason in the seventeenth century can stand as an exemplar for the ways that we need to be not only conscious about the presence of gender in our models of mind but also cautious in our analysis of these models. Lloyd follows Sandra Harding in distinguishing: *(a)* gender as a feature of our symbolic order, its operation as myth, metaphor, and symbolism (symbolic gender); *(b)* gender used to structure social arrangements (structural gender); and *(c)* the gendered characteristics of men and women (individual gender) (Lloyd 1993, 71). She also acknowledges that while the presence of gender in our models of the mind is certainly not new, analyzing its effect is a complex and uncertain task.

Lloyd's work first makes clear there is no necessary relation between explicit imagery and the presence of symbolic gender. Spinoza, for example, regarded reason as central to overcoming pity, which he described as "womanish" (Lloyd 1984). To understand reason as transcending emotion and sensibility (themselves explicitly associated with the feminine) is to identify reason as masculine by contrast, even if we do not picture it as a man. In fact Lloyd argues that the explicit presentation of reason as ungendered was also an implicit presentation of reason as masculine in a symbolic order where women represent sexual difference (Lloyd 1993). In Weininger's work, memory is obviously explicitly aligned with masculinity; it both represents and is definitive of many masculine values—for example, the value of having a life worth recording and recounting in all its detail, the kind of life that Catherine Weed generously attributes to Thurlow Weed (chapter 2). But part of what makes memory symbolically masculine in Weininger's account is also the description of femininity as the absence of memory. In Loftus's work, memory is explicitly represented as both a woman and an unruly child. It is also implicitly associated with women through a vocabulary of unruliness and suggestibility—used to talk about memory and women in therapy—and through marking a place for a contrasting masculine authority. I suspect that this authority is scientific reasoning.

Second, Lloyd's work points out that although relationships among symbolic gender, structural gender, and individual gender may be complex and difficult to sort, symbolic gender often interacts with structural and individual gender. For example, representations of reason as ungendered, even if symbolically masculine, did allow women to claim reason (reason was democratized in the early modern period); at the same time, women were barred from many of the disciplines of reason (structural gender), and individual women were thought to be less reasonable than men (individual gender) (Lloyd 1984). Though decoding the effects of symbolic gender is uncertain, we can at least mark concerns in the present case. The descriptions of women that animate Loftus's and Ofshe's accounts of memory are unflattering stereotypes of women as wanton and suggestible and as without individuality, respect for the past, or serious moral character. This imagery is used to offer a general account of memory. Nevertheless, stereotypes organize our moral perception: who we respond to and how. The imagery will obviously have dangerous consequences for structural gender, coloring testimonial authority and causing women's memory to be regarded as less credible than men's. As well, implying that a group has certain moral deficiencies because of its cognitive limitations is a powerful way of naturalizing stereotypes. The tendency of these writers to convey and naturalize stereotypes of women through a feminized description of malleable memory is grounds for deep concern about the effect of the imagery on structural and individual gender.

Third, Lloyd recognizes that to point out gendered symbolism is not sufficient to critique a model of the mind; in fact, the model might be a very good one and might bring important features of a faculty to light.[6] To critique a model because of its symbolism can, however, operate on two levels. We can, as illustrated, attempt to understand the real historical relations among symbolic dimensions of models and their effects on structural and individual gender—which is to critique a model of memory because of its likely effects on people. Second, we can move back to the effects of the imagery on our understanding of the faculty. We can try to ascertain whether the symbolic dimensions of models make only certain characteristics of a faculty salient and thus lead us to ignore or distort others. I have raised concerns about the amount and kind of attention now given to memory malleability and error. Imagining memory as unreliably feminine in a cultural context where many women's memories are regarded as suspect will very likely provoke increased attention to memory malleability. I elaborate this concern in the next section.

Finally, Lloyd claims that some masculine symbolism, for example, the idea of reason as transcendent of emotion, is deeply embedded in our understanding of reason. She contrasts this situation to one where imagery can be "shed without leaving us with nothing to say" (1993, 82). Ideas of the feminine as multiplicity form a deeply embedded cultural symbolism. "Woman" has symbolized "multiplicity as against one-ness, indeterminacy as against determination" (Lloyd 1993, 75). Moreover, this long history of regarding women as unreliably changeable is evident in the accounts of memory in both Weininger and the FMSF. Because of the connections between memory and identity, multiplicity has made it easy to repicture women as defective rememberers. Doing so in Weininger's account in fact helps symbolize memory as a masculine faculty. But the use of women's multiplicity to symbolize memory itself as unreliable seems relatively new. It is resistible, and there are good reasons to resist both this representation of women and the understanding of memory it directs.

MODELS OF MEMORY AND MORAL CHARACTER

This final section draws out and elaborates a particular thread in my analysis, one connected to the discussion of archival and reconstructive models begun in the last chapter. In previous sections, I have illustrated how certain views of memory are linked to character ideals and stereotypes, and I have shown how memory is sometimes animated and personified to represent the character of rememberers. We gain a more philosophically and politically astute perspective on current discussions of old and new memory models when we see that the intimate involvement of character norms with theories of memory serves as part of the history of our scientific and philosophical reflection on memory.

Our memory models appear to be in transition. Daniel Schacter claims that after centuries of philosophical reflection and after the slow scientific progress of over a hundred years, the last few decades have seen dramatic and revolutionary changes in our understanding of memory—changes away from the idea that memory is a single system and changes away from "the long-standing myth" that memory is like a family photo album of snapshots (1996, 5). Loftus claims that her research has helped to create "a new paradigm of memory," one away from the idea that memory is like a video recording (Loftus and Ketcham 1994, 5). Schacter and Loftus identify the archival model—the model of memories as original, discretely stored images or recordings that subsequent occasions of remembering reproduce—as a long-standing paradigm only recently challenged by science. We may believe that the archival model is in the process of being replaced by a better, more dynamic reconstructivist model that will encourage an understanding of, for example, the importance of narrative to memory competence.

I have already raised some caution about talk of a straightforward transition by suggesting that truth and accuracy in memory have remained aligned with the archival model. I now briefly discuss aspects of John Sutton's work on early modern theories of memory to elaborate the thought that commitments about values and about moral character shape how models of our mental faculties are offered, accepted, rejected, or countered and how they are deployed. Moreover, values are often expressed through the imagery and symbolism associated with models. As the previous section made clear, I follow many theorists in contending that we should not dismiss imagery as a "superficial accretion" of our models (Lloyd 1993, 70). Rather, I contend that imagery and symbolism can help determine, first, how a model directs our attention and research, and, second, how scientific research interacts with other social processes. Claims about a transition to a new and better memory model must be assessed with attention to the complex normative and symbolic dimensions to modeling the faculties of the soul.

Sutton argues that reconstructivist models are not new and that we need to understand archival models as in part defending against "cultural and psychological fear about loss of control" that these more dynamic models evoke (Sutton 1998, 13). Sutton's historical example involves the response to Rene Descartes' and Nicolas Malebranche's theory of corporeal memory.[7] For Descartes, sensation, emotion, corporeal memory, and imagination belong to the body as well as the mind; we can give an account of them as bodily process. To explain how information is received, processed, and stored in the brain, Descartes follows a very long tradition of identifying "animal spirits" as the bearers of neural information (ch. 3). In a conceptual era dominated by the dualism of body and spirit, animal spirits, as their name implies, were ontologically odd entities able to bridge distinct realms. They moved among world, body, and mind, making possible the causal interaction of the material and mental. Although animal spirits now seem occult and arcane, they dominated philosophical, medical, and literary treatments of the mind for centuries, helping to "embed cognitive function in the body" (46).

For Descartes, the spirits are corporeal, the finest and most refined part of the blood, like a lively and pure flame (44). They carry information by moving through the network of pores and filaments that make up our brain, opening pores and bending filaments. Passing through, they leave traces of their motion as dispositions for the reactivation of certain patterns and the activation of others. Descartes uses the analogy of a network of folds in a piece of paper. The folds determine how and in what ways the paper may be more easily folded in the future. The traces of spirit motions are our memories. Descartes pointed out that a single fold will be sufficient for all things that resemble one another, and Malebranche applauded the model's possibilities for efficient storage (63). Malebranche also saw, however, that the blending of traces, and the network of folds that would cause associated traces to be activated, could lead to confused memory.

Sutton claims that Descartes' model foreshadows contemporary connectionist models of memory. Connectionism represents the mind as a neural network in a state of constant activation. New inputs cause a shift in the pattern of neural activity. Previously activated patterns help constitute the dispositions of the network to be activated in certain ways. Thus, the system exhibits causal holism, meaning that the representations stored as dispositions are all implicated in the system's current behavior. Memory traces are both extended and superposed; that is, stored information is spread across a number of parts of the system, and, like the fold in the paper, the resources used to represent one memory are coextensive with the resources used to represent others. In other words, a memory is not stored as a discrete item at a single location. The model is described as distributive rather than *local*.[8] Because dispositions affect new patterns of activation and because new inputs have an inevitable effect on previous dispositions, we can make no firm distinction between storage and processing. Cognitive systems are "complexes of continuous, simultaneous, and mutually determining change" (Van Gelder 1995, 373; quoted in Sutton, 5). The system is extremely dynamic.

Regarding memory as this dynamic allows theorists to model many of its aspects, such as its efficient storage, the immediate relevance of background information to incoming information, creativity through new associations, and the easy production of prototypes and concepts through the system's capacity for superpositional storage. On the other hand, extended, superpositional storage creates some degree of confusion and error from the blending of traces, and it also makes their interference with one another an inevitable part of our lives as rememberers. Malebranche was clearly worried about the moral implications of the model. He feared that the activation of associated traces would cause men to become confused; women with their weaker brain fibers were even more at risk (Malebranche 1674/1997, vol. 2, 130; quoted in Sutton 1998, 110). It is worth noting that this version of a reconstructivist model gives an account of how memory is continuously transformed while making no reference at all to social influence.

Despite his worries, Malebranche nevertheless accepted the dynamic model; for a group of English critics, the possibilities of confusion were reason enough to reject Descartes' model of memory. Sutton summarizes their fear: "the ideas that memories are just patterned motions of the spirits through brain pores denies the systematicity, stability, and structure characteristic of true thinking, reducing all cognition to mere association and the chance fusion of jumbling motions" (Sutton 1998, 129). In criticizing an earlier model of memory as motions, Joseph Glanvill wrote, "our *memories* will be stored with infinite variety of divers, yea contrary motions, which must needs interfere, thwart, and obstruct one another: and there would be nothing within us, but Ataxy and disorder" (Glanvill 1661, 39; quoted in Sutton 1998, 141, emphasis his). Critics argued for local, archival models with discrete, well-ordered memories. Many theorists, however, followed Descartes. Sutton suggests that Locke did so reluctantly, recognizing that an animal-spirits physiology might make nonsense of his view that we have sufficiently faithful memory to guarantee psychological continuity and the stability of our identities.

Sutton's account is meant to provoke reflection on the relation between culture and cognition in "late twentieth-century worries about memory, science, and truth" (1998, 1), particularly those worries about reliable memory at work in the false memory debates. With the benefit of hindsight, he urges us to regard cultural and scientific disputes about how to model memory partly as a discussion about values; in Descartes' time, it was about the possibility and desirability of control over a personal past marked by an individual's ability to recall that past in a comprehensive, dependable, and orderly fashion. Sutton's account contains a number of insights, some quite familiar to philosophers of science, that can be applied to current debates about models, and I briefly develop five of the points in the next few paragraphs. My intent, as will be clear, is not to assess individual memory models hoping that one will be adequate, but to suggest how we should understand the import of our discussions about them.

First, Sutton argues that reconstructivist models, including models that conceive the brain as a net and memory as distributive and superpositional, are not new to memory science; we can therefore use history to reflect on their current deployment. We should be immediately skeptical of a linear narrative in which one long-standing model has given way to a new and better one as an inevitable result of steady scientific progress. That dynamic models have recurred is reason to think that they contribute to an understanding of important features of memory, but the presence of dynamic and archival models as both historical and more recent competitors raises the possibility that each draws our attention to vital aspects of memory. I will return to this latter point.

Second, Sutton's account illustrates that in deciding how to model memory, a choice that generates research programs and directions of inquiry, we make choices about what aspects of memory are worth attending to and we make decisions about what counts as normal memory functioning. Not all of these properties in the domain to be modeled are discovered subsequent to the model's adoption; otherwise, we would have no grounds for this adoption. Nor, typically, is a model proposed to simply represent a domain we already understand well. Models are usually adopted on either a preliminary understanding or an intuition about properties. They then direct our attention to possible additional similarities between features of the model and the domain. Models are typically research projects (Boyd 1980).

In assessing current discussions, we should be cautious of preliminary commitments about normal memory functioning. They will not always be obvious from the description of a model. For example, for Sutton, the term "reconstructive" simply means that the only things stored are "dispositions for the re-evocation of explicit patterns" (133). "What I have been calling 'reconstruction' is the change in state from implicit to explicit, the actualizing of a disposition" (154). Sutton's use of "reconstructive"—the idea that memories are dispositions that can be activated as occurrent rememberings—is carefully neutral on issues of memory distortion. The FMSF claim, however, that memories are reconstructive, rather than reproductive, is a commitment to a high level of change and distortion in memory. A single model may have different potentialities and may be adopted for different reasons, including pragmatic ones.

Because of the many relations of memory to moral character, we must also be mindful of what our preliminary commitments are about the character of rememberers. Our adoption or rejection of a model may have in part to do with the values that the model either makes possible or forbids. Recall that Haaken identifies Herman as holding a literalist account of memory because Herman wants to regard women as truth-tellers. Glanvill rejects models of memories as motion because they suggest a level of confused memory that he thinks is neither credible nor tolerable. In pointing out the centrality of ethical concerns to the historical evaluation of theories of memory, Sutton concentrates on the rejection of models: "If a theory of the mind/brain threatens established moral beliefs, the theory is in trouble" (269). My analysis in earlier parts of the chapter indicates that we must attend to the moral ideals or stereotypes that move people toward models. We cannot, of course, simply adopt or reject models because we like or dislike the view of rememberers on offer with no attention to how we are capable of functioning; any ethics of remembering must have realistic commitments about our psychological capacities. But considerations of value are reasonable prima facie grounds for challenging the directions in which some models take us. The moral qualities we are in fact capable of instantiating may make certain models of mind inadequate or misleading.

Third, the imagery and symbolism of certain models, or versions of them, may make some aspects of memory more salient to us, regardless of the reason that the model was adopted. Whatever Descartes' rationale for his theory, for centuries the spirits had been personified to give an account of all the ills of cognition, all the ways in which the body corrupts the life of the mind. Bernard Mandeville has a character describe the spirits as "volatil Messengers" which "rummage and ferret in the inmost recesses of brain" (1711/1976, 130; quoted in Sutton 1998, 23). They could be rendered unstable by wine, body temperature, or environmental conditions. Because of the roaming of the spirits and their theoretical function of bridging ontological difference, they disrupted any sense of clearly bounded distinct ontological realms (Sutton, ch. 2). In my view, animal-spirit imagery could not but help provoke or exacerbate anxiety about mental confusion and thus make that the most salient feature of a reconstructive model. Sutton's own book is an interesting example of the unconscious effects of imagery and symbolism. Despite its official neutrality and its outlining of the benefits of a connectionist treatment, both the false memory controversies and the spirits influence Sutton—who, like many contemporary theorists, consistently talks of the blending aspects of memory in terms of confusion and internal distortion rather than in terms of our capacities for abstract thought and creativity. This focus on distortion now dominates writing on memory, even though scientists agree that "serious errors and distortions occur relatively infrequently" (Schacter 1996, 5).[9]

Imagery can also be deliberately used to direct our attention. Loftus explains to juries evaluating eyewitness testimony that "memories don't sit in one place, waiting patiently to be retrieved" (Loftus and Ketcham 1994, 4). Searching, as she says, for more adequate metaphors, she asks them to imagine the brain as a bowl of water and each memory as a teaspoon of milk stirred in (3). She asks us to think of memories as drifting through the brain like clouds or vapor, as wind, breath, or steam that disappears when we try to touch it (4). Loftus picks imagery for her juries that leads them to focus on how memory is difficult to reliably access and on how it is easily confused. Memories disappear on touch and mingle like milk in water.

To summarize the import of these first three points for an analysis of false memory writings, the FMSF presents a reconstructivist model to the public as the result of new scientific work on memory. But we must consider that the opportunity to talk about a high degree of confusion, malleability, and memory error in women's memories of abuse—that is, the commitment to this view of women's abuse memory—has motivated the FMSF's promotion of a reconstructivist model (even though this model has other potentialities). These commitments are expressed in the imagery and symbolism, discussed in previous sections, which derive from an unacceptable stereotype of women as having a weak sense of self. This stereotype of women is reciprocally promoted through the symbolism. The model, as deployed by the FMSF, offers a misleading picture of the normal amount of distortion in memory and of the malleability of women's character, and these deficiences are connected. Moreover the memory debates and the anxiety-provoking imagery through which they are conducted seem to have had a pervasive impact on the current deployment of reconstructivist models. Schacter notes that the false memory debates have led to a great deal of "renewed interest in memory errors and distortion" (1999, 193). There is less interest in the potential for modeling good reconstructive memory; it is assumed, unrealistically, that attention to memory error will give us an account of good remembering. There is also little interest in other ways of modeling truth, accuracy, and order in memory.

Fourth, Sutton's study argues that one of the reasons early reconstructive models were often rejected is that they did not make adequate allowance for norms of epistemic responsibility. This reason raises the question of why reconstructive models are so readily accepted at present when memory is again being represented in the language of unruly mental processes—that is, of confusion, disorder, and a lack of responsibility. We must consider that personifying memory through unruly children or women offers imagery that does not threaten our character ideals of rationality and control; rather, the personification reinforces pernicious stereotypes of women.

Haaken notes that Loftus's imagery seems interestingly transitional, mixing the idea of archival storage ("the memory drawers") with unruly messy children who reconstruct memory. But is it transitional or merely mixed? A fifth and final important point of reflection encouraged by Sutton's account is that models of mind do not always replace each other—sometimes they are held in tension as representing different aspects of cognitive activity and as offering different views of moral character. Archival and reconstructive models coexisted at the time of Sutton's discussion, and they coexist in an odd way in our own. I have been nagged and puzzled by the fact that we are almost always offered these models together—one characterized as old or deficient, the other as new and promising. This happens in Loftus, in Ofshe, in Haaken, in Schacter, in Sutton, in almost every contemporary theorist I discuss in this book. Why are we always being offered two models if only one is any good? I argued in chapter 4 that these models coexist in our time partly because the archival model continues to be a placeholder for the values of truth and accuracy; the reconstructivist model gives us distortion, and we must look elsewhere for the standard. They are also sometimes offered together to enforce a linear narrative of progress. We are placed as naive adherents to a model of memory that, as good scientists, we must now move forward and reject, even when it's not clear that many of us have been naive about memory.

But in contesting whether this linear narrative is a faithful rendering of the history of modeling memory, we also have some flexibility to rethink the complete rejection of the archival model, and we have an opportunity to consider again the necessary public and social dimension to remembering. We do need to think of how we keep our pasts straight, and we need to model this practice in ways that do not depend on the idea of internal memory storage with rank-and-file ordering. Much of our ordering of the past is established and maintained through memory activities. Narratives, of course, offer rich possibilities of explicit ordering through our extensive temporal vocabulary as well as the occasions for the kind of rehearsal that prevents the degradation of memory. We obviously need to understand narrative activities as a more positive dimension of memory competence, but I do not conceive of doing so as a way to be rid of the imagery of memory as a storehouse or an archive.

When we think of the activities that define us as rememberers, the rejection of storehouse imagery becomes disturbing. We preserve the personal past in part by embodying it in a public social world, and we do so not only by narrating it but also by taking pictures, making videos, being diarists, keeping records of accomplishment at work, and so on—in other words, we do so by being archivists. I do not mean that remembering is simply flipping through a photo album filled with faces I no longer recognize, nor is the creation and use of an archive a mere aid to an activity that needs to be understood as internal mental processing. Taking pictures is part of how I decide what to remember and the point of view from which I will remember. Moreover such activity always shapes and stabilizes future contexts of retrieval. Thought of in this light, the rejection of archival imagery becomes another way of severing the discussion of memory from an understanding of the lives of rememberers.[10] Although, as Sutton points out, the use of the archival model is to defend against the ideas of excessive disorder or confusion, we needn't think of this point as the idea that memories are static mental items, preserved as dated snapshots in our mind. Some theorists who are not at all naive about memory have been unwilling to give up the imagery associated with the archival model (Park 1997, Hacking 1995), and I have argued that we should not give it up. Nor have I rejected reconstructivist models. Excessive disorder and confusion are not their inevitable commitments. If we attend appropriately to memory activities in devising our models, we will see that we need to make room for both archival and reconstructive dimensions to remembering.[11]

CONCLUSION

Intimate abuse forms what Laurence Thomas refers to as a type of "hostile misfortune" for women, one involving the agency and attitudes of others to members of a diminished social category (Thomas 1992–1993, 236). Thomas's account of hostile misfortunes that accrue to downwardly constituted social categories is useful for thinking about the ways in which groups of people can be cognitively undermined, and their status as persons diminished, as a part of the strategy employed to discredit their accounts of harm. Although false memory advocacy is not simply backlash, it has provided an opportunity to widely discredit incest survivors. The devaluation of memory as a core cognitive ability and the lack of respect accorded to others as rememberers is a type of hostile misfortune that affects nearly all downwardly constituted social categories. In thinking about political harms, we must learn to be sensitive to how particular historical and contemporary representations of groups specifically discredit them as rememberers. Discrediting strategies will not always be obvious; their discovery may require an exercise in detection. Weininger's *Sex and Character* is explicitly misogynist. I believe that the best that can be said for the FMSF writings I have examined is that through the figure of metonymic replacement of the woman by her eager, false, suggestible, malleable memory, they mean to invoke a figure of women as noncredible when they testify to abuse.

Many of us find it very difficult to resist the authority of scientific texts, fearing that, if we undermine scientific authority, we will be left with no methodology for getting at the truth. I repeatedly make the point in this study that we are responsible for being good critics of science. Our ability to assess the direction of scientific research on memory and the forces that shape this research is crucial to an adequate appreciation of what is at stake when people make claims about the past.

NOTES

1. Elizabeth Loftus's work, when it is addressed to her professional peers, contains a mix of the two vocabularies while her popular work (Loftus and Ketcham 1994) makes more extensive use of false memory vocabulary.

2. See, for example, D. A. Bekerman and J. M. Bowers (1983). For a philosophical critique of memory psychology that predates the current crisis, see C. A. J. Coady (1992, ch. 15). To Coady, one of the most disturbing aspects of psychology's critique of eyewitness testimony is the "messianic positivism" of the science (263).

3. This pamphlet was included with material mailed for the conference "Memory and Reality: Reconciliation (Scientific, Clinical, and Legal Issues of False Memory Syndrome)," Baltimore, Maryland, December 9–11, 1994, cosponsored by FMSF and Johns Hopkins Medical Institutions.

4. Multiple personality disorder (MPD) is now known as dissociative identity disorder (DID). In this study, I use the older name to better reflect the role of this disorder in the debate.

5. Iatrogenic: induced inadvertently by a physician, surgeon, medical treatment, or diagnostic procedures (*Merriam Webster's Collegiate Dictionary*, 10th ed.).

6. Relatedly, Genevieve Lloyd cautions about models of reason that attempt to disrupt masculine symbolism by describing reason in feminine imagery, thinking that doing so will make a reliable contribution to gender equality. Janice Haaken comes close to suggesting that Elizabeth Loftus's feminine metaphors for memory are in some way liberatory. I see no reason to agree with her.

7. Descartes' theory is presented in *L'Homme*, first published in 1662 in Latin; Malebranche's endorsement of it is in *The Search after Truth*, first published in 1674. I depend on John Sutton's reading of these texts.

8. It is memory information as dispositional and superposed that John Sutton finds in Descartes and Malebranche.

9. John Sutton's own account also remains individualistic—the social comes in as a force for accepting and rejecting models.

10. For a view of cognitive systems as encompassing parts of our environment and activities, see Andy Clark (1998).

11. Both dimensions are equally apparent and important when we think about collective remembering.

6

SUGGESTIBILITY, MISDESIGN, AND SOCIAL SKEPTICISM

I study memory and I am a skeptic.

—Elizabeth Loftus

HOW MUCH SKEPTICISM?

In the last chapter, I examined a representation of women with weak identities, one that plays a significant part in our current complex engagement with issues of memory suggestibility. In this chapter, I shift to the figure of the therapist. I also draw out and highlight a theme of previous discussions in this book: how we respond to women's memories depends a great deal on how we allow our imaginations to be engaged. Feminists have been cautious in their response to foundation activities and claims, and the restraint of this response helps direct my concerns. Despite recognition that the FMSF has been engaged in a serious and successful multitargeting of women's competence and epistemic authority, feminists have accepted much of the current framing of memory suggestibility and the dangers of therapeutic contexts.

Feminist critics of therapy have suggested that feminism has moved from public activism to private healing, making room for the FMSF's claim that women seek the status of "victim."[1] Feminist therapists, in reconsidering their practice, have been sensitive to charges of depoliticizing abuse, but they have also become preoccupied with the problem of suggestibility.[2] Finally, some feminists have adopted the FMSF's characterization of the debate as a polarized conflict between scientific skeptics and naive believers. They have suggested that we should transform this bipolarity by, to some extent, bracketing the conservative profamily and antifeminist rhetoric of the FMSF and by seeking a middle ground in a judicious caution about the malleability of memory, especially in therapeutic contexts. Shelley Park writes, for example:

> It is too facile, and ultimately unpersuasive, simply to denounce or deconstruct these views. Despite the conservative rhetoric of the false memory movement, empirical evidence suggests that pseudo-memories (including memories of limited traumas) can be created when subjects are exposed to misinformation by a trusted authority figure. . . . The malleability of human memory raises serious philosophical questions with which feminists must be prepared to grapple. (1997, 10)

Feminists have, on the whole, tried to be responsive to foundation concerns while maintaining a commitment to the reality of childhood sexual abuse, to the welfare of women affected by abuse, and to the necessity of feminist political engagement. Sara Scott argues, however, that feminist caution about women's abuse narratives amounts to a political paralysis and that we have failed to respond effectively to the "discourse of disbelief" promoted by the FMSF (1997, 33).

The false memory debate is a deep and troubling context for examining questions of influence in a social epistemology. The FMSF's writings and activities—as well as the institutional, public, and feminist responses to the FMSF—raise serious ethical/epistemological questions about the appropriate role of skepticism in inquiry and about the appropriate degree and kind of our epistemic reliance on others. In this chapter, I investigate the interdependence of these issues in writings endorsed by the FMSF.

I first describe the difference between feminist and foundation projects and argue that the intent of a skeptical discourse is often to effect a shift in project. Specifically, the FMSF means to promote a shift away from the practical project of women's trying to understand and clarify past harm, often in association with other women and with therapists, in favor of waiting for science to discover the truth of the mind. I then examine a key imagining used in false memory writings to effect the shift in project: namely, that we are the victims of suggestive therapy. This imagining has a surprising precedent in Descartes' *Meditations on First Philosophy*,[3] and it seeks to motivate a shift in epistemic project through promoting skepticism about our faculties. Invoking this level of skepticism, however, creates a dilemma for the FMSF, as it can also work to undermine the faith in science that the FMSF promotes. Thus, in the final two sections, I examine the FMSF's use of the discourse of suggestibility to target therapists and limit our skepticism to women's memories of abuse. I argue that suggestibility, as we now encounter it, is a compound of worries about relational influence that we must distinguish and examine. Consequently, the evaluation of memory suggestibility cannot be left to science.

My intent is to lift concerns about influence from their home in the FMSF's skeptical strategies and to subject them to a self-reflective examination. How have we been influenced by the foundation's strategies? In focusing on the thought experiments that guide our skepticism, I am particularly concerned to explore the role of imagination in shifting relations of epistemic dependence. That we become dependent on those with whom we share imaginings is the FMSF's accusation; to encourage our dependence through shared imaginings is also its objective.

SKEPTICISM AND OUR PROJECTS

A striking feature of the FMSF's writings is their explicit endorsement of the language of skepticism. The scientific advisors to the FMSF associate skepticism positively with the commitment to a scientific method characterized by impartiality and the demand for fully evidenced claims. That the FMSF links skepticism with the avoidance of bias and the search for objective truth should first direct us toward assessing the charges of bias in relation to our projects and their underlying values. The aim of a skeptical discourse that depends, in part, on accusations of bias can be to disallow the values that undergird certain practices by claiming that the practices themselves cannot be pursued in ways that would allow for epistemic norms of objectivity.

The following is a common example of the kind of deflection that concerns me. When students sometimes accuse my marking of bias, they may be urging me to greater fairness in my evaluations. In this context, my having biases may mean that I fail to show an appropriate fidelity to some set of norms or standards for a particular evaluative practice, where my failure manifests itself in treating one set of cases quite differently from a relevantly similar set of cases. If I accept this charge of bias, I am obliged either to exercise more caution in my procedures or to find better procedures that reduce or eliminate the possibility of unfairness. I can accept the charge of bias while continuing to endorse the practice of grading.

I sometimes suspect, however, that there are no procedures that would exonerate me from a student's charge of bias. I sometimes suspect that students are trying to get me to concede that I should not be evaluating their work. Such students may either doubt that grading can ever be objective, or they may object to the values that underlie the practice. They may object, for example, to my institutional authority to judge their work. For these latter groups of students, an invocation of objectivity through the charge of bias is both the strategy and the disguise of a skepticism about the practice of grading. Thus the charge of bias can challenge the adequacies of procedures within a practice; or, more seriously or extravagantly, it can challenge the practice itself.

Since its inception, the primary stated activity of the FMSF has been to publicize the prevalence of false memory syndrome and the conditions that cause it, namely, therapeutic practices, self-help literature, survivor support groups, and broader social influences, including feminist activism. The FMSF has claimed that those most directly responsible for the spread of false memory syndrome are therapists who believe and express in their practice that childhood sexual abuse is widespread and an ongoing source of trauma for those victimized. As feminist therapists clearly fall into this category, I will understand the FMSF's critique of therapy as significantly directed at feminist therapists. Although feminists have sometimes responded by attempting to distinguish their commitments and practice from those of the "recovery" movement (Enns et al. 1995, Russell 1986/1999), their attempts to describe responsible therapeutic practice have had little effect on FMSF writings. For example, FMSF board member Harold Merskey writes:

> the attempt to explain everything by one single mechanism is a good sign of the quack. In this regard, the women's movement has grossly over-emphasized the importance of sexual abuse with respect to mental illness. . . . In this respect, some caregivers are responsible for confusing the issues and their intemperate campaigning makes things far worse for the real victims. . . . The shame and disgrace of inadequate treatment of victims today rests substantially with those who claim to be defending them. (1997, 134–35)

Because feminist therapists are committed to providing a context in which women who have been abused can explore and articulate their experience, I will assume in this chapter that feminists have an interest in supporting responsible feminist therapy.[4]

The FMSF has accused feminist therapists of not paying adequate attention to science, particularly to work on the malleability of memory, the unreliability of testimony, and the inability to test for repression under laboratory conditions. Rather, the FMSF charges that feminist therapists have an ideological bias toward childhood sexual abuse as an explanation for the unhappiness of their clients. Therapists manifest this bias in too easily accepting the claims of clients who say they were abused and in encouraging clients to search for abuse in their pasts. They exert harmful and careless influence over vulnerable clients through suggestive therapeutic techniques, ranging from hypnosis to simply asking clients if they have been abused. The ideologically driven commitment of these therapists to prefer and suggest certain explanations over others that might be equally compatible with the evidence is said to lead to great social harm—the accusation of innocent parents and the "brutalization of patients in therapy" (Ofshe and Watters 1994, 13).

Richard Ofshe accuses many therapists of having "slipped the ties that bind their professions to scientific method and sound research" (Ofshe and Watters 1994, 5). Elizabeth Loftus dedicates her book *The Myth of Repressed Memory: False Memories and Allegations of Sexual Abuse* to "the principles of science, which demand that any claim to 'truth' be accompanied by proof" (Loftus and Ketcham 1994, v). Loftus not only identifies the important epistemic project as the scientific understanding of the malleability of memory; she divides the public into "Skeptics" and "True Believers." True Believers accept the existence of repression. Skeptics recognize that the notion of repression is "essentially untestable," and they talk of "proof, corroboration, and scientific truth seeking" (31, 32). Although many writers have been careful to distinguish repression from dissociation, Loftus makes clear in a footnote that she regards talk of problems of delayed recall that incest survivors might face as a commitment to repression, no matter what term therapists use (Loftus and Ketcham 1994, 141). So the FMSF charges that feminist therapeutic practices display bias, including partiality that causes therapists to ignore alternative compelling explanations for women's unhappiness and problems with evidence. Unlike my students, who can offer no alternative to grading, foundation advisors offer a different and familiar locus of objectivity in the scientific study of memory, and they offer the public an option of perspectives: science-minded skeptic or true believer.

I do not believe that the FMSF's charge of bias can be read as an injunction to exercise caution within the project of a therapy that would allow and take seriously a narrative of past abuse; the FMSF's work is more reasonably interpreted as committed to removing this context. Foundation advisors explicitly campaign against therapy that involves attention to a client's past and against therapy that regards childhood sexual abuse as sufficiently serious and widespread that the possibility of such abuse might be raised as a hypothesis for a woman's distress. Ofshe proposes that all mental health disorders be treated either by biomedical therapy or by "rehabilitative-focused psychotherapy," which concentrates on "identifying troubling behaviors and coping patterns" and requires "no assumptions . . . about the etiology of disorders" (1994, 298). Board member Hollinda Wakefield and former member Ralph Underwager favor "cognitive behavioral therapy" that pays "minimal attention to the feelings of the client" since its intent is to change behavior and "maladaptive thinking" (1994, 362–63). Loftus suggests that therapy that focuses on the present "would become less a self-centered process of withdrawal and retreat than an act of moving outward to embrace the concerns of the community, the culture, and the environment" (Loftus and Ketcham 1994, 267).

FMSF members and advisors have also endorsed third-party negligence suits against therapists that would hold therapists accountable for "foreseeable harm," including emotional distress to the families of clients. The likely effect of such suits is that therapists will be less willing to treat those women who struggle to understand abusive pasts (Vella 1994, Bowman and Mertz 1996). FMSF supporters have campaigned for consumer mental health protection acts on a state and federal level that would limit access to the types of therapy that support disclosures of childhood sexual abuse and acknowledge the problems survivors face with recall of the abuse. A call for funding to develop model legislation for New Hampshire in 1994 stressed the necessity of developing a rationale that would include an explanation of "why the 'scientific community' should police therapy methods and procedures" and of developing "a legal analysis comparing fraudulent and politicized psychotherapists to drunk drivers" (National Association for Consumer Protection in Mental Health Practices 1994, 7–8). The legislation would ideally involve rules of ethical conduct for all therapy professionals and would eliminate "political 'psychology' theories" (8). Clearly, such proposed legislation intends to target feminist therapists.[5]

Moreover, the division between "Skeptics" and "True Believers" argues for a replacement of psychotherapy by science and not a collaboration of the two. Foundation skeptics do not support research designed to lend credence to women's experience of problems in recalling abuse. They are emphatic in contending that repression is untestable and that its investigation is not a part of scientific truth-seeking. I see no reasonable grounds for this contention. For example, Jennifer Freyd (1996) has developed a testable model of traumatic forgetting that examines the effect of betrayal by those we must continue to trust. Freyd argues that in such circumstances forgetting is an adaptive response. Additionally, a large number of studies have examined amnesia for abuse using a variety of different empirical methodologies (Scheflin and Brown 1996). Ofshe warns that science is distorted when influenced by social movements. Nevertheless, foundation skeptics explicitly support a science of the malleability of memory whose effect is to challenge psychotherapy as a site of suggestibility and memory distortion.[6]

The FMSF, in effect, argues that the public should support a shift in project that excludes the woman with a troubled past from participating as an epistemic agent in an understanding of her past and in contributing to social knowledge of childhood sexual abuse. She is not a participant in the scientific project of understanding memory, and her coming to understand her own past has no place in this inquiry. Through charging bias and evoking scientific objectivity, the activities of the False Memory Syndrome Foundation instead attempt a skeptical destruction of one of the contexts that allows a woman to understand a troubled and abusive past. But her perspective is critical to any communal project of objective knowledge of sexual harm.

THE ARGUMENT FROM MISDESIGN

I believe that there is a disturbing philosophical story about this shift from her project to their project, the attendant obliteration of the possibility of her perspective, and the degree of public skepticism that the FMSF has ignited. Many factors are obviously at work in the success of the FMSF. In previous chapters, I have focused on the social structuring of testimonial positions and on the stereotypical presentation of women as deceitful and easily influenced. Here, my interest is in an FMSF strategy that has its prototype in the least discussed yet most powerful of Descartes' skeptical arguments in the *Meditations*, which I shall call the argument from misdesign.[7] I discuss this argument in order to show that, in attempting to move us from support of therapy and survivor narrative through an appeal to scientific objectivity, the FMSF invites us into a shared imagining about the malleability of memory. This imagining is meant to promote a shift in epistemic project and in relations of epistemic reliance; but, in fact, it promotes a metaphysical skepticism that leaves knowledge unavailable.

In the *Meditations*, Descartes wishes to undertake the project of establishing a certain foundation for his beliefs. To do so, he must withdraw assent from the opinions he has as the result of habit, education, and other prejudice. This shift in project away from practical activity and the epistemology of the trusting believer is difficult. It requires the proof of real errors to engage doubt, which doubt must then become sufficiently powerful to allow for the complete suspension of trusting belief. There is an antiskeptical momentum, however, to our ability to identify errors within a practice, for these identifications suggest we can develop our procedures and refine our practices to prevent future error. Descartes needs to find a ground for doubt that cannot be answered by the ordinary practical precautions we might take in circumstances where we know that making a certain kind of mistake is a possibility. Descartes begins with the argument from illusion where the grounds for doubt can be lessened by appropriate attention to perceptual circumstances. For example, if remote objects always look deceptively small, perhaps one should get closer before judging their size. He moves to reasons for doubting that cannot be resolved by pointing to the possibility of precautions against error: the argument from dreaming, which is meant to make us wonder whether we can be sure about the source of our perceptual ideas; and the argument from misdesign.

The argument from misdesign is the final skeptical argument of the *Meditations*. It is meant to bring all of Descartes' beliefs—even those, like mathematical truths, that are indubitable—within the scope of a doubt that will lead to Descartes' withholding assent from all the ideas he has previously acquired. The argument from misdesign is developed by Descartes precisely to make his doubt as intense as possible by bringing into question the adequacy of his reason to withhold assent from what has not yet been proven certain. Descartes needs to become sufficiently skeptical about the worth of his ideas to compel a lasting shift of attention away from practical concerns and toward an examination of his faculties. As he seeks, so he says, not action but knowledge, he believes he cannot yield too much to distrust.

In making the argument from misdesign, Descartes notes that he has observed that others are sometimes in error, even about that of which they think they have perfect knowledge. This observation leads him to contemplate that God, through imperfection or malice, may have made him, Descartes, constitutionally subject to deception and error, even about matters of which he is certain: "How do I know that he has not brought it about that there is no earth, no sky, no extended thing, no shape, no size, no place, while at the same time ensuring that all these things appear to me to exist just as they do now?" (CSM, vol. 2, 14). The argument is summarized in the sixth meditation as follows: "Since I did not know the author of my being (or at least was pretending not to), I saw nothing to rule out the possibility that my natural constitution made me prone to error even in matters which seemed to me most true" (CSM, vol. 2, 53).

Descartes concludes from the argument from misdesign that "there is not one of my former beliefs about which a doubt may not be properly raised. . . . So in the future I must withhold my assent from these former beliefs just as carefully as I would from obvious falsehoods" (CSM, vol. 2, 14–15). He then takes care to keep the doubt in his mind by setting for himself the project of imagining that some malignant demon, at once exceedingly potent and deceitful, has employed all his artifice to keep deceptive presentations before Descartes' mind:

> It will be a good plan to turn my will in completely the opposite direction and deceive myself, by pretending for a time that these former opinions are utterly false and imaginary. . . . I will suppose therefore that not God, who is supremely good and the source of truth, but rather some malicious demon of the utmost power and cunning has employed all his energies in order to deceive me. (CSM, vol. 2, 15)

The argument from misdesign is a form of skeptical argument specifically oriented to motivating a shift in our projects, a shift away from the possibility of taking precautions in certain circumstances in which we might err. The shift is effected by postulating an internal mechanism that is unreliable, one that may cause us to be in error and not know it. Because the problem is one of an internal mechanism, potential error in judgment cannot be guarded against by attention to circumstances that form the settings of our projects. We must move away from these projects to an examination of the problematic faculty.

"Shirley Ann Souza was a mother's dream" (Loftus and Ketcham 1994, 1). "Christine, who was twenty-six the year that she began therapy, had known all her life that she had not come from a perfect family" (Ofshe and Watters 1994, 16). These narratives begin Loftus's and Ofshe's accounts of suggestive therapy involving "false" memories of abuse and the destruction of decent families. Foundation advisors make liberal use of narrative to make vivid the dangers of therapy, and these narratives have a single theme: a therapist could persuade any one of us that we are a victim of childhood sexual abuse. I regard these narratives as invitations to our imagination. In making this point, I want to concede that some are probably fairly accurate representations of irresponsible therapy. I follow Alan White in the view that to imagine something "is to think of it as possibly so. It is usually also to think of it in a certain way" (White 1990, 184). The activity of imagining is independent of the truth or falsity of the content of the imagining.

My concern is that our imaginative participation in these stories, which we are meant to take as representative of feminist psychotherapy, follows the form of an argument from misdesign. Here is a very explicit example from Ofshe and Watters, *Making Monsters: False Memories, Psychotherapy, and Sexual Hysteria* (1994):

> Picture an elephant. Imagine an apple. Now spend a moment visualizing an image of being sexually abused by one of your parents. It is an often distressing trick of the mind that it will create any event regardless of our desire to visualize the event. What separates an imagined image from a memory image is not a simple matter, for even imagined events are themselves largely built from memory. . . . To create this image, we might use recollections of our parents' physical appearances and of ourselves as children. We might place the scene in the memory of our childhood room. To create the action of the scene, we might use memories of other people's descriptions of sexual assaults or of abuse scenes depicted in books or movie dramas. In the end, all the pieces of the imagined event would have something of the weight of memory. . . . Our innate ability to distinguish between memory and imagination is a precarious and, at best, an imperfect mechanism. (107)

The content of the shared imagining that we are to undertake as readers is here supplied by Ofshe. However, the text that follows the quoted passage makes clear that what we are meant to imagine in thinking about this passage is that we are asked to produce a visualization of abuse during therapy. We are to engage in this imagining by supposing that the visualization is suggested to us by a therapist. Ofshe continues: "faced with the first visualization of abuse . . . at the beginning of therapy, patients often attest that the image does not feel like a memory" (107).

I am not concerned with whether, as a thought experiment, the proposed visualization produces an imagining for any reader, let alone one that seems like a memory. It need not succeed at doing so. If it does not succeed, we are then to further imagine that the therapist accuses us of denial and subjects us to further techniques of influence. We are to hold this therapist in our mind. The type of therapist we are asked to imagine, labeled a "recovered memory therapist," is described by Ofshe as "poorly trained, overzealous, or ideologically driven" (5). Recovered memory therapists "without an understanding of the damage they have caused . . . have employed methods that blur the already perilously thin line that separates memory from imagination" (5). In the passage following the imagining, we are told that such therapists can "destroy the patient's ability" to distinguish between memory and imagination (108).

We are first, then, asked to imagine that we are not well designed, that we may be prone to damaging error that we cannot detect as error. Our sometime inability to distinguish a memory image from a visualization is characterized as being the result of a precarious and imperfect psychic mechanism. Second, we are asked to concentrate on the figure of a therapist as potential deceiver. We are asked to imagine that she supplies the content of the visualizations by which we are misled and will use all her power to persuade us that the visualizations before our mind are memories. To hold in mind the presence of the therapist as a potential deceiver is to keep the possibility of misdesign concrete and vivid. She is the device that we use in this thought experiment to remind ourselves of our vulnerability to false memories. As the figure that supplies our visualizations, her presence, like the demon's, also works to define the project that we must abandon. Finally, that we should take ourselves to be deceived also serves to keep us hopeful by reminding us that there is a truth to be discovered about memory.[8] Ofshe believes that our understanding of memory and our cultural ability to deal with major mental health disorders await "the painstaking, expensive and time-consuming application of science" (Ofshe and Watters 1994, 298).

The argument from misdesign is particularly suited to the FMSF's objective: first, it turns us from feminist therapy as a kind of project within which we could take reasonable precautions against suggestions of abuse; second, it casts doubts wholesale on the abuse memories of women who seek therapy. Motivating our participation in a misdesign imagining does not depend on getting us to recognize our own serious errors; it uses our own confidence or credulity against us by pointing to confident or credulous others who have been in serious error. Only a few serious and suspect cases involving perception, judgment, or memory are needed to motivate the argument; and these suspect cases do not need to come from our own experience. Many FMSF writings recycle the same cases, some now notorious, of dubious recovered memory while engaging the reader, often explicitly, in thought experiments about the possibility of her own misdesign.

Second, a misdesign imagining may be raised on the suspicion that a number of our or others' beliefs or memories are false, but the argument bypasses questions of whether individual beliefs and memories are in fact false. It is meant to raise skepticism about a whole category of thought.[9] We can be alarmed by the potential for confident, unwitting error without adequately pausing to consider whether particular traumatic rememberings might be accurate and whether dependence on a therapist might not sometimes be wise.

A willingness to doubt women's memories with no attention to whether the memories are true or whether the abuse happened is evident in some of the most disturbing legal and political affirmations of the FMSF's work. In 1994, Gary Ramona successfully sued his daughter's therapists for negligence. The jury was asked to decide whether Holly Ramona's therapists had inappropriately reinforced Holly's false memories without being asked to reach a determination as to whether the memories were, in fact, false or whether the abuse had taken place (Whitfield 1995, 193–200).[10] The justice department in Canada recently considered reviewing all cases involving recovered memory testimony in which men have been convicted. Alan Gold, the lawyer responsible for the initiative and a presenter at FMSF conferences, argued that "real or not, such alleged memories are too readily confused with the results of suggestion and confabulation to have any degree of reliability" (Gold, quoted in Bindman 1998). Gold's appeal to misdesign is meant to render ineffectual the reasonable position that cases of recovered memory can be individually assessed.

Finally, we need to grasp what is both tempting and problematic for feminists in being responsive to the FMSF's doubts while affirming the widespread reality of childhood sexual abuse. The FMSF does not ask us to disbelieve women's narratives, but it does advise caution about them—which may seem like an appealing middle ground. However, the misdesign imagining replaces the focus on belief with one on assent or acceptance, and it can be read as encouraging an even deeper shift in epistemic commitment than the withdrawal of support for survivor therapy.

For Descartes, to withhold assent from an idea is to treat it as false for the purposes of inquiry. Modern epistemologists are more likely to distinguish between belief and acceptance of a hypothesis, where, according to Bas Van Frassen, acceptance is "a commitment to the further confrontation of new phenomena within the framework of that theory, a commitment to a research programme, and a wager that all relevant phenomena can be accounted for without giving up that theory" (1980, 88).[11] Although we often believe and accept the same hypothesis, we may accept a hypothesis for the purpose of inquiring without thinking it is true; alternatively, we may think a hypothesis is true, but inadequate to direct inquiry. Feminists historically have not only believed women's testimony of abuse but have accepted this testimony as the foundation of our research and activism. This commitment has allowed recognition of child sexual abuse as a widespread and serious reality for women. The FMSF offers the seductive option of continuing to think that most women are probably telling the truth about their experiences of abuse while rejecting this testimony as adequate to direct our projects.

The FMSF, however, faces an obvious difficulty in utilizing misdesign imaginings to promote reliance on science as a substitute for projects that rely on memory testimony. The intent of a misdesign imagining is to move our attention from projects that depend on the use of our faculties toward an examination of these faculties. However, if the problem of misdesign cannot be solved by our caution within certain projects, then neither can it be resolved by abandoning these projects for other projects that rely on the faculties of those who are similarly misdesigned. The figure of the therapist in foundation arguments, like the demon in Descartes, acts to delimit circumstances that remain epistemically unsafe. The demon reminds Descartes of the unreliability of sense perception and its deficiency as a source of knowledge. The figure of the therapist reminds us of the unreliability of memory testimony and its deficiencies as a source of knowledge. Descartes can, perhaps, investigate reason while avoiding problematic uses of perception. We cannot, however, in our pursuit of the sciences of memory avoid reliance on memory. Researchers who study memory are tremendously reliant on their own memories and on the memories of their experimental subjects.

Metaphysical skepticism is the view that attaining knowledge of certain subjects—the external world, other minds, the past, and so on—transcends our powers. We have no way of improving our position for knowing the truth, and the reason has to do with the alleged fact that the truth transcends our faculties and methods. The distinctively metaphysical skeptic has to widen the gap between reality and our faculties/methods to ensure that even the most persistent and cautious use of our faculties/methods could not in principle close this gap. In offering the argument from misdesign, Descartes is a metaphysical skeptic. In offering the argument from misdesign, foundation authors are also metaphysical skeptics. Descartes moves back from metaphysical skepticism. Recognizing that he is not epistemically self-sufficient, he resolves his doubts about reason partly through trust in the goodness and power of the cause that produced him. When memory is the faculty devalued in a misdesign imagining, faith in science and scientists is, quite obviously, no remedy.

DISSECTING SUGGESTIBILITY

In the third meditation, Descartes characterizes the doubt raised by the argument from misdesign as slight. A benevolent God would not have left us prone to undetectable error; moreover, the imagined demon is a device to aid withdrawal of assent, but is no real deceiver. My students, however, find more power in Descartes' description of the demon than he might have anticipated. They frequently ignore Descartes' claim that the demon is only a device, and in doing so activate the real possibility of their own deception. Their reading converts the argument from misdesign into an imagining about suggestibility.

The power of the FMSF's misdesign imagining depends on our actual concerns about suggestibility in therapeutic contexts. Although the therapist is a figure in the imagining, she is meant to differ from the demon in being a real threat. In this section, I examine the sorts of worries expressed through an alarm about suggestibility. I want to question, perhaps tendentiously, whether suggestibility is the appropriate language in which to express concerns about influence in therapy; I also want to argue that, at the very least, we need more precision about the nature of these concerns. To aid this dissection, I introduce a Canadian legal case, *A.(L.L.) v. B.A.* (1995), where defense counsel sought a sexual assault complainant's confidential therapy records on the grounds that they might reveal suggestive therapy. Though the complainant had had continuous memory for a sexual assault that occurred when she was six years old, records were sought partly to determine "the method of extracting the information from her during the 14 months she underwent sessions prior to going to see the police" (Aboriginal Women's Council et al. 1996a, 464). Such legal cases were not uncommon in Canada in the 1990s, and in the next chapter I discuss them more fully.

Our current worries about suggestibility reflect our concern about relationships of influence. The power of suggestibility to evoke social alarm depends on how we picture or represent these relationships. In the representations deployed in false memory writing, women are portrayed as dangerously susceptible to the power of a group of therapists who deliberately or inadvertently use suggestive techniques to implant false memories that become new self-conceptions for these clients. This scenario models therapeutic influence on a classic representation of hypnotic power as a danger to the social order. And, in fact, it is the sometime use of hypnosis in therapy that has legitimated the language of suggestibility in FMSF writings. As used technically in the context of hypnosis, hypnotic susceptibility or suggestibility "refers to the subjects' level of responsiveness to test suggestions."

These suggestions describe a "'make-believe' or counterfactual situation" that is to be

> treated by subjects as if it were really happening and is to lead to the occurrence of a congruent overt response. . . . In short, suggestions implicitly invite subjects to suspend the tacit rules usually employed to differentiate imagined events from actual events, to define the ongoing situation in terms of imagined events and to enact behaviors implied by those imagined events. (Spanos 1986, 90)

Nicholas Spanos describes the situation of suggestibility as a shared project of imagining, where what is to be imagined is controlled by one of the parties and enacted by the other. Hypnotic susceptibility (sometimes called "primary suggestibility") is tested through responses perceived by the subject as involuntary and is carefully distinguished by researchers and practitioners from gullibility (sometimes called "secondary suggestibility") (Hilgard 1965, 273–74). That a person receives a high score on a test for hypnotic susceptibility gives no indication that he or she is gullible, dependent, weak-willed, or compliant. Nevertheless, the idea of one person's responses being controlled by another, derived from popular representations of hypnosis, has animated a long history of concern about suggestibility that pays little attention to the technical notion of hypnotic susceptibility.[12]

In their comprehensive psycholegal history of hypnosis, Jean-Roch Laurence and Campbell Perry remark that "the general public tends to equate hypnosis with the notion of suggestibility, which is a polite way of characterizing a person as gullible and weak-willed" (1988, xiv). Their work makes clear that the public has often had excessive and ungrounded fears of hypnotic power related to particular views about the moral weakness of hypnotic subjects, especially women. If we take the popular conception of hypnosis as our model for thinking about suggestibility, what moral fears are engaged?

It is worth noting right away that shared imagining is a feature not only of hypnosis but of a variety of valuable make-believe activities. Children learn a wide range of social, motor, and cognitive skills through make-believe games initiated by adults and older children. From childhood on, friends and family help us achieve our objectives by staging preparatory imaginary scenarios that allow us to anticipate obstacles and formulate responses. Moreover, philosopher Kendall Walton (1990) has argued that our ability to participate in shared imaginings that we do not control is at the root of our response to the representational arts. We can thus think of many cases in which following the imagining of another is benign, pleasurable, and useful.

The overriding concern historically evoked by hypnosis, however, is one of excessive dependence: that the person following the imagining is too much under the power of the suggester. According to Laurence and Perry, the history of response to hypnosis is dominated by concerns about hypnotic power and the will:

> From a very early period, there have been allegations that hypnosis . . . could be used to sexually seduce women, or more generally, to abolish the willpower of those who submitted to it. . . . (1988, xvi)

This concern about the autonomy of the hypnotized subject is actually a compound of three distinguishable worries, all of which are present in recent concerns about women in therapy.

First, the implication between Spanos's contrast between imagined and actual events might make it look as if what is to be imagined is always false. In fact, situations that we imaginatively engage with may be true or untrue, likely to come about or unlikely. But we think of hypnotic subjects as gullible because we often picture them as accepting and enacting false or absurd suggestions about themselves. In transferring this concern to women in therapy, we may think that the therapist will implant ideas that are false but will be believed—such as, for example, that a woman has been abused when she has not been. *A.(L.L.)* was presented to the public as a case where the defense sought her records "on the suggestion that counselors may have unwittingly coached her into developing false memories of abuse" (Vienneau 1995, A3).

Second, we worry about the effect of uncritical judgment on action. Laurence and Perry note that hypnosis is a situation in which one is "asked to set aside critical judgement, without abandoning it completely" (1988, xiv). More precisely, the worry is that some feature of the suggestive circumstances, typically the authority of the suggester, will encourage a person to unwisely enact an imagining while at the same time rendering that person unable to properly evaluate whether she should do so.[13] The concern about unwise action (action that is both unfortunate and uncritical) is central to the current alarm about the suggestibility of women's memories. Therapy is represented as seriously undermining women's critical abilities, thus causing them to make precipitous false accusations. In *A.(L.L.)* the defense implied that the complainant would not have contacted the police but for the influence of therapy.

Finally, we may fear that the projects and objectives that persons take to be important to who they are, their self-understanding and self-presentation, are too much under the control of another. According to Ofshe, "patients [in therapy] receive encouragement . . . to surrender their will" (Ofshe and Watters 1994, 120). In popular representations of hypnosis, the subject seems to be involved in a project of presenting the self, where the project's defining feature is that the self is presented as under the control of another. Throughout their study, Laurence and Perry refer to this third concern as the persistent concern that the hypnotized subject has become an automaton with no will of her own. In *A.(L.L.)* the complainant was presented by the defense as an instrument of the therapist's project rather than, as the record appears to show, a self-defining agent:

> The production order was made . . . notwithstanding there being no evidence that information concerning the assault was "extracted" by counsellors from the Appellant. To the contrary, the Appellant's evidence is that she brought up the issue of reporting the assault to the police, a decision she came to once she developed the strength to do and the insight to realize that the assault was not her fault. (Aboriginal Women's Council et al. 1996a, 465)

What is important to notice is that the ethical concerns I have outlined are distinguishable, and the importance of this point will be clear in the next section, when I examine the scientific understanding of suggestibility. Worrisome influence can, for example, take place through shared imaginings where the subject does not come to believe something that is false; such imaginings can even have an objective such as discovering something about the world. A case in point: my sixth-grade science teacher and school principal, Mr. Duckworth, vigorously explaining resistance to our class by bouncing his wooden yardstick off a linoleum floor, added, as an aside, that were Randy to run headfirst into the wall he, too, would bounce off. Whereupon Randy, caught up in the spirit of demonstration, stood up and, running the length of the classroom, took himself headfirst into the wall. Mr. Duckworth's authority encouraged Randy to act without thinking and to act unwisely, although Randy did not come to believe anything false. Mr. Duckworth might well also, of course, have worried about Randy's capacity for self-definition, his willingness or eagerness to be a prop in a sixth-grade science demonstration. But we might also worry about a person's capacity for self-definition in circumstances where that person does not come to believe falsities and does not act precipitously.

When framed through a model of hypnotic suggestibility, however, worries about influence are easy to activate: they mutually provoke each other and are difficult to contain. The suspicion that the complainant in *A.(L.L.)* had had suggestive therapy aroused public and legal anxieties about false belief and precipitous action and also about whose agency was in control of her complaint. Worries about who people become in their relationships with others are especially high for groups like women, who have been traditionally regarded as lacking autonomy. Unsurprisingly, women were regarded as particularly suggestible throughout the history of public response to hypnosis. Laurence and Perry's study demonstrates that moral alarm about the hypnotist's power often took the specifically gendered form of doubt about women's moral character—interestingly, not only over their alleged innate weakness of will, but also over their purported tendency toward hysterical pathologies and their inclination to lie about sexual assault.

Philosopher Diana Meyers has defined autonomy as a cluster of competencies, including skills of self-discovery, self-direction, and self-definition. Moreover, like many contemporary theorists, she defends autonomy as relational, acknowledging that the relevant competencies "can only be developed in the context of social relationships, practices, and institutions" (Mackenzie and Stoljar 2000, 17). What is intriguing is that, if we understand autonomy in the way that Meyers does, the complex of worries that comprise the alarm about women's suggestibility is a point-by-point denial of their autonomy: their abilities at self-discovery, self-direction, and self-definition. But the complainant in *A.(L.L.)* testified that she had never forgotten the abuse, had described it to others, had raised it herself in therapy, and had come forward when she heard that the respondent had assaulted someone else (Aboriginal Women's Council et al. 1996a, 459). In fact, she claimed that her counseling was actually autonomy *enhancing*, an experience that supported her skills of self-discovery and self-direction. And I find no reason to disbelieve her. She came to remember her past more accurately, as involving an assault that was not her fault, and she was able to take action that she considered right and necessary.

When we are told to be worried about suggestibility, we must be alert to the social forces and representations that shape our understanding of risk and of who is at risk. To model the therapist as a deceiver with dangerous hypnotic powers to which women are especially susceptible is an irresponsible representation. While it is appropriate and essential for therapists to realistically assess the influence they have on individual clients, I contend that in most cases we have no reason to accept the current construct of suggestibility as a description of this influence. This construct encourages us to impute exceptional power to therapists and to deny agency to clients. When we are told to be worried about suggestibility, we also have a responsibility to identify and disentangle specific kinds of concerns. We must look realistically and carefully at the relationships in which problematic influence on memory is suspected, and we must carefully disentangle a number of different kinds of concerns. In the next section, I offer a caution about how far our present reliance on science can aid in these projects.

SCIENCE AND SUGGESTIBILITY

I stated earlier that the argument from misdesign is meant to effect a shift in our projects away from those that involve the threat of undetectable error to an examination of the problematic faculty. The specter of suggestibility made vivid in Ofshe's misdesign imagining has given added authority to the FMSF's claim that we must shift away from the support of survivor therapy toward a science of the malleability of memory. A key strategy of the FMSF's replacement of testimonial contexts for survivors with scientific experiments about memories has been to raise fears about suggestibility and then reabsorb the analysis of suggestibility into a body of preexisting psychology research on the inaccuracy of recall, initially on the studies of eyewitness testimony devised by Loftus. The FMSF's organization of suggestibility as a problem for memory science has been growing in sophistication; it has more recently involved experiments designed to have subjects develop pseudomemories for trauma-like events when prompted by a trusted individual (Loftus and Ketcham 1994, ch. 7).

I have argued in previous chapters that we should resist the present intense focus on memory malleability, and in this section I offer additional reasons for my caution, which reasons are grounded in how scientists model suggestibility. This research inflames the particular concern that influence on memory inevitably leads to false belief; it tends to represent our relationships with trusted others as deceptive and problematic for memory; and it contributes to the present devaluing of therapy by representing it as a context in which remembering is dangerous and from which no knowledge of memory can be gained.

In a simple and typical experiment on memory suggestibility, a subject is shown a series of slides of a scene and then tested on her recall. The test questions incorporate misleading information by the experimenter: for example, when the slide shows a yield sign, the question may ask, "Did the car go through the stop sign?" The subject's answering yes will be taken as evidence that memory is suggestible.[14] Thus, first, when suggestibility is scientifically framed as the malleability of memory, there is an especially acute conflation of the issue of false belief with other effects of influence. Suggestibility is standardly operationalized by scientists as "the susceptibility to error when given false information or asked questions designed to elicit false information" (Fivush 1996, 152). As scientific tests for suggestibility are tests for false information, they easily lead to the conclusion that, insofar as we are influenced in our beliefs, we come to believe what is false.

In looking at the scientific treatment of suggestibility, we have some explanation for how therapist influence on clients has been used to organize a widespread fear of false belief. The FMSF, which depends primarily on Loftus for its understanding of suggestibility, has frequently made use of the results of a survey by Poole and colleagues (1995) that claims that up to 25 percent of therapists could be using suggestive techniques in therapy. The study has been widely quoted as evidence for the potentially epidemic nature of "false" memory. In fact, in the mid-1990s, the study was used to generate estimates of over one million cases a year (Pope 1996, 964).[15] The study, however, did not distinguish between techniques when they incorporate misleading information and these same techniques when they do not include misleading information. Nor did the researchers show that the techniques enumerated "are differentially associated with systematically supplying false or misleading information about child abuse" (Pope 1997, 1000). The study only supports a concern about "false" memory if the targeted techniques lead to false belief, and this reading uses the notion of suggestibility operationalized in memory science.[16]

Second, the scientific understanding of suggestibility is modeled on a situation invariably characterized by deceptive relationships. Subjects are misled by the experimenter. In Loftus's original "Lost in the Mall" experiments, which were designed to test whether whole false memories could be "implanted," her students deliberately deceived younger family members by persuading them they had been lost as small children when no such incidents had occurred (Loftus and Ketcham 1994, ch. 7). Scientific models of suggestibility can easily mislead us about the effect of influence on memory because of the way they represent relationships. In chapter 4, I referred to Janice Haaken's remark that, for scientists like Loftus, "emotional and social variables are introduced as factors that weaken and impair memory . . ." (1998, 51). If a background assumption on which experiments are designed is that memory is most accurate when there is no influence on it, then this memory research will obviously overlook the possibility that relational support may be vital to our abilities as rememberers. Moreover, because the assumption is built into the experimental design, it is itself not tested.

The difficulty with the scientific framing of suggestibility is not easy to see because scientists often represent their results as objective and value-neutral, as deriving from experiments carried out in carefully controlled circumstances designed to be unaffected by surrounding social–political biases and agendas. The artificiality of experimental design can itself lead to a certain criticism: namely, that because scientists study memory in a decontextualized manner, that is, outside the contexts in which remembering takes place, they therefore cannot give us much insight into these contexts. While it is true that science gives us limited insight into actual relational contexts of remembering, I do not attribute these limits solely to decontextualization. There is an additional level to the problem. Science is a social practice influenced by cultural ideals of individualism and autonomy in its study of memory. Scientific work on the suggestibility of memory does represent people as remembering in contrived relational contexts, portraying these relationships as wholly negative in their impact on memory. This representation is likely to be especially problematic for groups already represented as lacking autonomy.

Current research on suggestibility exemplifies that science is not independent of specific cultural influences such as the FMSF. The work of the

FMSF arose as a response to a legal problem—the increased possibilities for women to institute criminal proceedings related to historic abuse. The shift in Loftus's research, for example, toward using authority figures to implant "false" childhood memories in her subjects, attempts to structure a scientific understanding of suggestibility specifically for legal use in cases alleging sexual abuse where the complainant has been in therapy.[17] The generalized and gender-neutral language of empirical psychology, combined with its implicit commitment to individualism, has allowed the discussion of suggestibility as a threat to memory accuracy to spread to contexts where recovered memories are not at issue. In the next chapter, I look at the impact of suggestibility on legal cases that involve continuous memory for sexual assault. Nevertheless, because of the impact of false memory advocacy on scientific practice, the threat also remains to some extent bounded by worry about contexts like therapy. Even a scientist like Daniel Schacter, who is committed to a balanced and nonalarmist assessment of current controversies, contrasts the indispensable value of the laboratory, where "experimenters can control the events" that influence the development of memories, to therapy, where "it is impossible to make controlled comparisons" (1996, 276). As Schacter's remarks make clear, therapy has now entered scientific writing as an unreliable contrast to a laboratory setting since it comprises no controlled comparisons. But his comments also intimate the extent to which we are devaluing knowledge about memory that is gained from contexts like therapy.

Finally, then, we need to be critical and cautious, first, of how concerns about therapy have been absorbed into recent scientific research on suggestibility and, second, of how claims to scientific expertise implicitly exclude or denigrate alternative sources of knowledge. Psychotherapists know a great deal about individual memory experience and about the dynamics of remembering and forgetting that are difficult to model or test in the laboratory. They are nonetheless regarded by both scientists and a large segment of the public as less expert on memory than those engaged in laboratory research. This bias has been evident and troubling, for example, with regard to the difficult time clinicians and psychotherapists have had in gaining legitimacy for their knowledge of trauma-related amnesias. It is evident in charges that support for repression is purely anecdotal (see chapter 3). It is evident in Loftus's claim that any therapist's report of any incest survivor's delayed recall, whatever the terminology used, shows a commitment to repression, which is "essentially untestable."

Many of us have accepted that suggestibility is a problem that scientists are in the best position to define and study. This certainly seems to be the view of memory scientists who have been drawn into the false memory debates. Daniel Schacter writes: "The recovered memories controversy, though a complex affair that touches on issues of incest, family, social mores and even religious beliefs, is fundamentally a debate about accuracy, distortion, and suggestibility in memory" (Schacter 1996, 251). Even vigorous feminist critics of the FMSF have accepted that suggestibility is a problem amenable to scientific analysis. Therapist Laura Brown, for example, identifies two levels of the false memory debate: the level of science—what we can know and how we know it—and a political level of who owns the history of the family and childhood. Her discussion of suggestibility takes place under the heading of science (Brown 1996a). Because suggestibility marks a set of ethical concerns about autonomy and power, I have argued that we cannot concede the analysis of suggestibility to science. Scientists can provide valuable knowledge about the workings of memory, but only if we are confident of our ability and right to challenge the ways in which they frame problems and the claims to authority with which they sometimes do so.

CONCLUSION

The FMSF invites us into an imagining about suggestibility as a strategy of influence, and I initially set the question of how we might have been influenced by the foundation's skepticism. It may seem tempting and tidy to conclude from my analysis that through a bombardment of "false" memory imaginings, the FMSF has succeeded in suggesting that we are suggestible and that as a public we are unwisely enacting our role in this shared imagining. I do not accept this reading of FMSF influence. I do not believe that members of the public lack epistemic agency in relation to the FMSF. I do believe that the FMSF uses relatively powerful rhetorical strategies to shift our support away from women who have been abused. I have argued that the use of imaginings in the false memory debate is to influence the direction of inquiry and to configure relations of epistemic reliance. When we read the testimonials of incest survivors and when we read "false" memory writings, we are, in both cases, engaged in shared imaginings, where what is to be imagined is under the control of the authors of the texts. The imaginings to which we commit our assent will determine different kinds of epistemic projects. One is a political project of supporting the contexts in which women can explore and articulate their experience of harm. This project takes their testimony as fundamental to our own understanding of childhood sexual harm. The other is an equally political project of supporting the FMSF's science of a malleability of memory.

I have argued that the two projects are not compatible and that the FMSF seeks to shift our support from the first to the second. The FMSF project, however, is an invitation to uncontained skepticism; moreover, when a science of the malleability of memory is offered as an investigation of suggestibility, such a science encourages an ungrounded fear of widespread false belief. Finally, when we confront the doubts raised by an alarm of suggestibility, we need to address concerns about the appropriate degree and kind of our epistemic and practical reliance on others. It is important to realize that what is appropriate here does depend on our projects.

To raise an alarm about suggestibility is not just to advance the concern that through participating in imaginings, we come to believe what is false. It is a more complex grouping of concerns about who we become and what actions we take through our associations with others and their influence on us. Women who explore their pasts in therapy or with the support of other women may come to identify themselves as survivors, perhaps undertaking a radical change in self-presentation. They may act in ways that the FMSF was established to counteract. They may confront their families and even sue those they hold responsible for abuse. The change in women from dutiful daughters to the critics of patriarchal families has occasioned deep distress, and suggestibility must be engaged with as political criticism.

I believe that the context of therapy will remain problematic for feminists to assess and that the current debate directs us to incorporate a study of interpretive contexts like therapy more fully into our epistemologies. We need first an understanding of the influence of shared imaginings in a positive epistemology. Our ability to participate in shared imaginings is crucial to our response to art and to our moral ability to empathize with others. Susan Babbitt (1996) has argued that committed action on the basis of imagined possibilities is also necessary to bring about the social conditions that make possible objective knowledge. She acknowledges that commitment in advance of knowledge is always a risk but that it is often an epistemically necessary one.

Second, and relatedly, feminists who are committed to defending objective knowledge must critically evaluate the demands for transformative criticism in our current feminist accounts of objectivity.[18] Helen Longino (1994) and Naomi Scheman (1996) are among feminists who have argued for a view of objective knowledge as being the tentative product of "the critical workings of a sufficiently democratic epistemic community" (Scheman 1996, 231). Scheman's account stresses that to be sufficiently democratic is to be understood partly in that community's encouragement of marginalized or outlaw perspectives that challenge how privilege can be naturalized and justified. Facilitating the articulation of these perspectives requires "the cultivation of relationships of trust" and an understanding of "how we create the possibilities for meaningfulness in each other's lives" (233, 234). We require an account of objectivity that can endorse the contexts in which knowledge emerges only through relationships of trust, the influence of imagination, and the protection from premature criticism. The cost of supporting these contexts may indeed be uncertainty about whether our beliefs or commitments are fully justified; the cost of withdrawing our support from these contexts will be the silencing of these perspectives.

NOTES

1. For expressions and discussions of these concerns, see Louise Armstrong (1994), Laura Brown (1996b), Laura Brown and Erica Burman (1997), Carolyn Enns et al. (1995), Janice Haaken (1996), Celia Kitzenger (1993), and Carol Tavris (1993).

2. See especially, Carolyn Enns et al. (1995), Laura Brown (1996a), and Laura Brown and Erica Burman (1997).

3. References to the *Meditations* are by volume and page number to John Cottingham, Robert Stoothoff, and Dugald Murdoch, eds., *Descartes: Selected Philosophical Writings* (1988), vols. 1 and 2. Abbreviated in the text as CSM.

4. For an excellent discussion of responsible therapy, one attentive to the false memory debates, see Mary Gail Frawley-O'Dea (1999).

5. R. Christopher Barden directed this initiative.

6. Feminists, among others, have vigorously criticized the type of extreme positivism that is manifest in foundation writings: a demand for falsifiable hypotheses, a commitment to the neutrality of the context of justification, and little recognition of the role of social interests in the setting of scientific agendas. For an extended argument about the importance of feminist perspectives to objectivity, see Richmond Campbell (1998).

7. In my reading of this argument, I follow Rockney Jacobsen (n.d.). There has been much discussion about what the third level of skeptical doubt is in the *Meditations*. Jacobsen notes that only a few commentators have treated the argument from misdesign as importantly distinct from the use of the demon as a device.

8. I owe this point to Jan Sutherland.

9. In a persuasive questioning of the evidence for FMSF's claims about the nature of false memory syndrome and its alleged epidemic status, Kenneth Pope (1996) has challenged the FMSF and its Scientific and Professional Advisory Board to "report any available scientific data about the ability to diagnose false memory syndrome without meeting the person alleged to have the disorder" (962). Pope notes "that it remains unclear whether the protocol of any research purporting to validate the false memory syndrome diagnosis in large numbers of people used any criterion other than the decision rule that all recovered memories of abuse are inherently false" (959). The use of misdesign imaginings is the rhetorical strategy that supports this decision procedure. Disturbingly, to point out the dearth of evidence for false memory syndrome has seemed somehow beside the point in this debate, a weak technicality that does not address the ground of the skepticism.

10. See Cynthia Grant Bowman and Elizabeth Mertz (1996) for a feminist analysis of the Ramona case.

11. I am grateful to K. Brad Wray (1997) for drawing my attention to this article.

12. Ernest Hilgard writes "that for assessment purposes we may define susceptibility as the depth [of hypnosis] achieved under standard conditions of induction, the more susceptible becoming more hypnotized than the less susceptible when common procedures of induction are followed" (1965, 67). Items tested on suggestibility scales range from eye closure to posthypnotic suggestion, and responses are experienced as involuntary. Therapists are themselves often not careful to distinguish hypnotic susceptibility from other meanings of suggestibility. Most writers on hypnosis insist that the distinction is clear and justified on the basis of many kinds of experiments that have substantiated a lack of correlation between hypnotic susceptibility and other kinds of suggestibility. Therapists have also been affected by the current skepticism and have become somewhat uncertain as to how they should respond to a charge of suggestive therapy. Therapists need to understand the forces that are determining public alarm and to be clear about what they mean when they themselves use the term.

13. It may also simply be the need to take action. For example, social workers are sometimes instructed to be careful in speculating about a client's situation when that client is in crisis, to avoid saying, for example, "What would happen if you were to confront him about his abuse?" The worry is not that the client will develop false beliefs but that the need to take some action may be so great that the client is rendered unable to evaluate the consequences of acting, even when it might be unwise for her to act.

14. This example is based on Elizabeth Loftus's earlier research into the misinformation effect on memory.

15. Interestingly, uses of Debra Poole and colleagues' survey almost never note that the results include only those responses from therapists who had treated ten or more adult female clients in the two years before the study (Pope 1997, 1001). Using the study to talk about suggestive techniques implies that certain techniques are suggestive when they are used with women.

16. For a feminist concern about suggestibility that is insufficiently wary of the conflation of influence and falsity, see Carolyn Enns and colleagues' (1995) discussion of scientific research.

17. Elizabeth Loftus explains how controversies over abuse memories motivated her to devise new kinds of experiments, in chapter 7 of *The Myth of Repressed Memory* (Loftus and Ketcham 1994).

18. The description of transformative criticism is in Helen Longino (1994).

7

THE COSTS OF A STEREOTYPE: PROTECTING WOMEN'S CONFIDENTIAL RECORDS

In the final two chapters of this book, I move from a direct focus on false memory writing to a set of broader reflections on relational personhood and relational remembering. The present chapter is about relational personhood. If we ignore the range of people's dependent and interdependent relationships in a context where we have to understand capacities or deliberate values, we risk an incomplete and distorted account. I have been steadily developing this point in relation to women's memories. I now trace the influence of the false memory debates on a Canadian legal controversy that began in the 1990s. I expand on a relational notion of personhood and trace how its neglect in the false memory debates has distorted not only our understanding of rememberers but our grasp on other values as well.

In Canada, as elsewhere, one effect of false memory discourse has been an increased legal wariness of relationships between women and their therapists. Throughout the last decade, this wariness has been reflected in frequent defense counsel demands for access to women's confidential records in sexual assault cases so that they can scrutinize client–therapist interactions. The controversy over women's therapy records first displays a portion of the cost of reanimating a stereotype of women with weak identities. In cases where purported recovered memory was rarely at issue, the potent stereotype of women's suggestibility activated by false memory discourse nevertheless helped license serious violations of women's confidentiality. Examining the role of false memory advocacy shows in a very concrete way how alarm about women's relationships can flourish in contexts where no realistic attention is paid to the relational dimensions of selfhood.

More optimistically, I show that moving to a relational view of persons can be an effective strategy for resisting the described stereotype and its costs. I concentrate on two sets of legal deliberations. In the companion decisions

R. v. *O'Connor* (1995) and *A.(L.L.)* v. *B.(A.)* (1995),[1] the Supreme Court of Canada first formulated procedures for records production. The majority did express concern about therapeutic relationships and thereby set a low standard for assessing the relevance of records. At least one judge interpreted the decision "as meaning that the majority of the Supreme Court of Canada accepts that therapeutic records will often be relevant (but not always) in cases of this type, or indeed the statement may even be read as meaning that such records will only rarely not be relevant."[2] Feminists regarded *O'Connor* as a disaster for women's equality.

In the later *R.* v. *Mills* (1999),[3] however, the Supreme Court upheld the constitutionality of amendments to the Canadian Criminal Code that replaced the *O'Connor* regime with a more restrictive approach to records access. In other words, the court changed its mind. The obvious difference between the decisions is that the majority in *Mills* attended to the equality rights, as constitutionally guaranteed to Canadian women, while the majority in *O'Connor* remained silent about these rights. I shall argue that this difference required a second difference and led naturally to it. *Mills* used a relational representation of persons while *O'Connor* did not. In *Mills*, the majority, in fact, recognized the importance of therapeutic relationships to women's recovery from sexual harm. Examining the shift in the court's reasoning is an opportunity to outline the importance of a relational conception of persons to issues of political equality.

The third aim of my investigation is to show that social practices such as violations of confidentiality significantly constitute women's real lack of relational boundaries. False memory writings have often promoted a stereotype of women as without boundaries, and we have allowed this stereotype to affect women's political and legal status. We need to radically alter our approach to this issue and to argue for the right to set relational boundaries as a condition of genuine equality. I begin by defending the premise that promoting equality requires a relational understanding of people's lives; I draw in particular on Christine Koggel's *Perspectives on Equality: Constructing a Relational Theory* (1998). I then examine the Canadian response to records disclosure and the changing representation of persons required by the Supreme Court's commitment to women's equality.

RELATIONAL SELVES AND EQUALITY

In defending equality, liberal political theorists have generally offered or utilized a description of "persons" that focuses on what we have in common on the basis of which we should all be accorded equal concern and respect.[4] The power of a liberal approach lies in its insistence that certain basic similarities among persons constitute a sufficient ground for demanding their equal treatment, while its persuasiveness often depends on persons recognizing one another for what Seyla Benhabib refers to as "generalized others": "[T]he standpoint of the generalized other requires us to view each and every individual as a rational human being entitled to the same rights and duties we would want ascribed to ourselves. In assuming this standpoint, we abstract from the individuality and concrete identity of the other" (1984, 87).

Despite the attractiveness of a view of equality supported by a reasonable appreciation of what we all share, feminist theorists have argued that we make a mistake in our approach to equality when we represent persons as generalized others and when we found discussions of substantive equality on the ability to identify with others as like ourselves. First, such discussions often fail to provide a detailed understanding of circumstances of inequality, because doing so is not their focus; and, unfortunately, this failure affects their ability to ground appropriately contextual specifications of the values at issue. In a political context characterized by substantive inequalities, we cannot say what it is to treat persons with concern and respect without knowing quite a lot about the circumstances of their lives, including the specific ways they have been disadvantaged. We may have a general idea of autonomy as the ability to direct one's life or of privacy as limited accessibility, but we need to understand how to give content and support to these ideals within specific contexts. To do so, we require information about persons' identities, self-concepts, and circumstances. Second, representations of these values will in fact necessarily be developed around assumptions about people's lives that move away from what we have in common and that may leave some people outside their range. As described, a value may even harm them. Finally, such approaches to equality require that we imagine ourselves into very different lives, making judgments about what others do and should value and what counts as valid reasons for so doing. We have little assurance that we can imagine others' lives with any fullness or accuracy.[5]

The question for theorists who argue that positive formulations of equality require a comprehensive understanding of inequalities is: How do we achieve this understanding? How do we come to understand not only the mechanisms by which values are shaped but also the real effects of how values are institutionally embodied in the lives of those with whom we stand in moral community? Feminists such as Christine Koggel (1998), Susan Sherwin (1998), Diana Meyers (1989), Susan Brison (1997), and many others have argued that we must attempt to think of persons distinctively and concretely rather than generically; and doing so requires paying attention to the variety of relationships in which people's lives, self-concepts, capacities, and values are actually formed. We develop and live our lives as persons within complex networks of institutional, personal, professional, interpersonal, and political relationships—both chosen and unchosen. We are shaped in and through our interactions with others in ways that are ongoing; and we develop cognitive and moral capacities and skills, including skills of moral reflection, in relational contexts that not only give these capacities and skills specific content but also offer methods of evaluation and self-evaluation. We come to understand our lives through how others respond to us, and our relational histories are significant determiners of the tenor of our responses to others. Moreover, feminist theorists have argued that in the context of substantive inequalities, we must pay particular attention to relationships that undermine persons, their self-concepts, abilities, and opportunities, and that shape values and structure continued interactions in ways that entrench, rather than ameliorate, inequalities.

To illustrate the difference between an equality analysis that uses a generalized other and one that attends to persons as concrete others with specific relational histories, I will consider two different approaches to privacy, one of the values most seriously at stake in the production of women's personal records. In using privacy as an example in this discussion, I assume that concern and respect for persons sometimes requires that we value their privacy and thus that privacy is, at least sometimes, necessary to equality. Later, I link the importance of privacy to the representations of women's suggestibility that I discussed in chapter 5.

In his classic liberal analysis of privacy, "Privacy, Freedom and Respect for Persons" (1984), Stanley Benn assumes that an exploration and defense of the value of privacy is best conducted from the standpoint of the generalized other. He writes:

> [A] general principle of privacy might be grounded on the more general principle of respect for persons. . . . To *conceive* someone as a person is to see him as actually or potentially a chooser, as one attempting to steer his own course through the world, adjusting his behavior as his apperception of the world changes, and correcting course as he perceives his errors. It is to understand that his life is for him a kind of enterprise like one's own. (228–29, his emphasis)

Benn contends that "to *respect* someone as a person is to concede that one ought to take account of the way in which his enterprise might be affected by one's own decision" (229, his emphasis). As "a man's view of what he does might be radically altered by having to see it, as it were, through another man's eyes" (242), this respect for persons requires a prima facie obligation not to alter the interpretive circumstances of their choosing by the intrusion of uninvited or unwanted observation.

As the quoted description indicates, in order to engage with Benn's defense of a prima facie obligation toward privacy, we focus on basic similarities among persons, on our status as self-directed choosers who regard our lives as our own. In other words, Benn's chooser is explicitly represented as a generalized other to whom we relate through an attitude of reciprocal respect for one like ourself. In order not to compromise the generality of the description, the chooser is represented as unembedded in a social context—we know little about his social location or the networks of relationships that structure his life and sense of himself.

The central insight of Benn's account—that one's perspective on one's own life has value and is often worthy of protection—is one that I endorse and will defend. However, Benn's own strategy for defending this value cannot secure it in the contexts within which we need it, and this problem is at least partly due to his representation of persons. First, the description of persons as unembedded leads to a distorted idea of what is even possible with regard to our practices of noticing and attending to our environment. Jeffrey Reiman (1984) points out that, as Benn is aware, Benn's principle (i.e., no unwanted or uninvited observation of the circumstances of my choosing) is unacceptably wide; it would, for the most part, forbid us to pay attention to what is going on in the world. However, as Reiman also argues, Benn's attempt to set limits to this principle is unsuccessful. Benn simply stipulates that privacy is especially important when the observation is of what I take to be central to my identity (Reiman 1984, 309). The strategy of Benn's defense of privacy represents persons in a way that denies the inherent sociability of human life. Even if we agree with his insights, we are left with the issue of defining the kinds of circumstances within which limited accessibility to others is an important value. But for this defense, we need a full and realistic understanding of what counts as harmful accessibility to others.

Second, to represent a person in a wholly generalized way is impossible. Representing a chooser as unembedded in the social world in fact represents him as someone whose enterprise and sense of that enterprise are independent of his relations and thus highly self-directed. Benn's chooser appears in the text quoted as the captain of his own fate, responsible by himself for perceiving his errors and for directing and redirecting his course.[6] In other words, affirming the importance of privacy involves identifying with Benn's chooser as autonomous in the sense of being independent of others. The assumption of independence becomes part of Benn's description through the representation of an allegedly generalized other. We do not know how to proceed on Benn's analysis when we are considering the nature and importance of privacy interests for people: *(a)* whose circumstances are such that they cannot conceive of their lives as substantially self-directed or *(b)* whose values do not condone the degree of independent self-directedness of the chooser in Benn's example (Sherwin 1998). Nor do we know how to proceed if we do not find ourselves in Benn's description. The strategy of the analysis does not encourage us to move outside of thinking about the generalized other in our exploration of privacy, even while the actual details of his analysis do represent a particular kind of person. As records disclosure will show, the effect of privacy invasions can have differential and serious consequences for groups whose members' lives have been subject to previous continuous invasions of privacy in relationships of inequality. These consequences cannot be understood without paying attention to the histories of these people's lives.

In "Women and Their Privacy: What Is at Stake?" (1983), Anita Allen offers a contrasting style of analysis of privacy, understood initially as limited accessibility involving dimensions of secrecy or confidentiality, anonymity, and solitude (238). Allen does not seek to give greater definition to this value through the representation of a generalized other; rather, as her title suggests, she provides a detailed analysis of the interest women have in privacy. Her analysis is mapped through an understanding of how women's relational histories may compromise informational privacy and anonymity, and how they may render solitude impossible. She discusses the ways in which women are subject to systematic unwarranted invasions of informational privacy through inappropriate questioning about their personal lives, martial status, or sexual histories in their relations with the courts, with potential employers, with welfare officials, with banks, and with teachers or professors. She discusses women's distress at such invasions and the injuries to women's careers, financial stability, and self-esteem. She considers the anonymity and informational privacy invasions "commonly experienced by women in public places," where women "come to accept . . . being questioned about personal matters by strangers . . . and being singled out by strangers" (241). She discusses women's responses to these invasions: for example, how many "come to believe they are 'fair game' if they venture into public places into which men may go to find repose" (241). She attends to how women lack solitude, especially at home, where their caretaking functions allow them little time for themselves. Moreover, Allen's work is sensitive to how privacy has developed as a politically inflected value, one that has related people unequally—for example, by exposing women to harm in designated places of state noninterference, such as the home.

Allen directs us to think of how privacy has taken shape as a value in political and relational contexts where women's concrete needs for types of limited accessibility have not been addressed. Another way of putting this point is that the social construction of women's identities as subsumed, as a function of or for the identities of others (chapter 5), denies women opportunities to set relational boundaries. I will go on to apply this kind of analysis, one that takes into account women's experience of relationships, to issues of records disclosure. I conclude this section by focusing attention on some of the moral dimensions of relating to others in ways that I have endorsed as a theoretical imperative: that is, relating to persons as concrete others with specific relational histories. My discussion provides a route to thinking once again about the importance of testimonial positions, but this time it is from within a broader discussion of political equality. To protect testifiers from exploitation, we need to ensure their ability to set limits on when and with whom they will share their perspectives.

Allen's account attends to structures of interpersonal and institutional relationships and to women's *responses* to invasions of privacy. Koggel remarks that "when we focus on the network of relationships, we begin to notice patterns both in the stories told by individuals with concrete histories and identities and in the social and legal structures that make the stories possible, patterns that make us attend to the inequalities experienced by concrete others in specific contexts" (1998, 107). Because we cannot assume that we are all the same or that we can understand people's lives through conceiving of them as generalized others, a relational analysis directs us to attend to the perspectives of those who are marginalized, those whose equality we are attempting to defend. But attending to others' perspectives within a commitment to equality raises questions about how to do so in ways that support equality.

Laurence Thomas (1992–1993) points out that the different patterns of injustice endured by those in disadvantaged social locations will have a profound effect on their self-concepts, structures of memory, and emotional configurations. He argues that no amount of goodwilled imagination on the part of those whose lives have not been subject to these patterns of injustice will provide access to the perspectives of those who have been systematically disadvantaged. Thus, in order to be morally responsive to groups affected by systemic injustice, we must defer to their accounts of their experiences. Thomas is not claiming that those who are marginalized cannot be wrong about the character of their experiences; rather, he is claiming that there should be a presumption in favor of their accounts—a presumption that is warranted because they are speaking from a vantage point to which the more advantaged do not have access. Thomas's view requires that the socially dominant, if they want to be morally responsive to inequality, must trust the accounts of those treated unequally when they say what it is like to be in their situation. In other words, Thomas argues that we must regard those marginalized as testifiers. However, the dominant must also act in ways that enable those who have been treated unequally to trust the former with their perspectives and to see value in providing them with their accounts.

This last point is particularly important in considering records production. A relational account of persons stresses the importance of gaining access to the perspectives of those treated unequally. However, those concerned about equality must guard against how easily the perspectives of those treated unequally can be exploited in order to do further harm. Elizabeth Spelman, in

"Treating Persons as Persons" (1977–1978), elaborates this concern by differentiating treating a person as a bearer of rights from treating her more fully as a person. The latter involves "respond[ing] to someone as the person she is . . . more exactly, the person whom, someone takes himself or herself to be" (151). To treat people as persons in this sense is to attend to their self-concepts, "to respond to the ways in which they choose to be seen and not through our favored ways of perceiving them" (151). Responding to people through attending to their self-concepts does not mean simply accepting their view of themselves. Here Spelman agrees with Thomas. It does, however, involve respecting that they have a perspective on their lives and trying to understand what that perspective is. But Spelman points out that our self-concepts also mark points at which we are particularly vulnerable. If you know how I regard myself, what facts about me I take to be the most important to who I am, what kind of affective orientation I have toward the world—what causes me joy and what causes me shame, as well as whom I hope to become—then you know a great deal that can harm me. Those concerned with equality must understand the self-concepts, perspectives, and emotional configurations of those disadvantaged by current arrangements while they protect and promote the circumstances in which people can form self-concepts without their exploitation.

To capture the importance of not exploiting others' perspectives on their lives, I shall define as a positive value the ability to develop a self-concept and perspective on one's life and experiences within relational contexts that support rather than undermine this development. How to treat persons respectfully as persons raises issues of what persons should and should not be obliged to share with others; their ability to set boundaries and develop a perspective and sense of self in relationships based on equality; and the ability to protest, avoid, or sever relationships that undermine or exploit them. As we lack an adequate term for the positive value of having one's own perspective on one's life, I shall refer to it as the value of the "personal." The personal as a value is obviously linked to issues of privacy and confidentiality, but it also assumes a relational, rather than an unembedded, self. After reviewing the Canadian response to records production, I will show that the exploitation of others' perspectives in circumstances of inequality is one of the chief harms of this practice.

THE CANADIAN RESPONSE TO RECORDS PRODUCTION

In the 1990s, a defense strategy for contesting women's credibility in sexual assault trials changed. It went from directly questioning a complainant about her sexual past—an option restricted, though not foreclosed, by rape-shield legislation—to attempting to gain information about a complainant's personal past via seeking disclosure of a wide range of records about her life. Records sought often included notes made in the context of therapy or counseling.

The shift in defense strategy was dramatic in terms of the frequency of requests for records, the undiscriminating volume of material about women's lives that was subpoenaed, and the range of records requested. The Ottawa Rape Crisis Centre in Ottawa, Ontario, did not receive a single request in its first eighteen years of operation, but it received nine in 1994 (McPhedran 1995, 1505). In 1995, "two hospitals in Toronto, Ontario, along with two legal-assistance organizations and a community agency for women, received pre-trial subpoenas to produce all their records for the last 5 years. The subpoenas did not even mention the name of the rape complainant" (1502). In some cases, "the accused sought access to virtually every document ever written on the complainant" (Busby 1997, 162). Records requested have included not only any sort of therapy or counseling record but child welfare records, public and residential school records, personal diaries, records from social service organizations, Children's Aid societies, prison and detention centers, immigration offices, witness-assistance programs, alcohol recovery centers, and so on (149).

Personal records have been of little interest to the defense outside of cases of alleged sexual harm. Records production has been a gendered practice, and the easy availability of information about women's lives supports sexual assault as a practice of gender inequality. In order for the assumption of women's sexual accessibility to be maintained in a social context in which everyone agrees that women must consent to sex, there must be mechanisms for devaluing women's claims that they have not consented. The unique accessibility of records in sexual assault cases provides a mechanism. If records are commonly held to be far more relevant in these cases than in others, the implication is that exceptional measures must be taken in such cases before the court can conclude that a woman has not fabricated charges or has not acted in such a way that her lack of consent is irrelevant to her accessibility.

Women's personal records have been used in sexual assault cases to try to find anything in a woman's past that might scare her off or discredit her testimony. Although records have been sought for many mundane reasons—for example, to try to find inconsistent statements—in many cases records have been produced when the defense has offered no grounds for saying why the information contained in them would be relevant. Lawyers have certainly been aware of the effect of records production on complainants. Lawyer Katharine Kelly noted that the defense counsel she interviewed said they examined records "for evidence that the primary witness is not credible, or for inconsistencies in her account or for material that embarrasses her or humiliates her enough to convince her not to proceed" (Kelly 1997, 187). One defense lawyer, who was an early advocate for the strategy, was quoted in *Lawyer's Weekly* (May 1988) on the advantages of attacking the complainant at the pretrial stage: "You have to go in there as defence counsel and whack the complainant hard . . . get all the medical evidence, get the Children's Aid Society records . . . and you've got to attack with all you've got so that he or she will say 'I'm not coming back'" (quoted in McPhedran 1995, 1505).

Allen's work on privacy presents a picture of women as disturbingly accessible to others—physically, psychologically, and emotionally. That violations of informational privacy are often a viable defense strategy in sexual assault cases is therefore not surprising, given the history of women's accessibility. But there are particular social forces that have licensed the act of records production as the most recent form of this violation. In Canada and elsewhere, the strategy has been partly enabled by the growing concerns about women's suggestibility and malleability, as promoted by the FMSF and discussed in previous chapters. Throughout the period of greatest ease of access to women's records, distrust of women's therapeutic relationships in particular was aggressively encouraged by the advocacy work of the FMSF; and we can see the influence of the false memory debates interwoven throughout the legal and public response to records disclosure.

We need to recognize that, in the period when suspicion of therapeutically contaminated memory was most influencing the practice of records production, few Canadian records cases actually involved recovered memories. In her excellent 1997 study of the discriminatory impact of records production, Karen Busby surveyed the forty cases referenced on Canadian legal databases where records were requested in the eighteen-month period preceding Canadian Supreme Court deliberations about the practice in *A.(L.L.)* and *O'Connor*. In only two were complaints laid subsequent to purportedly recovered memory, and in one of these, "the evidence specifically indicated that the memories were restored" without therapeutic intervention (Busby 1997, 166).

Nevertheless, the discourse of women's suggestibility activated by the FMSF clearly facilitated access to women's confidential records. In a pre–*O'Connor* article in the *Medical Post*, records production was described wholly in terms of the threat of false memory syndrome through quoting a defense lawyer who used the language of implantation: "The false memory syndrome is something that has been noted and accepted by our courts as a potential defence. . . . It has been legitimately used in cases where it has been suggested that there has been a memory implanted by a therapist." The attorney said that in such a case: "I want to see your records. I want to see exactly what you wrote down during those therapeutic sessions, and whether it could be suggested that you in fact assisted in some way in enhancing or developing this memory" (quoted in Fitz-James 1995, 18). After *O'Connor*, defense lawyers remained blunt about their intent to use therapist influence on memory as a reason to demand records:

> In cases where a rape complainant has gone to therapy, and the accused's position is "I'm innocent, she was never raped," you have to have those records to see whether or not the counsellor was encouraging her false beliefs or solidifying them. . . . We're talking about a kind of indoctrination where a therapist encourages a belief in the victim, hardening the memories or filling in the blanks. These people have no concern about the presumption of innocence and the possibility of convicting innocent people. ("Rock Must Modify Court's Rape Ruling" 1996, A16)

It should be noted that this justification for records production does not involve reference to memories recovered in therapy, but simply to any case where a complainant has had therapy and where the accused denies the rape. In seven of the cases Busby surveyed, suspected improper therapy influence was, in fact, offered by the defense as a rationale for seeking records.

The threat of suggestive therapy also critically affected assessments of the potential relevance of records in higher court decisions, even when no evidence was offered to bolster this concern. In *A.(L.L.)*, as discussed in chapter 6, recall that the defense sought counseling records partly to determine "the method of extracting the information from her during the 14 months she underwent sessions before going to the police" (Aboriginal Women's Council et al. 1996, 464). In *O'Connor* (1995), Bishop Hubert O'Connor, former principal of a native residential school, was charged with four sexual offenses involving four different women, all former students who were subsequently employed at the school under O'Connor's supervision. He was also their priest. The women were ordered to authorize release of all residential school records and all medical, psychiatric, and counseling records that related to the incidents. The defense made no allegation of improperly suggestive therapy.

In *O'Connor*, the Supreme Court instituted a two-stage procedure involving a context of disclosure and a context of production. At the first stage, the judge would assess the likely relevance of the records to the defense. If the judge determined that an initial relevance threshold was met, the records would be ordered disclosed to the court and examined by the judge to assess their probative value. The judge was enjoined to weigh the constitutional right of the accused to make full answer and defense against the privacy interests of those referred to in the records, particularly the complainant (para. 22; para. 30, 31). If the judge determined that nonproduction would constitute a reasonable limit on the ability of the accused to make full answer and defense, the records would be released to the accused.

Although *O'Connor* was a reaction to the burgeoning demand for women's personal records and an attempt to regulate the practice, the decision was widely seen as having opened access to records at the disclosure stage: one, because of the majority's silence on women's equality; and, two, because the majority offered little guidance on when records might not be relevant to the accused. The court stated explicitly that at the first stage, the onus on the accused to show relevance "should be a low one" (para. 24). The majority held that the "sheer number of decisions in which such evidence has been produced supports the potential relevance of therapeutic records" (para. 27). Moreover, they speculated that "generally speaking, an accused will only become aware of the existence of records because of something which occurs in the course of a criminal case" (para. 26), suggesting, in somewhat unclear language, that there would be a presumption of materiality if the accused were aware of the existence of the record. Finally, the majority gave three examples of when the records would be relevant, but no indication of when they might not. They stated that records "may reveal the use of a therapy which influenced the complainant's memory of the alleged events," referring to this danger as "the problem of contamination" (para. 29). They also expressed concern about records made close in time to a complaint, implying that such records might show influence on the complainant to bring the complaint, the defense's suggestion in *A.(L.L.)*. *O'Connor* and *A.(L.L.)* did involve claims about historic events. The majority concern about inappropriate therapy cannot, however, be grounded in the facts of these cases; nor do the cases leading up to *O'Connor* and *A.(L.L.)* support the court's concerns about memory influence.

In 1997, the Canadian Parliament finally moved to restrict access to complainant records in sexual violence cases, affirming a woman's right and need to seek therapy after assault without thereby compromising the success of a claim against her assailant. Bill C-46, which amends sections 278.1 to 278.91 of the *Criminal Code*, balances the potential relevance of the records to the accused's constitutional right to make full answer and defense with both the equality and privacy rights of the complainant. It requires that judges provide written reasons for production or nonproduction of records. It also singles out eleven assertions that are no longer sufficient in themselves to establish the likely relevance of a record, including that the record relates to medical or psychiatric treatment, therapy, or counseling that the complainant or witness has received or is receiving; and that the record may relate to the reliability of the testimony of the complainant or witness merely because the complainant or witness has received or is receiving psychiatric treatment, therapy, or counseling. In *R.* v. *Mills* (1997)[7]—a decision again showing the influence of the FMSF—Belzil J., Alberta Court of Queen's Bench, declared C-46 unconstitutional. He reduced the issue of probative value of records to one of avoiding "recovered memory syndrome": "It is acknowledged that some therapists may 'contaminate' the process of recovered memory through suggestion, and the records would have to be examined in order to determine whether a recovered memory is in fact valid" (para. 34–35). The case did not involve an adult woman and did not involve recovered memory.

Belzil's decision was reviewed by the Supreme Court; and subsequently, in *Mills* (1999), the Court reconsidered its earlier position in light of the equality provisions of the Canadian Constitution. It upheld C-46 and characterized the notion that "consultation with a psychiatrist is, by itself, an indication of untrustworthiness" as an "invidious" myth (para. 119).

RELATIONSHIPS IN *O'CONNOR*

My interest in the transition from *O'Connor* to *Mills* is in the representation of women in these decisions; it is in the extent to which a greater concern for equality involved a shift from a fundamentally nonrelational view of women's lives to a relational view. In this section I examine the lack of relational analysis in *O'Connor*. Feminist intervenors to *O'Connor* and *A.(L.L)* framed the issue of records production as the court's responsibility, as well as the court's subsequent failure to pay attention to the specific inequalities associated with sexual harm to women. I shall interpret feminist concerns as targeting the court's failure to attend to women as concrete others with specific relational histories.

In what Karen Busby has categorized as a series of "stunning oversights" (1997, 174), the majority in *O'Connor* failed to mention any of the history of institutional and interpersonal relationships of inequality that characterized the context of the case. The case involved Aboriginal women who had been put into native residential schools and thus had relational histories that had involved enormous previous invasions of personal and informational privacy. The majority did not reflect on these histories to consider how records production would have disproportionately invasive consequences for women who suffer intersectional oppressions. These women are not only more vulnerable than others to sexual assault but they also have lives more vulnerable to scrutiny and recording. *O'Connor* increased their vulnerability to sexual assault through making them yet more vulnerable to invasions of personal and informational privacy. Busby also pointed out that the accused was related to the complainants along multiple axes of social power: white–Aboriginal, male–female, teacher–student, employer–employee, and priest–parishioner. Someone in the dominant position on all these axes of power would be in a very strong position in sexually exploiting women to compel their silence or discredit their testimony.

That sexual assault might be a sort of violation leading to a heightened privacy interest was considered by the majority in *O'Connor* only in the context of records in possession of the Crown, where it was dismissed by suggesting that the complainant had given up her privacy interests in such records (para. 7). That the accessibility of personal records might reproduce some of the emotional harms that are the effect of sexual violation was not considered at all. The majority gave no reflection to the importance of counseling after assault to women who might be involved in generally unsupportive relationships; nor did they consider the effects of producing records on counseling relationships.

Both Benn's and Allen's accounts of privacy make clear that our discussions of values are shaped by assumptions about persons and how they are or are not related to each other. The presence of such assumptions needs to be kept in mind when assessing the majority's critical discussion of relevance. The history of sexual assault jurisprudence is one in which access to assumed relevant information about women's lives has been judged by later courts to depend on and to entrench discriminatory stereotypes and beliefs. As one would thus expect the court to be careful in its deliberations on relevance, I find the majority's distorted representation of women at this point in the decision particularly disturbing—women are represented as without previous specific histories of institutional or interpersonal relationships. It is in this context as well that the court made its most explicit remarks about suggestive therapy. Although the majority opined that the sheer number of cases in which records are produced supports the assumption of relevance, the frequency of production is more arguably a reflection of women's relationships with the legal system in their role as complainants in sexual assault cases—an alternative interpretation that the majority did not even consider. In taking the accused's awareness of a record as a reason to suspect its materiality, the majority evoked the imagery of an accused and a complainant who are strangers to each other, rather than, as is most often the case, people who have had some relationship to each other prior to the events that brought them before the courts. The courts know full well that most assaults are not committed by strangers. (In only one case of the forty studied by Busby were the accused and complainant unknown to each other.) Given the long-term, complex relationships between the complainants and the accused, and given that the accused may have had a hand in producing the very records he sought, *O'Connor* seemed like a particularly odd context for the imagery of stranger assault.

Moreover, although therapeutic records are among those most frequently requested, the majority offered no thoughtful reflection about the nature of therapeutic relationships and how that might bear on such records. No context was given for concerns about suggestive therapy, which left the issue open to the reading that to suspect contamination would always be appropriate. No attention was paid to the exploratory or interpretive dynamics of therapeutic relationships, nor was any attention paid to the interpretive dimensions of note-taking. In one notorious case, *R.* v. *Osolin*, a young woman had consensual sex with two men earlier in the day at a third man's trailer. She was later attacked by two more men who had heard she was easy and who thought that they could all have a turn with her. During the trial, the complainant had to undergo a grueling cross-examination about her interaction with the men; afterward, she found herself facing a further delay in her trial. During this time, months after the incident, her therapist noted that "she is concerned that her attitude and behaviour may have influenced the men to some extent and is having second thoughts about the entire case."[8] These remarks were used to affirm the relevance of the women's records to assessing her motive in bringing complaint, but this notation is the therapist's, and we have no idea what the client actually said. In summary, neglect of the relational dimensions of women's lives caused the court to be inattentive to a number of harms associated with records production, and it also allowed for an unsubstantiated estimation of relevance—something that could only encourage the practice of production.

I now turn to a specific effect of records production in promoting relationships of inequality. Records production has been described as a compensatory strategy for gaining information about a complainant's past—a strategy that had been lost through rape-shield legislation—and many commentators have pointed out that the idea of false memory syndrome provides a timely replacement for stereotypes of women as outright liars about sexual assault (Bronitt and McSherry 1997, 259). Earlier, however, I argued that a relational account of persons directs us to attend to the self-concepts and perspectives of those treated unequally, to recognize that these self-concepts are themselves relationally formed and that they can easily be exploited. When we consider the exploitation of women's self-concepts, records production differs in disturbing ways from questioning a complainant about her sexual history; in addition, false memory discourse, in my view, helps activate a representation of women that makes them especially vulnerable to the disrespect of and exploitation of the persons they take themselves to be.

The Aboriginal Women's Council, intervening in *O'Connor*, wrote:

> [A]n equality respecting justice system would treat individual complainants as individuals not as types. It would view such individuals' history of mental health treatment or sexual assault not as a justification for extra-invasive disclosure, but as reason for caution, sensitivity, and a heightened vigilance about the purpose and effect of records disclosure. (1996b, 435)

I read this remark as echoing Spelman's concern about how to treat a person, first of all, as the person she is, rather than as filtered through our favored ways of seeing her. It is to treat her as having a self-concept and a perspective on her life, and an emotional affective orientation toward her life. It is to recognize that only she can articulate this perspective, and it is to relate to her through attention to it (although this does not mean simply accepting it). It is to take into account that self-concepts are formed in and through relationships with others, and it is to recognize the importance of relational resources that contribute to the possibility of having a self-concept that has not been consistently damaged and undermined by oppression. It is to recognize that whom a person takes herself to be can make her particularly vulnerable, and it is to be obliged not to use her self-concept or emotional–affective configuration against her in ways that damage her equality. I have described this orientation to the perspective of others as a concern about the personal as a positive value, and this deep dimension of respect for persons reveals some further very disturbing aspects of records disclosure.

First, when records made by others are represented as defining the complainant in court, she has little control over her self-representation in the very context within which her credibility and character are being tested. Her articulation of her perspective is preempted, as she is represented first through the interpretation of whoever made the record and, second, through the interpretation of the defense who seeks to represent her as noncredible. Nevertheless, her records, and especially her therapeutic records, may contain considerable information about how she views her life. Thus, second, she is unable to set relational boundaries concerning with whom she will share herself. Moreover, as the records are produced to the accused, their production has the potential to make her life history available to the person who may have assaulted her. Records production has the potential to re-relate her through a dynamic of shame and humiliation to her assailant. Relationships with therapists and counselors are a type of relationship in which a woman may give others considerable access to whom she takes herself to be. The production of her counseling and therapeutic records may involve the betrayal of her trust in this relationship when she is particularly vulnerable and may inevitably cause additional emotional harm. In addition, it may involve betraying her trust in the very relationship to which she has turned in an attempt to reestablish herself as a person with boundaries—a person who has some control over when and to whom she's accessible. Thus, records production may re-relate her in a damaging way to her complainant while, at the same time, it destroys the more positive context within which she has chosen to try to reunderstand her life after the assault. Production may also undermine her by leading her to doubt her judgment in having made herself vulnerable within therapy. It may then undermine self-trust, which is necessary to her sense of herself as autonomous. She is particularly likely to feel she has betrayed herself if she has engaged in self-recrimination about the assault, as any such recrimination will certainly be used to suggest her responsibility. Because dominant understandings of sexual assault have historically involved prescriptions of women's taking particular responsibility for men's sexual interest (regardless of its circumstances), it is not uncommon for a woman to feel some responsibility for her own assault.

Finally, records production involves trying to get as much information as possible about a person's perspective on her life precisely to use it against her. In *Osolin*, the complainant had been cross-examined extensively about consent and about a difficult relationship with her parents that the defense presented as a motive to fabricate. The records offered no new information; rather, they offered indications of self-doubt, confusion, and self-recrimination, all of which could be used to undermine her. Information may be sought about who the person is precisely in order to support a stereotypical understanding of her life; this aspect is true of *Osolin* as well. One of the most disturbing aspects of *O'Connor* was the majority's failure to recognize the potential of records production, first, to create or shape relationships of exploitation and emotional harm through allowing others to gain access to a complainant's perspective on her life and, second, to use her perspective against her in a situation characterized by substantive inequality.

The issue of records production has been rife with allusion to false memory and suggestive therapy. In a context barren of thoughtful representation of women's relationships, one relationship, that of a woman to her therapist, has been repeatedly singled out as a justification for records production. The purported suggestibility of women, and their consequent susceptibility to false memory syndrome, has been an important legal justification and perhaps the primary public justification for records disclosure. It is important to understand its power in this context.

False memory syndrome has played the role of a new social harm, one that can override expectations of privacy or force a renegotiation of duties of confidentiality. As the fact about records production that catches the attention of the public, false memory syndrome allows for an elision of the differences among cases, obscures the amount and array of records ordered, and thus also obscures the ways in which records production particularly targets women whose lives have been heavily documented. It perversely allows for a repetition of the theme that when complaints of sexual harm come before the courts, someone has an honest but mistaken belief about what went on. In one case, counsel for the defense argued that the complainant's memories of abuse were "either fabricated or honest but mistaken recollections" (Brady 1996, 82). The use of the syndrome allows the defense to raise issues of both competence and credibility: it is presented as a personality disorder that renders memories of sexual harm unreliable, or it at least represents women as too easily influenced to be reliable witnesses.

Records production is the attempt to gain maximal access to a person's self-concept and perspective on her life in order to use this information against her. Most significant to understanding some of the harm associated with records production is that false memory syndrome represents women as no longer having appropriate psychological boundaries that others need respect. A woman's personal memories are crucial to whom she takes herself to be. False memory syndrome is presented as a disorder in which the memories fundamental to a sense of self are not only false, but implanted. As a woman's identity, personality, interpersonal relationships, and lifestyle allegedly become centered on these memories, she no longer has her own perspective or an autonomous self-definition. She is presented not just as easily influenced or as lacking full psychological integrity, but as having a self-concept that has been constructed by someone else.

In the FMSF representations discussed in chapter 5, women are without individualized perspectives, and they lack the capacity for self-definition. This representation of women as lacking psychic integrity, ego boundaries, and individuality has been a particularly damaging and effective stereotype in the context of records production. First, confidentiality as a value depends on a respect for privacy. As Benn's writing shows, traditional accounts of the value of privacy have been predicated on individuality and autonomy as key virtues. Philosophical and legal commentators have argued that the function of privacy is, variously, to protect our own point of view on our activities; to protect our ability to hold unpopular opinions and act without undue interference; or to give us a sense of moral self-ownership, a recognition of our capacity to shape our own lives (Benn 1984, Gavison 1984, Reiman 1984). To represent women as without autonomous individuality has put them outside the range of considerations that typically engage people's defense of privacy. Second, women's lack of psychological boundaries constitutes a public danger that must be contained by overseeing their relations of dependence—hence, a positive reason to override women's expectations of privacy. The FMSF presentation of a woman in therapy opens to scrutiny what she might think of as most personal about her life—her feelings, memories, perspectives, and sense of identity—because it is no longer properly hers. False memory discourse and records disclosure combine to present a potent stereotype of women as without relational boundaries used to justify a practice that in fact deprives them of the ability to set such boundaries.

RELATIONSHIPS IN *MILLS*

I have argued throughout this study that we can only resist current stereotypes and alarms about suggestibility through a realistic attention to persons as relationally constituted. In *Mills*, the Supreme Court of Canada was able to resist the powerful representation of women's malleability that contributes to women's present lack of relational boundaries through violations of their confidentiality. I believe that its shift away from the distorted and damaging presentation of therapeutic relationships, which has haunted the debate on records production, is the consequence of a much broader and more detailed focus on women's lives as relational. Given my defense of the personal as a value, I am particularly interested to see the court's struggle for a new relational understanding of privacy, one that does not leave women outside its range.

According to Christine Koggel, "what we need to do is sketch a conception of the relational self that demonstrates the importance of all kinds of relationships . . . to justice and equality" (1998, 146). Women appeared as relational selves in *Mills* whereas they had not in *O'Connor*, and the decision, in general, is replete with the language of relationality. The majority in *Mills* positioned itself as in an ongoing, lively, and positive dialogue with the Canadian Parliament. It also recognized that Parliament was attending to relationships of horizontal inequality—inequality that results from acts of individuals and groups, rather than from acts of the state. In doing so, it immediately expanded the relational considerations at work in its deliberations. This point is important, given that concern about equality in Canadian criminal law has been nearly wholly dominated by considerations of "power imbalances as between the state and the accused" (McInnes and Boyle 1995, 347). *Mills* characterized Parliament as a valuable ally to the vulnerable. It also recognized horizontal equality concerns would have an impact on women's relationship with the courts (para. 59). It acknowledged and discussed the fact that women whose lives had been heavily documented in their previous relationships with institutions would have special equality concerns in records production.

One of the most interesting developments in *Mills* was the court's commitment to talking about values both contextually and relationally. A relational approach to equality is one in which the values that embody respect for persons must be shaped by the attention to details of particular contexts. Koggel writes that such an approach

> cannot provide general conditions for satisfying equality of respect in all contexts or for all times. These conditions can only be settled dialogically in concrete contexts by taking account of the perspectives of everyone involved under conditions that promote a presentation of diverse views and that enforce mechanisms for giving and assessing justifications for current and proposed policies. (Koggel 1998, 245)[9]

The court reaffirmed an approach to rights and values that does not see them as competing but as coexisting in particular contexts where the nature of the context will shape the definition and scope of the rights and values. It stated that "rights . . . often inform and are informed by, other similarly deserving rights and values at play in particular circumstances" (para. 61) and that a contextual analysis of rights requires attention "to the factual content" of particular contexts. A commitment to examining context could not help but move the court toward a more attentive assessment of the relevant institutional and interpersonal relationships in sexual assault litigation. For example, delineating the appropriate contextual understanding of full answer and defense in a context where women's equality rights are at play required the court to attend to how women have been historically subject to discriminatory biases and stereotyping in their position as sexual assault complainants. The court concluded that full answer and defense must be understood with careful attention to how myths and stereotypes distort the truth-seeking process. Moreover, the commitment to a realistic understanding of sexual assault compelled the court to reflect on the complainant–therapist relationship. *Mills* included an extensive analysis of the value of such relationships to victims of sexual assault, categorizing "the notion that consultation with a psychiatrist is, by itself, an indication of untrustworthiness" as a "recent" and "invidious" myth about the unreliability of women's testimony (para. 119).

The majority pointed out that privacy, as well as full answer and defense, falls under fundamental justice and that both sets of rights must be understood as informed by the equality provisions of the Canadian Constitution. I am particularly interested in the evolution of the court's view of privacy, and I will conclude with this discussion. Feminist intervenors to *A.(L.L.)* stated that the issue in records production is not principally one of privacy but equality (Aboriginal Women's Council et al. 1996a, 460). I believe this assessment reflects the fact that privacy has traditionally been seen as a value that must often give way to other values. However, what is important in thinking about privacy in this context is how accessibility is related to discriminatory practices. On a contextual approach to values, we have no reason to suppose that privacy as adequately informed by equality should give way to full answer, rather than help to shape it.[10] Although the personal as a positive value is not the same as privacy, a contextual understanding of privacy informed by equality can help prevent the particular kind of undermining of the personal at stake in records production, and I take the court to be moving toward such an understanding of privacy.

The court noted in *Mills* that it had previously "characterized the values engaged by privacy in terms of liberty, or the right to be left alone by the state" (para. 79). The court noted as well that it had understood privacy in terms of the ability to protect a core of information relating to one's "individual identity" (para. 80)—information, for example, about lifestyle, intimate relationships, and religious and political views from the state. The court thus located the idea of the personal primarily in the kind of information any individual might want protected from dissemination to the state. In *Mills*, the court explicitly signaled that it was moving away from what is often characterized in the privacy literature as an individualist notion of privacy to an approach that stresses the role of privacy in creating certain relational possibilities. It stated that "privacy is . . . necessarily related to many fundamental human relations" (para. 81), and it moved beyond case law to cite philosophical treatments of privacy by Charles Fried and James Rachels, who argue that privacy, as control over whom one shares information with, is a value that is necessary for the development of certain relationships.

Fried (1984) is interested in the conditions necessary for developing relationships of love, friendship, and trust (211). The development of such relationships, he argues, requires that we be able to withhold certain information from most people in order to share it with particular chosen others, thereby constituting the intimacy of these chosen relationships. Fried claims privacy allows us to accumulate "the moral capital" that we spend in friendship and love. Rachels's version of the view is more generalized. Different patterns of behavior characterize different relationships. Moreover, "*however* one conceives one's relations with others, there is inseparable from that conception, an idea of how it is appropriate to behave with and around them, and what information about oneself it is appropriate for them to have" (1984, 295, his emphasis). Rachels concludes that "our ability to control who has access to us, and who knows what about us, allows us to maintain the variety of relationships with other people that we want to have" (295). Although, for Fried, privacy is a functional value, it is not "just a possible social technique for assuring this or that substantive interest" (Fried 1984, 205); rather, it is conceptually related to the relationships that it serves. Moreover, according to Fried, and quoted in *Mills*, this ability to form intimate relationships "is at the heart of our notion of ourselves as persons among persons" (para. 81), and so privacy gains fundamental importance as a value.

The majority in *Mills* recognized that its previous approach to privacy was inadequate to the task of shaping an understanding of privacy informed by equality in the context of records production, and I see in their use of Fried a struggle to find an account of privacy adequate to this task. I first want to point out obvious problems with Fried's view and then comment on what I take to be the value of the court's deliberation.

Jeffrey Reiman, in criticizing Fried's account of informational privacy as necessary to intimate relationships, argues that it is not the sharing of information that is important to intimacy but the context of caring that makes the sharing of information significant (1984, 305). Moreover, Reiman finds Fried's view of intimate relationships, as symbolized by the expression "moral capital," distastefully economic in spirit. I believe, first, that Reiman is right that the nature of relational context, and how people care for us or do not, determine the importance of our ability to share or withhold information from others. This point is obvious in the case of records production. Moreover, in categorizing Fried's view as overly economic, Reiman points to a persistent tendency in the privacy literature—a tendency that Fried does not escape—to talk in terms of the secure possession of a self that is shared or not shared. Privacy theorists ignore the continuous development of identities and self-concepts through relationships that form and change us. Finally, neither Fried nor Rachels pays attention to relationships of inequality; and the relationships they discuss, as well as Fried's focus on exchange, may reinforce the assumption that privacy as a value is tied to "relationships of voluntary (economic) exchange, of intimacy, and of domesticity" and that these relationships "[are] not about power" (Ackelsberg and Shanley 1996, 215).

Fried and Rachels do have the important insight, however, that patterns of access configure relational possibilities, and this understanding can be extended to relationships of inequality and equality in the contexts of records production. Marilyn Frye has argued that differences in power are manifested in asymmetrical access. For example, "The president of the United States has access to almost everybody for almost anything he wants of them, and almost nobody has access to him. . . . The creation and manipulation of power is constituted by the manipulation and control of access" (Frye 1983b, 103). We need to understand and shape the values through which we regulate patterns of access in concrete contexts to encourage or discourage certain relational possibilities, and privacy is the primary value through which we regulate access.

I contend that the majority used Fried because they saw potential in his account to link privacy to the creation of positive possibilities for relationships through allowing people to control access to personal information in some contexts. Two sorts of positive possibilities are at issue. First, the court was concerned to protect relationships in which women can recover from sexual assault, which the court has characterized as a complete denial of women's equality. As most victims of sexual assault seek counseling, the court was particularly concerned to protect access to therapy. The court characterized therapeutic relationships as relationships of trust, "an element of which is confidentiality" (para. 82). However, the court moved from Fried's remarks on intimate relationships to their remarks on therapeutic relationships without much indication of what these relationships have in common or why Fried's account applies.[11] The connection seems to be this: these relationships are all relationships in which we typically choose to let others treat us as maximal persons in Spelman's sense. We sometimes give others a lot of access to our self-concepts and perspectives, and in doing so, we give others the power to affect how we view our lives and the power to undermine us, should they so choose. We hope that in therapeutic relationships, as well as in relationships of love and friendship, we can explore aspects of our lives that make us vulnerable; we trust that our doing so will not be used to undermine us by the persons to whom we express our lives or by their revealing or being forced to reveal this information to others. We count on our lovers and friends not to make us vulnerable to others by revealing information that they could predict might be used to harm or undermine us. In the context of sexual assault, women's formal ability to restrict informational access to some opens up possibilities for others to treat them as maximal persons in ways that enhance rather than undermine equality.

I have argued that we have a political responsibility to make sure that people's perspectives on their lives are not easily accessible to others in order to entrench, promote, or excuse relationships of inequality. More specifically, I have argued that persons should not be obliged to reveal their perspectives, doubts, hopes, and confusions about their lives to those who will use their doing so to treat them unequally. Further, when a person's sense of self has been damaged by practices of inequality, they should have access to relational contexts where they can attempt to repair this damage. The court used Fried to make a connection between these imperatives. Although I do not think that, even in *Mills*, the court recognized how the extent of potential exploitation to records production is a practice incompatible with respect for women as persons, it did recognize the importance of allowing women control over informational accessibility in order to protect opportunities for them to deal with the harms of inequality.

Second, I have argued that those concerned about equality must, in fact, have access to the perspectives of those treated unequally, without allowing the exploitation of these perspectives to exacerbate inequality. The court recognized that if the defense can obtain counseling records easily, women who do seek counseling will be less likely to report assaults. As women can only be protected against sexual assault if they are willing to speak about being assaulted, the court recognized that a relationship with women that supports their equality before the law depends on greater protection of their personal records.[12]

O'Connor was recognized as a disaster for women's equality. The announcement that the constitutionality of C-46 had been upheld in *Mills* was thus initially greeted as a remarkable victory. The contrast between these decisions, however, is not this stark. Feminist intervenors sought an absolute prohibition on records production. *Mills*, like *O'Connor*, leaves records decisions to judicial discretion and thus did not adequately recognize records production as a practice of gendered inequality. Moreover, like *O'Connor*, *Mills* offers little real guidance about relevance, and this omission is especially disturbing given that we are in the grip of a renewed cultural skepticism toward women's claims of sexual harm. Finally, I have described the change in the court's reasoning from *O'Connor* to *Mills* as the court's move toward an understanding of inequality that recognizes the necessity of attending to the diverse networks of relationships that structure people's lives, experiences, and self-concepts. But this understanding is implicit, rather than fully articulate, in *Mills*. For it to take hold requires that it be given a more reflective and explicit affirmation.

CONCLUSION

In this chapter, I have shown that when we follow the seepage of false memory discourse, we find deep fissures in the structures that we rely on to promote and defend women's equality. To find and repair these fissures, we must learn to reconceive our values through attention to the relationships and practices that give them their actual character. How we treat people as rememberers has implications, for example, for their access to other values, like privacy or confidentiality, values that we must re-vision to reflect and express the relational nature of persons and their lives. In the next and final chapter of this philosophical excavation, I consider for the final time what it might mean to rethink the value of memory by attending to the relationships in which we conceive a personal past.

NOTES

1. *R.* v. *O'Connor*, [1995] 4 S.C.R. 411, [1995] S.C.J. No. 98, online: QL (SCJ). Hereafter *O'Connor*. *A.(L.L.)* v. *B(A.)*, [1995] 4 S.C.R. 536. Hereafter *A.(L.L.)*. References in the text are to paragraphs of these decisions. I discussed *A.(L.L.)* in chapter 6. In this chapter, I focus on *O'Connor*, which contains the detailed specification of procedures for records access. *A.(L.L.)*, released at the same time, simply refers to *O'Connor* for these procedures.

2. *R.* v. *Mills*, [1997] A.J. No. 1036 at para. 57 (Alta. Q.B.), online: QL (AJ).

3. *R.* v. *Mills*, [1999] S.C.J. 68, online: QL (SCJ). Hereafter *Mills*. References in the text are to paragraphs of the decision.

4. The following discussion is in general indebted to Christine Koggel's account. I have simplified many of her insights to put her theory to use in this context. My understanding of relational personhood has also been influenced by many years of discussions with my colleague Susan Sherwin.

5. We have little reason to believe that the emotional understandings, values, and expectations that we imagine would be those of the person herself. Further, our epistemic norms may simply reflect our own bias about what counts as a good reason for her choices. We have no way of testing our perspective without engagement with hers.

6. Stanley Benn, in the more concrete examples he uses to illustrate the application of the principle, makes mention of President Johnson, candidates to the Supreme Court, and a famous conductor—all examples of people who would seem to others to have lived exceptionally self-directed autonomous lives, who symbolize those who direct others rather than those who are directed by others.

7. *R.* v. *Mills*, [1997] A.J. No. 1036. (Alta. Q.B.), online QL (AJ).

8. *R.* v. *Osolin*, [1993] 4 S.C.R. 595, [1993] S.C.J. No. 135, online: QL (SCJ). Para. 150.

9. Christine Koggel also stresses the necessity of offering justifications that can stand as reasonable and fair "to all parties," including "those whose perspectives have been absent or ignored." In my view, the court endorsed this approach through expressed concern "that due regard is given to the voices of those vulnerable to being overlooked by the majority." Moreover, it reiterated that a range of different perspectives were legitimately involved in determining whether a trial process was fair—not only the perspective of the accused, but also those of the community and the complainant.

10. It is important to see how full answer is both shaped and protected in *Mills*. It "does not include the right to evidence that would distort the search for truth" (para. 76). Where information contained in a record "is part of the case to meet or where its potential probative value is high," the right to full answer will be centrally implicated (para. 94). In cases where it is not clear whether the information is necessary to meet full answer and defense "the judge should err on the side of production to the court" (para. 132).

11. Charles Fried's own specific remarks on trust are an extension of his views on privacy, and they involve our ability to withhold information about ourselves as necessary to others' trusting us and thus to relationships of reciprocal trust. Monitoring prisoners, for example, as an option to incarcerating them, removes the possibility of error and so does not make trust an applicable value. These remarks do not seem to provide any argument for the confidentiality of therapeutic records.

12. The court's remarks on mental integrity also showed awareness of how perspectives on lives are shaped through relational interactions. It recognized that in the context of sexual assault litigation, relationships with the courts can easily exacerbate the complainant's sense of violation and affect her mental integrity. They recognized that relationships of dependency and trust are often necessary to preserving or restoring the mental integrity of individuals violated by assault (para. 85).

8

A SINGULAR AND REPRESENTATIVE LIFE: PERSONAL MEMORY AND SYSTEMATIC HARM

Although philosophers often discuss contemporary issues in their writings, there has been little philosophical engagement with "the memory wars." An important exception to this neglect is Ian Hacking's influential constructivist account of memory and multiple personality disorder in *Rewriting the Soul: Multiple Personality and the Sciences of Memory* (1995). Hacking's work on early memory science is, like John Sutton's, partly provoked by the false memory debates. But while Sutton merely references the debates as a rationale for his historical study, Hacking engages them more fully.

Hacking's ambitious aim in *Rewriting the Soul* is to complement Michel Foucault's account of modern power as the disciplining of the body and the control of populations with an account of the secularization and regulation of the soul through the nineteenth-century sciences of memory. There are two key times in Hacking's account. The first is the present that motivates the account—a time when our politics is dominated by "front line memory confrontations" (4). The second is the past that Hacking reviews in the book—the "radically formative" period in the history of memory science that he suggests has made the confrontations nearly inevitable (4). In the late nineteenth century, the meaning of "trauma" was extended from physical to psychological wounding, giving rise, Hacking argues, to a conception of traumatic forgetting as key to the development of the modern psyche. Our selves are secret, hidden, formed through forgetting, and accessible, if at all, only through the expert recuperations of psychoanalytic practice. According to Hacking, our cultural acceptance of traumatic forgetting has allowed women to become suggestible to renarrating their pasts as involving forgotten child sexual abuse.

I use Hacking's sophisticated work on "memoro-politics" (143) to conclude my discussion of the memory debates and to raise a final issue for theorists who are concerned about their legacy. Like many theorists represented in this study, Hacking orients a more general account of remembering through reflection on the suggestibility of women's memories of abuse. His discussions of the mechanisms of suggestibility and of change in memory meaning are thoughtful and provocative. He appears careful not to conflate issues of false belief with other ethical concerns about memory influence. Nevertheless, the problematic tendency of memory theory that has preoccupied me in this study—the devaluing of the social and relational—is also at work in the writings of this careful philosopher. Hacking designates women's memories as personal in contrast to communal memory. This distinction frames his ethical discussion of women's memories, and it has slipped by unremarked by commentators on his work.

Hacking's use of the term "personal" as a contrast to the term "communal" is quite different from my own use of "personal" as involving a perspective on one's life that need not exclude more collective perspectives (chapter 7). As I shall argue in detailing his view, Hacking's understanding of personal is enmeshed with two problematic notions of privacy: one, a notion of social privacy that I reject as damaging to women's equality; two, a notion of psychological privacy that I reject as damaging to an account of memory. My objective is to test Hacking's account of experiential memory as personal against our understanding of a particular type of harm of which child sexual abuse in an example.

Oppressive harms are harms suffered by individuals qua members of oppressed or marginalized groups. We understand whether individuals have been harmed and how through hearing their accounts of the past. The nature of oppressive harms can only be adequately understood if we regard the person who relates the harm as part of a group that is subject to certain harms, and if we interpret their account of the past as somewhat representative of what might be endured by people in that group. Moreover, many groups subject to oppressive harms themselves desire to come to a shared understanding of the meaning of the past and to have the unjust nature of this collective past acknowledged. They thus wish their memories to be understood as part of the collective memory of a certain group.

Collective memory involves experiential memory, but it is more than a collection of individual memories. Collective memory requires the meaning of a group's past to be shared, and to be understood as shared, among at least some group members. This shared meaning in turn may require reinterpretation of individual pasts by members of the group. David Middleton and Derek Edwards write: "people reinterpret and discover features of the past that become the context and content for what they will jointly recall and commemorate" (1990a, 7).

I see no prima facie conflict in regarding someone's memories as personal as well as either representative of collective interests or an expression of collective memory. Toni Morrison describes the slave narratives that have influenced her writing not only as personal but also as representative and as collective memory. She states that these narratives were written to say: "This is my historical life—my singular, special example that is personal but that also represents the race" (1987, 104–5). Yet this study has exposed a complex tendency to theorize about personal memory in ways that exclude shared or collaborative interpretation of the past as viable personal memory. In Hacking's work, we see this tendency quite explicitly through his distinction between personal and communal memory, and we can assess some of its broader ramifications. Hacking's implicit assumption that communal understandings compromise the value and integrity of personal memory is especially problematic when we look to groups whose perspectives on the past are already politically marginalized.

I first describe Hacking's ethical worries about women who now remember childhood sexual abuse. I then raise a political objection to the scope of his worry about memory suggestibility: that important new understandings of systematic harm to those marginalized seem, without adequate justification, most crucially at issue. I contend that Hacking's text evades recognition of the problem of scope through a distinction between personal and communal memory that marks off women's memories as only personal. Hacking does not fully or fairly explore their collective dimensions and their contribution to a collective understanding of child sexual abuse. Were he to do so, he would recognize that the recognition and redress of political subordination require interaction between our personal and communal perspectives on the past. As women's memories are the only ones at issue in his text, Hacking also does not see the problematic ramifications of his view for our general understanding of oppressive harms. Reflecting on Hacking is a final opportunity to visit some of the relational dimensions of remembering that we must liberate from theoretical neglect.

HACKING'S ACCOUNT OF SUGGESTIBILITY

Although Hacking characterizes himself as a skeptical or neutral spectator to contemporary debates about memory (3, 17), he in fact has deep ethical misgivings about the ways that women now remember their pasts. Hacking contends that Western European culture has too easily accepted a framework for reviewing the past that licenses suspicion of child abuse via allowing traumatic forgetting. Women have thus now become suggestible to the thought that their present unhappiness might be due to forgotten or unacknowledged childhood sexual abuse. When a woman is encouraged to review her personal past through a narrative of forgotten abuse, she is deprived of the opportunity for the kind of self-knowledge that comes from an honest and rigorous individual assessment of the past. I do not, in this chapter, assess Hacking's account of the origins and development of the idea of psychic trauma; my concern is with his analysis of present-day suggestibility. Hacking discusses different mechanisms of memory suggestibility and offers a contrasting notion of autonomous self-knowledge. I concentrate my analysis on the key mechanism of memory suggestibility, which he labels "semantic contagion," and I also refer to a mechanism that he does not label, which I will call "narrative determinism."

Hacking endorses a reconstructivist account of remembering, one that allows for change in memory meaning as a normal part of reviewing our past. He points out that human actions can be described in a variety of ways. My present action is one of typing, working on a manuscript, and keeping my partner waiting for dinner. Moreover, our understanding of the past, its significance to us, changes as we evolve new interests, gain knowledge, or shift circumstances. Next week, I may remember this activity as tiring. Later, if I lose the chance to do philosophy, I may remember it as exhilarating. We frequently reinterpret our past, especially as it involves human action, through new descriptions and categories. We use these redescriptions to make sense of our lives and to construct a self-concept that is partly narrative in form. Narrative self-construction, however, while an ordinary and necessary part of human activity, gives rise, Hacking thinks, to a threat of chronic suggestibility and thus to the need for an ethics of remembering that confronts this threat.

According to Hacking, when we view our past under a new generic description, we will recall incidents as specifically fitting under this description and call to mind more such incidents: "When we think of an action of a certain kind, our mind runs to other acts of that kind" (238). Hacking refers to our tendency to specify the past through actions that fall under a new interpretive category and to think of similar actions or incidents as "semantic contagion." For example, if I begin to think of my past as one of "wasted opportunity," I will start to pull out actions and incidents that admit of this description. Moreover, Hacking thinks we are especially prone to use categories that are associated with social narratives that can be easily adapted as well-structured self-narratives. We are particularly attracted to narratives that purport to offer clear causal links between the past and present (257). I refer to this second mechanism as "narrative determinism." Women who suspect childhood sexual abuse as an explanation of their adult unhappiness—particularly, but not exclusively, those women who are diagnosed with multiple personality disorder—have been suggestible to reinterpreting their past as a specific type of harm narrative: "A certain picture of origins is imparted to disturbed and unhappy people, who then use it to reorder or reorganize their conception of their past. It becomes their past. . . . this picture becomes disseminated as a way of thinking of what it was like to be a child and to grow up" (88–89).

Our suggestibility through semantic contagion and narrative determinism is contrasted by Hacking with "our best vision of what it is to be a human being" (267). We need to understand that our end is to become self-aware, that we are our memories, and that we are Kantian agents, autonomous and responsible for the moral selves that we become (264). In order to pursue a vision of responsible remembering, one that respects others and ourselves, we need a sophisticated analysis of the risks of semantic contagion, of the way it may lead us to misunderstand crucial issues of individual responsibility. First, we may distort or exaggerate the meaning of the past in order to mold it into new categories. Second, our memories may imply that agents acted with blameworthy intentions that were not, in fact, the intentions with which they acted. Third, if we think of our pasts as determined while we are all the while reinterpreting them through social categories, we may lack adequate self-understanding. We may be prone to the conceptual error of thinking of the past as having caused our present without taking sufficient responsibility for how we are "making up ourselves" through remembering (94).

You and I have problems. You leave. Reading novels afterward of women who have been abandoned by their lovers, I come to think of myself as abandoned. Moreover (I reason) I could not be this distraught unless you had abandoned me. Perhaps I am distorting the account of the breakup—I forget that I shouted at you to go. I may think you intended to abandon me when you did not. In accounting for my distress, I may neglect that how I have interpreted the breakup—as an act of abandonment—is a causal factor. Hacking concludes that we need to avoid any "glib patter that simulates an understanding" of the past (266)—one that simulates an *understanding* because there is a causal explanation for whom we are becoming, but one that only *simulates* an understanding because we do not recognize what our own contribution is. Hacking thinks that all of this may happen and that it may still be true to say that you abandoned me. The truth of our descriptions about the past does not inure us from the moral failings that are a consequence of our suggestibility.

In analyzing suggestibility, Hacking is especially concerned with the contagious aspects of what he calls "new descriptions," like "sexual harassment" or "child sexual abuse." It is, of course, women's memories of abuse that motivate his general reflections on suggestibility. Hacking believes that the use of new descriptions easily provokes the issue of inappropriate blaming. Reinterpreting my past to include, for example, sexual harassment may involve a morally problematic simplification of my own agency, but it may also give rise to problematic moral condemnation of others. Interpreting the past through new social categories may imply that agents acted under descriptions that were in fact unavailable to them, as the social understandings of such harms had not yet been formulated. Sexual harassment did not achieve institutional recognition as a harm until the mid-1970s. In remembering the times I was sexually harassed at work in the 1970s, I may be holding others responsible for intentional harassment when they would have understood their actions as mere flirting. Hacking's focus on new social descriptions of harm, however, creates confusion for the scope of his account of suggestibility.

THE SCOPE OF CONTAGION

Given the generality of his account of suggestibility, I am concerned about the scope of Hacking's analysis of ethically problematic memory—his focus on women's memories of abuse and more broadly on new categorizations of harm. The scope of the analysis is difficult to determine from the text, and I want to pose three issues about semantic contagion. First, is there a kind of remembering itself that is ethically problematic, or does a kind of remembering create opportunities for irresponsible remembering that we can nevertheless avoid? Second, do all women's memories of childhood sexual abuse fall within the scope of semantic contagion? Third, is there anything about women's memories of childhood sexual abuse that makes this kind of memory especially likely to exemplify contagion?

Hacking uses "semantic contagion" as the description of a "mental mechanism" (249), an "internally prompted suggestion" (256). When we encounter a new interpretive category for our past, "semantic contagion" marks our tendency, first, to remember incidents in our past as specifically falling under this category and, second, to think of more and more such incidents. The infectious agent is a category newly used to understand the past, but the cause of the category infecting our past is the way memory works. Thus, Hacking proposes a memory mechanism that is itself problematic in making bad consequences very likely.

I turn now to the second issue of scope. Because Hacking's account of semantic contagion is general enough to raise worries about *coming to interpret the past through a moral category*, a fortiori, it is general enough to raise concerns about most memories of child abuse. Hacking begins *Rewriting the Soul* with a concern about the forgotten: "the forgotten event, that when it is brought to light, can be memorialized into a narrative of pain" (214). His account of mechanisms of suggestibility, however, subtly shifts his concern to the remembered but interpretable past, and it draws in the memories of all who reinterpret their past through child sexual abuse. For example, in discussing reinterpretation of the past, Hacking is interested in the case "of today's adult, who did not have these descriptions when she was a child, but who now looks at the past and recalls episodes that, she now thinks, fall under those descriptions. She was abused, although not flagrantly, as a child" (240–41).

Finally, although I find inconsistences in the text, Hacking does, at certain points, want to restrict the scope of contagion to certain groups of memories—those that involve recently legitimated social understandings of harm. Because Hacking thinks child sexual abuse is a fairly new description of harm, the restriction makes women's memories of child sexual abuse an especially likely case of suggestibility. Hacking's description of semantic contagion seems to give it a very broad scope. It sometimes seems offered as a general worry about interpreting the past: "There is no canonical way to think of our own past. In the endless quest for order and structure, we grasp at whatever picture is floating by and put our past into its frame" (89). Yet at other points—especially in a discussion of new social understandings—Hacking identifies his interest as "memories that arise by mental mechanisms different from more straightforward recollection, whatever that may be" (249). This discussion of scope sets the following problem for Hacking's account. On the one hand, he presents contagion as too global in scope to be persuasive as a worry; on the other hand, there seems no reason to limit its scope to new social understandings of harm.

In adducing a suggestibility mechanism with sufficient range to cover contemporary memories of childhood sexual abuse, Hacking offers a description of problematic remembering broad enough to capture nearly all morally significant memory. We should note that Hacking begins his discussion of suggestibility with remarks on epidemics, and he is almost certainly aware, from his own work on Foucault, of the implications of the epidemic imagery evoked through "contagion." To paraphrase Linda Singer, the construct of epidemic is used to produce anxiety about the uncontrollable proliferation of something dangerous in the social body, which proliferation demands and justifies special intervention and management (1993, 29). To suggest that our memories are systematically subject to contagious change is to raise the image of an uncontrolled proliferation of morally problematic memories, where a memory mechanism itself is the problem. The concern about suggestibility, however, seems insupportable at this level.

That memory is in general associative and that we reunderstand our past in light of our present needs and concerns is an explanation of the pragmatic value of memory. In chapter 3, I referred to the meaning of memory as the significance of the past to the present. Memory is not only selective in terms of what significance something has for us at the time of attending; how and what we remember also depends on the concerns, interests, and associations contributed by our present environment. Our understanding of the past, its significance to us, changes as we evolve new interests, gain knowledge, shift circumstances, and enter new relationships. Hacking grants that we do not always remember the same events in our pasts in the same way, that "there is no canonical way to think of our own past" (1995, 89). But he has too little say about the significance of this point for the moral agents that we become.

As I argued in chapter 2, our capacity to reinterpret our pasts is essential to our developing responsible moral agency and cannot be thought of as a unilateral threat to it. The social practice of taking responsibility for our actions requires that we can become aware of them as now fitting certain normative descriptions that we may have been unaware of at the time we acted. Moral learning and ongoing responsibility thus require shifts in the meaning of memory. I develop morally by coming to reunderstand and reexperience a piece of behavior undertaken innocently as thoughtless and mean. I come to understand I was thoughtless because adults encourage or compel me to reflect on my behavior. The process of moral understanding is not one where I remember the experience in exactly the same way but merely describe it differently. If this is what I do, I have made little moral progress. Unless I am able to not only frame the experience through different concepts but re-remember it experientially—now with shame or regret, for example—I could not develop as a moral agent affected by this re-remembering. In addition, I must reflect not only on the incident under question, but on others that may be like it.

I agree with Hacking that it is possible to adopt a category of harm, stretch it over one's past, and construct a pat deterministic narrative that may inappropriately proportion responsibility while leaving one with little self-understanding. But the kind of associative mechanism Hacking describes is compatible with reflective judgment and a responsible assessment of one's past, and must be compatible in order for us to become responsible rememberers. Hacking agrees that the past is legitimately subject to interpretation. As such, interpretation will often, in fact, involve shared social understandings of how to characterize events, these kinds of social understanding cannot in general be incompatible with the unsentimental self-understanding that Hacking endorses, if it is a real possibility.

If this kind of remembering results in no uncontrollable contagion, what makes Hacking's worries compelling about women's memories? I do not see anything in the mechanism of semantic contagion that can explain Hacking's proposing it as a new memory mechanism or his attempting to limit its application to newly legitimated categories of harm. The ethical issues Hacking raises for responsible remembering are issues for any moral reinterpretation of the past. But if proper understandings of our past are made through the use of social categories, why aren't these the kinds of understandings women are typically engaged in?[1] Hacking is pressed to offer an account of ethical reinterpretation; such an account is especially important given the kind of category he targets.

Hacking has a special concern about new understandings of harm—our current understandings of sexual harassment and child sexual abuse, for example. He thinks that such categories raise a metaphysical puzzle about the past: "These redescriptions may be perfectly true of the past. . . . And yet, paradoxically, they may not have been true in the past" (249). Because my focus is on Hacking's description of memory suggestibility and its likely bad consequences for responsible remembering, I will not enter into a discussion of whether the past is ever indeterminate in the sense that puzzles Hacking. I do not think it necessary to do so in order to raise questions about Hacking's concentration on these categories. I would point out that the fact that understandings are newly legitimate does not mean that they are new. Moreover, the point of many new conceptualizations of harm is to make long-standing types of social interaction apparent, and this point is important for understanding oppressive harms. Accounts of oppressive harms, including child sexual abuse and sexual harassment, will often involve newly legitimated social understandings. Oppression involves an interrelated system of institutional structures and norms that subordinate one group to another. Understanding a harm as oppressive requires looking at it in context to judge whether it is part of an oppressive structure. Moreover, oppressive systems are usually naturalized and normalized through comprehensive ideologies involving folk understandings, authoritative theories, and systems of cultural representation. Thus oppressive systems are often not recognized as oppressive by those involved in them.

Making oppressive harms apparent often requires a shift in social power and considerable rethinking of the conceptual schemes through which such harms have been naturalized. Hacking's account of suggestibility should be of deep concern to those who need an account of oppressive harms. Presumably, there must be good ways of understanding the past through new collective understandings of harms, or we would otherwise make little progress in coming to an understanding of oppressive harms. I am especially disturbed by the suggestion in Hacking's work that we avoid irresponsible remembering by practicing strong skepticism about the use of social understandings as a prophylactic against contagion:

> The current (1994) wisdom in the multiple personality and recovered memory movements is that therapists must ensure that they do not suggest memories to their clients. . . . I fear this is simplistic. We have very little grasp of the workings of "suggestion." . . . Many clients in therapy belong to numerous self-help groups or at least read the self-help books. After you have filled in the questionnaires and proved that you satisfy at least the minimum requirements for disorder X, it requires a certain robustness not to suspect that you do have disorder X. The best cure is to complete all the questionnaires for every disorder. When you discover that you may suffer from every dysfunction, a certain skepticism may set in. Few have the stamina for that type of cure. (255)[2]

Moreover, Hacking's primary ethical concern about the use of new categories is the issue of inappropriate blaming, and accounts of oppressive harm are needed to address such concerns. Oppressive harms have their character as harms through a complex interrelation of structures that all work together to subordinate the individuals of a group. They are often unrecognized and unintended under the descriptions by which they are understood as oppressive. For individuals socialized within oppressive structures, questions of responsibility and blame are very complex. An adequate account of oppressive harms will not increase the tendency to see oppressive harms as intended under oppressive descriptions, but it will address some of these complex questions.

What I want Hacking to do is elaborate on and distinguish when a shared understanding of the past through a new categorization of harm is legitimate and when it is not. In my view, Hacking evades and closes this inquiry by categorizing women's memories as personal. This categorization works to both mystify and privatize the kind of harm women are trying to understand. It seems to open women's memories, in particular, to the concerns about suggestibility that dominate Hacking's ethics of memory. But finally, like other work I have examined, Hacking's use of "suggestible" women as rememberers also damages his resultant picture of memory.

COMMUNAL AND PERSONAL MEMORY

The last four chapters of *Rewriting the Soul* contain Hacking's substantive philosophical and ethical critique of women's memories, and this critique, as outlined above, is framed by a distinction between personal and communal memory. Hacking writes that there are "perhaps two kinds of politics of memory," the personal and the communal (210). Communal memory is exemplified by Jewish memory of the Holocaust, the only example of communal memory in *Rewriting the Soul*:

> A large photograph is captioned: "Horror Unforgotten: The Politics of Memory." Communal memory has always played a major role in group identity. . . . Holocaust memories are unusual in that they are directed both inward and outward. Inward, to the group whose memory of suffering it is, and outward to Gentiles especially Westerners who must never forget that their culture (my culture) must take responsibility for the genocide. Yet despite the fact that the memory of each people has its own character, we shall not be misled if, briefly, we think in anthropological terms, and hold group memories to be among the ways in which group identity and difference are cemented. (210–11)

The politics of personal memory, the subject of *Rewriting the Soul*, is fixed by contrast:

> The politics of personal memory, is, in contrast, relatively new. . . . In no way do I deny that there are interconnections between group memory and personal memory. One obvious link is trauma. . . . But this seems to be a one way projection. That is, holocaust memories would have become part of group memory and there would have been an associated politics, even if traumatology never existed, and even if there had never arisen, late in the nineteenth century, the politics of memory. But the politics of personal memory, I contend, could not have arisen without those sciences. (211)

Hacking specifies no sense in which the politics of personal memory has a communal or collective dimension. The lack of a collective dimension to women's memories is sharpened by Hacking's prose: "Individual factual claims are batted back and forth, claims about this patient, that therapist, combined with larger views about vice and virtue" (211–12).

It is first important to note that Holocaust memories occupy the space in Hacking's text for legitimate communal understandings of oppressive harm, and that women's memories are labeled as self-evidently personal in contrast to communal. Hacking acknowledges that his account of memory is one-sided; however, as women's memories are not communal, they will not benefit from a fuller analysis of communal memory. I approach Hacking's contrast in two ways. First, what makes women's memories personal is not articulated by Hacking with the same degree of richness as what makes Jewish memories communal; therefore, we need to understand Hacking's account of communal memory and see how women's memories differ. Second, I want to challenge Hacking's use of this contrast. I argue that we can understand women's memories as collective (a broader term than communal), and in doing so we gain insight into the nature of the memories and of the harm remembered. This alternative understanding is compatible with women's memories being personal, and it raises troubling questions about Hacking's use of the personal as a contrast to communal.

Several features seem to have explicitly influenced Hacking's choice of Jewish memory of the Holocaust as exemplifying communal memory.[3] It is for most of us a clear, serious, and uncontestable case of collective memory; but other aspects to Hacking's use of it are equally important. Hacking chooses a titled photograph of a monument, a memory artifact that displays three layers of commemorative representation. He identifies the Holocaust not only as contributing toward group identity, but also as contributing toward the memory of a people who have long had an identity and who have been engaged in "an almost timeless communal practice of remembering" (211). This practice of communal remembering involves chronicles, odes, and tales of origins, and it is encoded in ritual. It is the memory of cultural traditions preserved and transmitted through practices of inscription (texts) and bodily incorporation (ritual). In summary, communal memory is the memory of a shared past that can be or has been memorialized, that contributes to cultural identity, and that is in a tradition of practices of collective remembering for that cultural group.[4]

Women do not form a distinct cultural or ethnic group or people, and women's memories are obviously not communal in this sense. Moreover many practices of women's specifically commemorating women's pasts are relatively recent, and women have had difficulty obtaining access to resources of commemoration. Few memorials are dedicated to women's lives, and there has been particular social resistance to establishing memorials and commemorations of women's experiences of harm. For example, although a number of memorials have been established to commemorate the shooting of fourteen women at the Ecole Polytechnique in Montreal, Quebec, commemorative ceremonies on December 6 have been and continue to be the subject of resistance and countermemory.[5] So women's memories do contrast with the type of communal memory that Hacking identifies. But what is the import of contrasting personal to communal memory, and why does Hacking draw the contrast where he does?

In choosing a culture or ethnic group as the relevant level of group life for a discussion of communal memory, Hacking sets a contrast that discourages us from asking how understanding women's group affiliations is relevant to understanding their memories of harm. In chapter 2, I used the work of Elizabeth Waites to argue that we are always situated as rememberers. Memory is inherently selective, and what is salient for us will depend on interests and concerns that are seldom ours alone. Moreover, what we remember depends not just on our past social environment but on our present one—on the shared sets of interests, concerns, and consequent ways of attending that characterize the various social collectivities to which we belong (Halbwachs 1950). In order to understand experiential memory, we must always look at someone's memory experience relationally.

Two sorts of group affiliations seem relevant to understanding the nature of women's memories, and they may give us insight into the harm of child sexual abuse. The first group is the family. Women's memories of childhood sexual abuse are memories of their family life; and theorists of collective memory, beginning with Maurice Halbwachs (1925/1950), have seen family memory as a particularly important kind of communal memory. As I have argued previously, what we attend to as needing remembering and how this should be remembered are the result of explicit socialization; and it is the family that initially socializes us as rememberers. To look at women's memories through the frame of family memory does not require that all family members share a view of the past. An understanding of collective memory for a group will include an analysis of the conflicts and negotiations through which certain viewpoints may come to dominate.

Regarding women's memories as family memories is important in understanding child sexual abuse. How family members associate in their attempts to form, maintain, enforce, and transmit a shared understanding of the past may tell us much about women's experience in the family relevant to understanding such abuse. The vulnerability of children to harm depends partly on their status as apprentice rememberers. Children lack developed capacities as autonomous rememberers, and when they are abused, they often face powerful suggestions to forget what has happened to them "or to recall it as a dream, a fantasy, or unreal" (Brown 1996b, 12). They have little testimonial authority. Moreover, Jennifer Freyd's work on betrayal trauma (chapter 6) is premised on the insight that, when we investigate the inhibitory mechanisms of memory, we must here as well look to the distinctive circumstances of differently situated rememberers. In chapter 3, I also pointed out that adult women have special responsibilities as family rememberers, responsibilities to celebrate and sanitize family life. This role may add to our resistance in accepting their testimonials of family harm; it may therefore actually increase women's vulnerability to such harm. The hostile misfortunes to which a group is subject may depend on their situation as rememberers.[6]

Second, a woman might enter a certain group with whom she shares a kind of experience, and she might adopt particular frameworks to talk about the experience; thus, she helps to form collective memory for that group. The consciousness-raising and activism groups that have characterized contemporary feminism are examples of such groups. Consciousness-raising is an activity that is both knowledge-producing and personally transformative. Individuals with some understanding of the dynamics of oppression come together to reassess their pasts and to recognize the commonalities and the differences in experiences they may have regarded as private or personal. As new understandings become socially acknowledged, they form the occasion for more women to conceive of themselves, their pasts, and their relation to others differently, thus contributing to individual identities, group identities, and social understandings of harm.

The effects of child sexual abuse, themselves, contribute to a dynamic of privatization. Such abuse isolates individuals. It privatizes their experience through shaming, traumatization, and social skepticism; and it often leads to adult patterns of substance abuse and consequent social isolation. It is difficult for women to rehearse and credit their own memories of abuse, to contribute them to social understandings, or to integrate them into self-understandings.

Judith Herman has argued that public acknowledgment of categories of harm facilitates individual memory: "To hold reality in consciousness requires a social context that affirms and protects the victim" (Herman 1992, 9). Richard Ofshe considers such a claim remarkable (Ofshe and Watters 1994, 11). But that some women have come to see a shared meaning to the past has allowed others to remember their pasts as abusive and to credit these memories. Victims and survivors of sexual abuse have collectively contributed a great deal to our understanding of this kind of harm. Women have also collectively been able to analyze the dynamics of privatizing their lives that make them vulnerable to certain harms. Some of this analysis has centered on the political maintenance of a domestic sphere as a realm where women have been unprotected from sexualized harms.

I have said that our understanding of oppressive harms requires viewing people's accounts of the past as representative and understanding our own pasts as shared, and I hope to have indicated how viewing memories through a collective frame contributes to our understanding of child sexual abuse. As Janice Haaken's study indicates, thinking of women's memories collectively can also aid our understanding of childhood sexual abuse narratives when no abuse has occurred. Though Hacking raises communal memory in his text, he does not consider the ways in which shared or conflictual memories may be identity-determining for the family as a social group; nor does he consider what role women's and children's memories play in this dynamic. In addition, he does not consider the communal remembering that women have engaged in to politically analyze their oppression. In the next section, I offer some plausible conjectures for why Hacking fails to see women's abuse memories as any kind of social memory. I also return to the theme of how our representations of rememberers and of memory are co-constitutive.

PRIVATIZING WOMEN'S LIVES AND MEMORIES

The way that Hacking does regard the family and the way that he describes women's groups reveal a complex meaning to "personal" in his study of women's memories. Hacking tends to talk about the family as traditionally private: "Child abuse, especially when it has sexual contents or overtones, seems to be the greatest evil in private life" (58). I would suggest that Hacking categorizes women's memories as personal in contrast to communal, partly because the memories are about events in the family, the traditionally private sphere. Moreover they are about sexual, hence deeply private, matters. Hacking does not conceal his distaste for current controversies over women's memories. He regards us as "voyeurs" to people's family lives (113). In accepting women's life in the family as private, Hacking loses and neglects a certain level of analysis of their memories and of the kinds of harms to which they may be subject. He also risks further normalizing a way of understanding women's lives that makes them subject to certain harms. However, because Hacking does not see women's memories through shared feminist understandings that include a critique of the privatization of women's lives, he misses this level of analysis. This point directs me to the question of why Hacking does not see the tradition of feminist consciousness-raising and public–political activities of desilencing—teaching, writing, holding forums and speak-outs, and lobbying for resources and memorials—as a kind of collective remembering.

Hacking makes a distinction that is fundamental to the way he analyzes memory and that once again relies on the language of privacy:

> I am fascinated by the dynamics of the relation between people who are known about, the knowledge about them, and the knowers. That is a public dynamics. There is also a more private one. The theory and practice of multiple personality today is bound up with memories of childhood, memories that are to be not only recovered but redescribed. . . . I have to discuss not only making up people but making up ourselves by reworking our memories. (6)

Though he makes a reference in this passage to childhood—and so, again, implicitly the family—he connotes a second meaning to "privacy." Memory is private according to Hacking when it has to do with self-creation, the creation of our identities through recollection in contrast to a public dynamic of knowledge production. This passage disturbs me. Knowledge of women does not seem to involve women themselves as epistemic agents on Hacking's account; nor is the creation of their identities a public, partly epistemic matter. A woman's reinterpretation of an abusive past is a "personal" identity project.

Like many of the theorists I have surveyed in this study and despite his purportedly general account of suggestibility, Hacking sees group resources as grounds for intense worries about suggestibility in the case of women's memories in particular—regardless of whether the groups are "expert," knowledge-producing groups or feminist groups. Because of his concern about suggestibility, he does not reflect on the important, legitimate, reciprocal contributions of individual and collective viewpoints when women reinterpret the past. Although Hacking states that the child sexual abuse movement "is the most important piece of consciousness-raising of the past three decades" (66–67), he has no positive analysis of consciousness-raising; and he consistently presents groups in which women share accounts of the past either as dangerous sites of suggestibility or as opportunities to wallow in personal victimization. I have quoted a passage where Hacking describes the contagious nature of self-help groups. Hacking's chapter on the gendered dimension of MPD ends through recommending the perspective of Doris Lessing's Alice in *The Good Terrorist*: "Communes. Squats. If you don't take care, that's what they become—people sitting around discussing their shitty childhoods. Never again. We're not here for that. Or is that what you want? A sort of permanent encounter group. Everything turns into that, if you let it" (Lessing 1986, 34; quoted in Hacking 1995, 80).[7]

I have described consciousness-raising as a dynamic that is both knowledge-producing and personally transformative. Through participation in collective remembering, a woman helps to generate knowledge of child sexual abuse and thus comes to understand her own life and self differently. Hacking wants to separate producing knowledge about child sexual abuse (a public dynamic) from using these new understanding to remember the past (a private dynamic). Women who remember are involved only in the private dynamic, each singly and solely on a journey of individual self-creation through a narrative of harm. Moreover, once Hacking identifies women's memories as personal in the sense of being used for personal identity creation, he invokes a *philosophical* tradition of thinking about memory, one that excludes others' contributions to one's understanding of the past by counting them as cases of memory distortion; and I conclude with a discussion of this tradition. This third sense of memory as personal will show for a final time that we must be careful of how we let our representations of rememberers inform our accounts of remembering. For although Hacking's own explicit account of memory is antithetical to the philosophical tradition that I indicate, he does not overcome its influence.

Our heritage in thinking about memory, especially in relation to the self, is empiricist, and Mary Warnock identifies the most influential element to this heritage as the view that memory is a special kind of self-conscious experience: it is experience that copies and resembles sensory perception. Philosophers have often claimed that memory experience is first personal, in the sense of exhibiting or repeating the rememberer's position on the remembered event, where "position" is most easily understood perceptually. In remembering seeing the lake for the last time this summer, I reexperience what was in my frame of perception at the time. The memory is personal in representing my unique perspective, and the nature of this image does not change as long as I continue to remember seeing the lake for the last time this summer. You cannot share my memory as memory because you did not occupy my unique perspective. Moreover, memories are a special kind of conscious experience, exhibiting consciousness of the self as part of the object of remembering. In remembering the lake for the last time this summer, I remember myself seeing the lake. My memories are personal because they are about me.

Finally, philosophers have often proposed a causal condition to distinguish cases of my genuinely remembering from cases in which I was present at an event and seem to remember, but, in fact, am confusing as memory what someone told me about the events. For example, the seeming memories I have for events of my childhood, events for whose occurrence I may have adequate evidence, may really be my recollections of what others have said about my past. Genuine memory must be causally dependent on my past in the normal sort of way. The way in which this condition is often understood is that the source of my memories must derive *wholly* from my own past. Mary Warnock writes: "The derivation of memory must be, in some non-complicated sense causal. I must know the past is as I say it was *because* I experienced it and not through the operation of any other cause" (1987, 30). The causal restriction on memory is meant to provide a kind of objective criterion—one not available from introspecting experience—that ties memory reliably to the past; and this condition has been thought compatible with a range of views of memory and perception. Warnock, following Elizabeth Anscombe, identifies this type of causality as informed by the metaphor of source. In evaluating the status of a claim as a memory claim, we are engaged in a specific brand of causal inquiry about how it came into existence. If I justify a memory claim by saying "I witnessed the event," I have answered the question and given "a causal explanation of a perfectly familiar kind" (1987, 50). Warnock points out that part of what makes this familiar *causal* talk is that, like mechanical metaphors and the metaphor of a causal chain, the metaphor of source stresses continuity; we can visualize the history that has taken us from one state of affairs to another. "We will not think of the spring as the source of the river unless we believe that somewhere, even if invisible . . . the water is continuous with the water we later identify as the river" (51).

This causal requirement sharpens the sense of my memories as personal through sealing my unique perspective on the past. My perspective on the past is free of the influence of others' present perspectives. Other people and their past perspectives on events frequently form part of the content of my memories, and through the information that they have and I lack, others may contribute toward my general understanding of the past. However, their present perspectives on my past do not help form and do not alter my memories of this time.

This reading of experiential memory offers a powerful picture of memories as individual, unique, self-referential, self-sufficient representations—ones unshareable as memory and beyond the legitimate influence of new collective understandings of the past. Because these features have been offered as or used in an elaboration of the nature of experiential memory, they have sometimes been treated by philosophers as analytic features of such memory, as part of what it means to remember the experiences of one's own past. It is easy to see how Locke could think that the mere having of experiential memories gives rise to personal identity, a sense of my life as uniquely mine.[8] I hope by now to have rendered this view of experiential memory wholly implausible.[9]

I acknowledge that our causal interest in memory is sometimes motivated by the need to determine whether others' contributions to my account of the past rule out my justifying certain claims by reference to my memory. But the source metaphor fails to account for the causal influence of the present. What is now salient about the past and the categories through which I remember are contributed by my present environment. Moreover, while supposedly independent of a commitment to a memory impression, the standard reading of the causal condition is as a causal restriction in which no other cause accounts for how or what I remember but my past. Such a restriction is only plausible on the assumption that memory is an impression or imprint of experience and is not, in general, inherently interpretive. Thus many philosophers continue to think of experiential memory in a way that excludes reinterpretation through shared perspectives from being compatible with memory integrity.

Hacking's philosophy of memory is explicitly reconstructionist. Like most contemporary philosophers and scientists, he makes the now familiar point that memory does not work like a camcorder, which reproduces experience. He emphasizes that most of our significant memories involve human activity, which is subject to changing interpretation; there is no canonical way to think of the human past. Hacking, rightly, holds that there is no original memory experience of human activity that further remembering either matches or distorts. A memory experience is an experience of recalling the past on subsequent occasions where the nature of the occasions will help determine how the past is recalled.

Hacking's account of women's memories as private in the sense of self-constituting, however, at least invokes a way of thinking about memory where memories themselves are unique, private experiences that have integrity through their being immune to the influence of other perspectives. Consciousness-raising, on this traditional view, would not be a legitimate memory activity; moreover, indications suggest that Hacking himself has not fully rejected the influence of more static accounts of memory.

Hacking, as I have noted, uses the idea of indeterminacy to express his concerns about interpreting the past through new categories, and there is slippage in the way he conceives indeterminacy. Hacking's claim is that it might not, for example, have been determinate in the past that a certain behavior was sexual harassment—even if we can truly retrospectively categorize it as such—because it was not determinate that we would come to understand behaviors in this way. But there is a difference in saying *(a)* that our interpretations of the past change and hence it is not determinate how we shall come to remember it; and *(b)* that there is something indeterminate about the nature of a memory that we distort when we remember determinately through a new description. Although Hacking is committed to the first point, he sometimes talks as if he means the second. "Let a scene be recalled, an uncomfortable scene now recalled in terms of abuse. Although the scene may have some prominences, it is also clouded; it has long been buried" (254). Hacking's wording suggests that one experiences an original and now vague memory presentation. And our interpreting such scenes determinately is often linked by Hacking to distorting the past. In illustrating indeterminacy through imagining what might have been true of a disputed historical case, Hacking speculates that perhaps "Bernice's father did abuse her, but in less flagrant ways than Bernice seemed to remember; when she acquired a set of new descriptions in the form of horror stories at the home for wayward girls, semantic contagion went to work" (247).

Although Hacking rejects the notion that memory copies sensation, he is unpersuaded by recent narrative accounts of memory and suggests that memory is better thought of "as dwelling on a *scene*" (251, his emphasis). "I want briefly to suggest the merits of a vulgar point of view; memory is in some ways comparable to perception, as long as we do not demand images" (251). Replacing the image with the scene is meant to be compatible with the changing significance of the past. A laudable feature of Hacking's account is that it refuses to oppose archival and reconstructive models. But even sophisticated returns to the archival model may be motivated by an implicit commitment to the truth of memory as its mirroring of the past.

When Hacking writes about interpretations through new descriptions, he has the disturbing tendency, as in the Bernice example, to do so in terms of distortion and inaccuracy, rather than in terms of changing and more accurate interpretations of the past. This tendency is especially problematic in the last chapter of Hacking's book, "False Consciousness," a chapter that he describes as bringing "to the fore . . . difficult moral questions [that] have been in the background" of the account (257). Although Hacking has offered an astute and subtle account of how ethical problems in our understanding of the past are compatible with the truth of our past claims, the chapter begins by asking: "Does it matter whether what we seem to remember really happened, more or less as we remember it?" (258). Hacking pursues cases of inaccurate and false memory throughout the last chapter, suggesting that the problems with memory interpretation are consistently problems of memory distortion. The best explanation I can think of for the consistent slippage toward distortion is a continued commitment to a memory impression that must be sealed from the effects of contagion.

CONCLUSION

Hacking's ethics of memory is dominated by an intense worry about memory suggestibility, a social inheritance of the false memory debates. It is difficult to see how we can come to an understanding of oppressive harms if we accept this framework. As soon as we begin to conceptualize and socially acknowledge such harms, semantic contagion is activated and we distort the past in trying to understand it.

Disturbingly, Hacking intimates that the solution to influence is to practice a committed skepticism of the use of social resources in reviewing our pasts. Withdrawal from the social, however, is neither a viable nor an ethical response to concerns about problematic influence. We cannot, of course, withdraw from collective understandings; we are already always remembering through perspectives that are shared as well as individual. If our circumstances provide us with adequate relational resources, we can learn how to check our perceptions and interpretations of the past with others, how to contribute our perspectives to group recollection, and how to use our own memories to correct the memories of others. We become responsible rememberers. Our skills and capacities as rememberers are not separable from our autonomy competencies, our abilities to trust appropriately, and our capacities for self-trust—all themselves socialized. True, we are often under tremendous pressure as children and later as adults to remember both a personal and collective past as those more socially powerful want it represented; and our abilities to withstand these pressures and act as autonomous rememberers are lifelong developmental tasks that require social support.

Hacking, however, isolates women's memories as personal, denying them these resources on threat of contagion. He fails to offer an investigation of women's memories through the lens of whether they already express a shared view of the past, and he fails to consider how they contribute to collective understandings. Hacking's contrast between communal and personal memory blocks these investigations. It removes our attention from the dynamics of how women's memories are formed, and at the same time, it prevents a serious treatment of the collectives that women themselves form in an attempt to understand their pasts and produce social knowledge. Moreover, the contrast obscures the complex meanings of the personal in Hacking's account. Some of the meaning reflects a tradition of viewing women's lives as personal. The personalizing of women's lives and relationships, the privatizing of the family, and the denial of women's testimony as productive of knowledge make women vulnerable to certain sorts of oppressive harm, a problem that Hacking's account helps normalize by personalizing their memories. Hacking's account of women who remember abusive pasts as involved in personal identity projects also draws on a philosophical tradition of understanding experiential memory as uniquely personal. A person's life is revealed as uniquely hers through memories that encode and repeat the singular perspectives of her perceptual position in the world. Hacking's focus on women's memories, complexly overdetermined as personal, deprives us of the conceptual framework required for an adequate theory of oppressive harms.

My intention in this study has not been to deny the existence or importance of personal memory. I believe that memory contributes to a special sense of our lives as unique and our own; and if we are relatively favorably situated, then we can gain great benefit from these important values. However much the meaning of some memories depends on group interaction and socially determined salience, our memories are associatively linked in ways unique for each individual and thus have meaning not captured or exhausted by their collective dimensions. The value of personal memory, however, requires a fuller account that does not sever the personal from the collective.

We can be denied many of the benefits of personal memory when we are denied appropriate opportunities or resources for understanding the past. We can be exploited, our self-concepts can be damaged, and our sense of responsibility can be undermined when relationships either offer us faulty conceptual resources for understanding the meaning of our past or mislead us about when seeming memory should or should not be trusted. Obviously, to point to the crucial social dimensions of successful remembering is in no way to deny that our understandings of the past may be harmfully distorted through our associations with others.

Notice, however, that the lawyers and judges who were concerned about women's memory in the context of records production spoke of memory influence solely in terms of notions such as implantation and contamination. Any influence on women's memory was thought of *only* in terms of memory distortion. While this contemporary concern about suggestibility appears to acknowledge social dimensions to remembering, it in fact endorses an implicit model of memory purity: namely, the idea that when others influence our memory, they do so only harmfully. I have argued that this misconception is widespread and that it has affected philosophical accounts of memory like Hacking's, as well as court decisions about confidentiality and scientific models of memory accuracy. It is shaped and exacerbated by an unacceptable stereotype of women's dependency, itself related to a false ideal of autonomy as complete independence. We must resist this negative alignment of memory influence solely with memory contamination, and we must work for a more balanced view of memory as an inherently relational capacity. A relational account of memory is central to providing an adequate and coherent account of our skills as rememberers and moral agents, of our "best vision of a human being."

Finally, it is only in more fully understanding the complex social dimensions of personal memory—how memories are formed, supported, undermined, narrated, and tested in a variety of relational circumstances—that we can engage in an informed and intelligent conversation about influence.

NOTES

1. Even if one were to agree with Ian Hacking that a diagnosis of MPD has a tendency to encourage some of the ethical concerns he raises, given the reported incident rate of child sexual abuse, we would still need an account of why most women who understand their pasts as containing abuse are not properly understanding their pasts.

2. See also: "My very neutrality makes me cautious about even the name of our topic. Names organize our thoughts" (Hacking, 16–17).

3. Many writers have discussed the difficulty of representing the Holocaust, and some have explicitly raised the question of whether the Holocaust can find a place in collective memory. But Ian Hacking is not the only writer to choose the Holocaust to exemplify collective memory in order to frame investigation of women's memories of abuse. In *Searching for Memory* (1996), Daniel Schacter also finds it natural to map the terrain of contemporary memory debate by first referring to an attempt of revisionist groups to "recast society's collective memory of the Holocaust" (8). Reference to the memories of Holocaust survivors as cases of traumatized memory in feminist discussions has angered many writers who see this as an attempt to appropriate serious and uncontested examples of traumatic harm in order to bootstrap women's memories into a weighty moral category. But I am also disturbed that these memories are the sole representative of collective memory in Hacking's account, as I take part of the implied contrast to be the seriousness of such memories as compared with women's memories. This example emphasizes a credibility and authority to shared accounts of the past. For Hacking, the politics of personal memory has none of this credibility. He refers to it as a "brouhaha."

4. For a critique of standard ways of thinking about communal memory, see Paul Connerton (1993).

5. Countermemory can take the form of men's using December 6 as an occasion to remember aspects of their relations with women. David Lees, for example, reflects at a December meeting of Metro Men Against Violence (Toronto): "I sat in the back row trying to stay in the shadows and wondering what I could say . . . that twice I have struck a woman in each case to stop the woman from striking me; that my truly vicious gift for silence and distance was taught to me by my mother. 'Domestic violence' presents itself to me as an unfaded, 30-year old image of a man standing in a kitchen with blood from a hammer blow pouring down his face, asking a woman to be more reasonable" (1993, 46–47). In a 1998 article in a student newspaper (Halifax, Nova Scotia), Stephen Brown wrote: "I am not going to feel guilty anymore that I used my virginity on the anniversary of Marc Lepine's murder of fourteen women at Montreal Polytechnique. . . . I am not going to feel guilty anymore that I have been with differ-

ent women in different ways. . . . I am not going to feel guilty anymore that each of them was raped before and after me . . . because I did not rape them. I am not going to feel guilty anymore that I did use them because they did use me. That's what it's all about, right" (1998, 9).

6. As another obvious example, the efficiency of assimilating native peoples to colonial cultures by placing native children in residential schools also depends on the vulnerability of children as young rememberers.

7. Because of a Foucauldian influence, Ian Hacking is concerned with the expert classifications through which we get kinds of people—specifically, the association of a categorization of child sexual abuse with the rise of multiple personality disorder as a way of being a person. Still, it is a disturbing fact about his account, which is an account of the social dimensions of knowledge, that he generally fails to see women as knowledge-producers or to see that the work of feminist therapists is dependent on and situated in collective feminist understandings.

8. That each memory is itself thought to be personal is indicated through philosophical thought experiments in which the progressive transfer, one by one, of one individual's memories to a second individual is imagined to be a transfer of the first person's psychology—independently of the history of associations that these memories have exhibited or how they may have been formed or cued in environments never encountered by the second individual (Parfit 1984).

9. The traditional empiricist account of memory has been subject to considerable criticism, however—particularly the commitment to an original and lasting memory image that copies a perceptual experience as the core of what it is to remember. Accounts of memory that defined it through the experience of an original memory datum or a secondary perception encountered persistent difficulties saying what linked this image to the past (Anscombe 1981, Malcolm 1963); moreover, the extent to which people experience memory as imagistic varies widely. Nevertheless, many contemporary philosophers continue to model memory broadly on perception, stressing the importance of the causal condition.

BIBLIOGRAPHY

Aboriginal Women's Council et al. 1996a. "Factum for *A.(L.L.) v. Beharriell*." In *Equality and the Charter: Ten Years of Feminist Advocacy before the Supreme Court of Canada*, Women's Legal Education and Action Fund. Toronto: Edmond Montgomery.

———. 1996b. "Factum for *O'Connor* v. *The Queen*." In *Equality and the Charter: Ten Years of Feminist Advocacy before the Supreme Court of Canada*, Women's Legal Education and Action Fund. Toronto: Edmond Montgomery.

Ackelsberg, Martha, and Mary Shanley. 1996. "Privacy, Publicity, and Power: A Feminist Rethinking of the Public-Private Distinction." In *Revisioning the Political: Feminist Reconstructions of Traditional Concepts in Western Political Theory*, ed. Nancy Hirschmann and Christine Di Stefano. Boulder, CO: Westview Press.

Ackerman, Diane. 1996. *A Natural History of the Senses* (excerpt). In *The Anatomy of Memory*, ed. James McConkey. Oxford: Oxford University Press.

Alcoff, Linda. 1991–1992. "The Problem of Speaking for Others." *Cultural Critique* 20: 5–33.

Alcoff, Linda, and Laura Gray. 1993. "Survivor Discourse: Transgression or Recuperation?" *Signs: Journal of Women in Culture and Society* 18 (2): 260–90.

Allen, Anita. 1983. "Women and Their Privacy: What Is at Stake?" In *Beyond Domination: New Perspectives on Women and Philosophy*, ed. Carol Gould. Totowa, NJ: Rowman and Allanheld.

Allen, Barry. 1997. "The Soul of Knowledge." *History and Theory* 36 (1): 63–82.

Anscombe, G. E. M. 1981. "Memory, 'Experience' and Causation." In *The Collected Philosophical Papers of G. E. M. Anscombe, Vol. II: Metaphysics and the Philosophy of Mind*. Minneapolis: University of Minnesota Press.

Aquinas, Thomas. *Commentary on Boethius' De Trinitate*, qu. 3, art. 1.3.

Armstrong, Harvey, et al. 1997. "Response to the CPA Position Paper on Memory," in PAR-L@hermes.csd.unb.ca (listserv). Cited September 16, 1997. Available from PAR-L-SERVER@unb.ca.

Armstrong, Louise. 1994. *Rocking the Cradle of Sexual Politics*. New York: Addison-Wesley.

Babbitt, Susan. 1996. *Impossible Dreams: Rationality, Integrity, and Moral Imagination*. Boulder, CO: Westview Press.

Baier, Annette. 1985a. "Cartesian Persons." In *Postures of the Mind: Essays on Mind and Morals*. Minneapolis: University of Minnesota Press.

———. 1985b. "Mixing Memory and Desire." In *Postures of the Mind: Essays on Mind and Morals*. Minneapolis: University of Minnesota Press.

Bartky, Sandra. 1990. "Shame and Gender." In *Femininity and Domination: Studies in the Phenomenology of Oppression*. New York: Routledge.

Bass, Ellen, and Laura Davis. 1994. *The Courage to Heal*. 3rd edition. New York: Harper Perennial.

Bekerman, D. A., and J. M. Bowers. 1983. "Eyewitness Testimony: Were We Misled?" *Journal of Experimental Psychology: Learning, Memory, and Cognition* 9 (1): 139–45.

Benhabib, Seyla. 1987. "The Generalized and Concrete Other." In *Feminism as Critique*, ed. Seyla Benhabib and Drucilla Cornell. Minneapolis: University of Minnesota Press.

Benn, Stanley I. 1984. "Privacy, Freedom, and Respect for Persons." In *Philosophical Dimensions of Privacy: An Anthology*, ed. Ferdinand Schoeman. Cambridge: Cambridge University Press.

Berliner, Lucy, and Elizabeth Loftus. 1992. "Sexual Abuse Accusations: Desperately Seeking Reconciliation." *Journal of Interpersonal Violence* 7 (4): 570–78.

Beverley, John. 1992. "The Margin at the Center: On Testimonio (Testimonial Narrative)." In *De/colonizing the Subject: The Politics of Gender in Women's Autobiography*, ed. Sidonie Smith and Julia Watson. Minneapolis: University of Minnesota Press.

Bindman, Stephen. 1998. "Can Recovered Memories Be Trusted? Justice Minister Rejects Call for Inquiry." *Ottawa Citizen*, May 4.

Borland, Katherine. 1991. "'That's Not What I Said': Interpretive Conflict in Oral Narrative Research." In *Women's Words: The Feminist Practice of Oral History*, ed. Sherna Berger Gluck and Daphne Patai. New York: Routledge.

Bowman, Cynthia Grant, and Elizabeth Mertz. 1996. "A Dangerous Direction: Legal Intervention in Sexual Abuse Survivor Therapy." *Harvard Law Review* 109 (3): 540–639.

Boyd, Richard. 1980. "Metaphor and Theory Change: What Is 'Metaphor' a Metaphor For?" In *Metaphor and Thought*, ed. A. Ortony. Cambridge, England: Cambridge University Press.

Brady, Erin. 1996. "False Memory Syndrome: The Female Malady." *Dalhousie Journal of Legal Studies* 5: 69–93.

Brewer, William F. 1998. "Memory for Randomly Sampled Autobiographical Events." In *Remembering Reconsidered: Ecological and Traditional Approaches to the Study of Memory*, ed. Ulric Neisser and Eugene Winograd. Cambridge: Cambridge University Press.

Brison, Susan. 1997. "Outliving Oneself: Trauma, Memory and Personal Identity." In *Feminists Rethink the Self*, ed. Diana T. Meyers. Boulder, CO: Westview Press.

Brister, Jude, Ellen Bass, and Louise Thorton, eds. 1983. *I Never Told Anyone: Writings by Women Survivors of Child Sexual Abuse*. New York: Harper and Row.

Bronitt, Simon, and Bernadette McSherry. 1997. "The Use and Abuse of Counselling Records in Sexual Assault Cases: Reconstructing the 'Rape Shield'?" *Criminal Law Review* (Camden) 8 (2): 259–91.

Brown, Daniel P., Alan W. Scheflin, and D. Corydon Hammond. 1998. *Memory, Trauma Treatment and the Law*. New York: W. W. Norton.

Brown, Laura S. 1996a. "On the Construction of Truth and Falsity: Whose Memory, Whose History?" In *The Recovered Memory/False Memory Debate*, ed. Kathy Pezdek and William Banks. San Diego: Academic Press.

———. 1996b. "Politics of Memory, Politics of Incest: Doing Therapy and Politics That Really Matter." *Women and Therapy* 19 (1): 5–18.

Brown, Laura S., and Erica Burman. 1997. "The Delayed Memory Debate: Why Feminist Voices Matter." Editor's introduction to "Feminist Responses to the 'False' Memory Debate." *Feminism and Psychology* 7 (1): 7–16.

Brown, S. 1998. "Take Back the Bullshit." *Picaro* (Halifax, Nova Scotia), September 29.

Brownlie, E. B. 1999. "Lies, Secrets and Silence: Substantiated Memories of Child Sexual Abuse." In *Fragment by Fragment: Feminist Perspectives on Memory and Child Sexual Abuse*, ed. Margo Rivera. Charlottetown, PEI: Gynergy Books.

Busby, Karen. 1997. "Discriminatory Uses of Personal Records in Sexual Assault Cases." *Canadian Journal of Women and the Law* 9: 148–77.

Campbell, Richmond. 1998. *Illusions of Paradox: A Feminist Epistemology Naturalized.* Lanham, MD: Rowman and Littlefield.

Campbell, Sue. 2003. "Relational Remembering: Suggestibility and Women's Confidential Records." In *Confidential Relationships: Psychoanalytic, Ethical, and Legal Contexts*, ed. Christine Koggel, Alannah Furlong, and Charles Levin. Amsterdam: Rodopi Press.

———. 2002. "Dependence in Client-therapist Relationships: A Relational Reading of *O'Connor* and *Mills*." In *No Person Is an Island: Personal Relationships of Dependence and Interdependence*, Law Commission of Canada. Vancouver: UBC Press.

———. 2001. "Memory, Suggestibility and Social Skepticism." In *Engendering Rationalities*, ed. Nancy Tuana and Sandra Morgen. New York: SUNY Press.

———. 1999a. "A Singular and Representative Life: Personal Memory and Systematic Harms." *Canadian Journal of Philosophy*. Supplementary, vol. 25, *Civilization and Oppression*, ed. Catherine Wilson.

———. 1999b. "Framing Women's Testimony." In *Fragment by Fragment: Feminist Perspectives on Memory and Child Sexual Abuse*, ed. Margo Rivera. Charlottetown, PEI: Gynergy Books.

———. 1997. "Women, 'False' Memory, and Personal Identity." *Hypatia: A Journal of Feminist Philosophy* 12 (2): 51–82.

———. 1993. "Autobiography and the Conditions of Personhood." Presented at the Canadian Society for Women in Philosophy, September 1993, University of Calgary.

Campbell, Terence. 1998. *Smoke and Mirrors: The Devastating Effect of False Sexual Abuse Claims*. New York: Insight Books.

Carstensen, L., et al. 1993. "Repressed Objectivity." *APS Observer* (March): 23.

Chu, James A., Lisa M. Frey, Barbara L. Ganzel, and Julia A. Matthews. 1999. "Memories of Childhood Abuse: Dissociation, Amnesia and Corroboration." *American Journal of Psychiatry* 156: 749–55.

Clark, Andy. 1997. *Being There: Putting Brain, Body, and World Together Again*. Cambridge, MA: MIT Press.

Clausen, Victoria. 2000. "Memory Debate Rekindled." *The Press* (Christchurch), August 9.

Coady, C. A. J. 1992. *Testimony: A Philosophical Study*. Oxford: Oxford University Press.

Code, Lorraine. 2000. "The Perversion of Autonomy and the Subjection of Women: Discourses of Social Advocacy at Century's End." In *Relational Autonomy: Feminist Perspectives on Autonomy, Agency and the Social Self*, ed. Catriona Mackenzie and Natalie Stoljar. New York: Oxford University Press.

Connerton, Paul. 1994. "The Revenge of the Repressed." Parts 1 and 2. *New York Review of Books* 41 (19): 54–59; 41 (20): 49–58.

———. 1989. *How Societies Remember*. New York: Cambridge University Press.

Crews, Frederick. 1995. *The Memory Wars: Freud's Legacy in Dispute*. New York: New York Review of Books.

Criminal Code, R. S. C. 1985, c. C-46.

Culbertson, Roberta. 1995. "Embodied Memory, Transcendence and Telling: Recounting Trauma, Re-establishing the Self." *New Literary History* 26: 169–95.

Danica, Elly. 1988. *Don't: A Woman's Word*. Charlottetown, PEI.: Gynergy Books.

Dennett, Daniel. 1991. "The Origin of Selves." In *Self and Identity*, ed. Daniel Kolak and Raymond Martin. New York: Macmillan Publishing.

———. 1978. "The Conditions of Personhood." In *The Identities of Persons*, ed. Amelie Rorty. Berkeley: University of California Press.

Descartes, Rene. 1662/1998. *L'Homme (The Treatise on Man)*. In *Descartes: The World and Other Writings*. Trans. and ed. by Stephen Gaukroger. Cambridge: Cambridge University Press. First published posthumously as *Renatus Descartes de Homine*.

———. 1641/1984–1991. "Meditations on First Philosophy." In *Philosophical Writings of Descartes*, vol. 2, ed. John Cottingham, Robert Stoothoff, and Dugald Murdoch. Cambridge: Cambridge University Press.

Dillon, Robin. 1992. "Self-Respect and Emotion." Unpublished manuscript. Revised and published as "Self-Respect: Moral, Emotional, Political." *Ethics* 107 (2): 226–49.

Dixon, Greg. 2000. "Psychological Warfare—Can the Horror of Childhood Abuse Resurface Later?" *New Zealand Herald*, August 26.

Enns, Carolyn Zerbe, Cheryl L. McNeilly, Julie Madison Corkery, Mary S. Gilbert. 1995. "The Debate about Delayed Memories of Childhood Sexual Abuse: A Feminist Perspective." *The Counselling Psychologist* 23 (2): 181–279.

Epp, Jennifer. 2002. *Helpful Harms: Advocacy and Its Relation to Autonomy*. Master's thesis, Dalhousie University.

False Memory Syndrome Foundation. 2000. "Are Undergraduates Learning about False Memories?" *FMS Foundation Newsletter* 9 (1). Online edition. Accessed Jan. 15, 2000.

———. 1994. *False Memory Syndrome*. Pamphlet.

Felman, Shoshana, and Dori Laub. 1992. *Testimony: Crises of Witnessing in Literature, Psychoanalysis, and History*. New York: Routledge.

Fentress, James, and Chris Wickham. 1992. *Social Memory*. Oxford: Blackwell.

Fitz-James, Michael. 1995. "Sexual Abuse Cases Raise Tricky Issues of Records Disclosure." *The Medical Post* (September 12): 18.

Fivush, Robyn. 1996. "Young Children's Event Recall: Are Memories Constructed through Discourse?" In *The Recovered Memory/False Memory Debate*, ed. Kathy Pezdek and William Banks. San Diego: Academic Press.

Fivush, Robyn, Margaret Ellen-Pipe, Tamar Muracherver, and Elaine Reese. 1997. "Events Spoken and Unspoken: Implications of Language and Memory Development for the Recovered Memory Debate." In *Recovered Memories and False Memories*, ed. Martin Conway. Oxford: Oxford University Press.

Foucault, Michel. 1978. *The History of Sexuality, Volume 1: An Introduction*. Trans. Robert Hurley. New York: Pantheon.

Frawley-O'Dea, Mary Gail. 1999. "Society, Politics, Psychotherapy and the Search for 'Truth' in the Memory Debate." In *Fragment by Fragment: Feminist Perspectives on Memory and Child Sexual Abuse*, ed. Margo Rivera. Charlottetown, PEI: Gynergy Books.

Freyd, Jennifer. 1996. *Betrayal Trauma: The Logic of Forgetting Childhood Abuse*. Cambridge, MA: Harvard University Press.

———. 1993. "Theoretical and Personal Perspectives on the Delayed Memory Debate." Presented at Foote Hospital's continuing-education conference "Controversies around Recovered Memories of Incest and Ritual Abuse," Ann Arbor, MI, August 7, 1993.

Freyd, Peter. 2002. "Paul McHugh and FMSF." FMS-News@saul.cis.unpenn.edu (listserv). July 25, 2002.

Fried, Charles. 1984. "Privacy [A Moral Analysis]." In *Philosophical Dimensions of Privacy: An Anthology*, ed. Ferdinand Schoeman. Cambridge: Cambridge University Press.

Frye, Marilyn. 1983a. "A Note on Anger." In *The Politics of Reality: Essays in Feminist Theory*. Freedom, CA: The Crossing Press.

———. 1983b. "On Separatism and Power." In *The Politics of Reality: Essays in Feminist Theory*. Freedom, CA: The Crossing Press.

Gavison, Ruth. 1984. "Privacy and the Limits of Law." In *Philosophical Dimensions of Privacy: An Anthology*, ed. Ferdinand Schoeman. Cambridge: Cambridge University Press.

Glanvill, Joseph. 1661/1970. *The Vanity of Dogmatizing*. Ed. and intro. by Stephen Medcalf. Brighton, UK.: Harvester Press.

Goldstein, Eleanor, and Kevin Farmer. 1993. *True Stories of False Memories*. Boca Raton, FL: Social Issues Resources Series.

Good, Michael I., August Piper Jr., Harold Merckelbach, and Russell A. Powell, et al. 2000. "More Questions about Recovered Memories: Dr. Chu Replies." *American Journal of Psychiatry* 157 (8). Accessed online.

Guha, Martin. 2000. "Review of Janice Haaken, *Pillar of Salt: Gender, Memory, and the Perils of Looking Back* (New Jersey: Rutgers University Press, 1998)." *International Journal of Social Psychiatry* (Winter).

Haaken, Janice. 1998. *Pillar of Salt: Gender, Memory, and the Perils of Looking Back*. Piscataway, NJ: Rutgers University Press.

———. 1996. "The Recovery of Memory, Fantasy, and Desire: Feminist Approaches to Sexual Abuse and Psychic Trauma." *Signs: Journal of Women in Culture and Society* 21 (4): 1069–94.

Hacking, Ian. 1995. *Rewriting the Soul: Multiple Personality and the Sciences of Memory*. Princeton, NJ: Princeton University Press.

Halbwachs, Maurice. 1950. *La Mémoire collective*. Preface by Jean Duvugnaud. Introduction by Michel Alexandre. Presses Universitaires de France. English translation published 1980 as *The Collective Memory*. Introduction by Mary Douglas. New York: Harper and Row.

———. 1925. *Les Cadres sociaux de la mémoire*. Les Travaux de L'Année Sociologique. Paris: F. Alcan. Reprinted 1952 by Presses Universitaires de France.

Halifax Chronicle Herald (Nova Scotia). 1993. May 1, A1–2.

Harrowitz, Nancy, and Barbara Hymans. 1995. "A Critical Introduction to the History of Weininger Reception." In *Jews and Gender: Responses to Otto Weininger*. Philadelphia: Temple University Press.

Harvey, J. 1999. *Civilized Oppression*. Lanham, MD: Rowman and Littlefield.

Herman, Judith. 1992. *Trauma and Recovery*. New York: Basic Books.

Heywood, Carter. 1993. *When Boundaries Betray Us: Beyond Illusions of What Is Ethical in Therapy and Life*. New York: HarperCollins.

Hilgard, Ernst R. 1965. *Hypnotic Susceptibility*. New York: Harcourt, Brace and World.

Hill, Kim, and John Read. 2000. National radio transcript (New Zealand). August 8, 2000.

Horn, Miriam. 1993. "Memories Lost and Found." *U.S. News and World Report*, November 29, 52–63.

Jacobsen, Rockney. n.d. "Descartes on the Misdesign of the Mind." Unpublished manuscript.

James, William. 1890/1950. *The Principles of Psychology*. Vol. 1. New York: Dover Publications.

Keller, Helen. 1902/1988. *The Story of My Life*. New York: Bantam.

Kelly, Katherine. 1997. "You Must Be Crazy If You Think You Were Raped: Reflections on the Use of Complainant's Personal and Therapy Records in Sexual Assault Trials." *Canadian Journal of Women and the Law* 9: 179–95.

Kitzenger, Celia. 1993. "Depoliticizing the Personal: A Feminist Slogan in Feminist Therapy." *Women's Studies International Forum* (16): 487–96.

Klein, Viola. 1946/1971. *The Feminine Character: History of an Ideology*. London: Routledge.

Koggel, Christine. 1998. *Perspectives on Equality: Constructing a Relational Theory*. Lanham, MD: Rowman and Littlefield.

Laidlaw, Toni Ann, and Cheryl Malmo. 1990. *Healing Voices: Feminist Approaches to Therapy with Women*. San Francisco: Jossey-Bass Publishers.

Laing, R. D. 1967. *The Politics of Experience*. London: Penguin Books.

Laurence, Jean-Roch, and Campbell Perry. 1988. *Hypnosis, Will, and Memory: A Psycholegal History*. New York: The Guilford Press.

Lees, David. 1992. "The War Against Men." *Toronto Life* 26 (18): 34–39, 98–104.

Lessing, Doris. 1986. *The Good Terrorist*. New York: Vintage.

Lindsay, D. Stephen. 1994. "Contextualizing and Clarifying Criticisms of Memory Work in Psychotherapy." *Consciousness and Cognition* 3: 426–37.

Lindsay, D. Stephen, and J. D. Read. 1994. "Psychotherapy and Memories of Childhood Sexual Abuse: A Cognitive Perspective." *Applied Cognitive Psychology* 8: 281–338.

Lloyd, Genevieve. 1993. "Maleness, Metaphor and the 'Crisis' of Reason." In *A Mind of One's Own: Feminist Essays on Reason and Objectivity*, ed. Louise A. Antony and Charlotte Witt. Boulder, CO: Westview Press.

———. 1984. "The Man of Reason." In *Women, Knowledge, and Reality: Explorations in Feminist Philosophy*, ed. Ann Garry and Marilyn Pearsall. Boston: Unwin Hyman.

Locke, John. 1993. "The Reality of Repressed Memories." *American Psychologist* 48: 518–37.

———. 1690/1961. *An Essay Concerning Human Understanding*. Selected and edited by John W. Yolton. London: J. M. Dent and Sons.

Loftus, Elizabeth F. 1997. "Creating False Memories." *Scientific American* (September), 277.

Loftus, Elizabeth F. 1993. "The Reality of Repressed Memories." *American Psychologist* 48, 518–537.

Loftus, Elizabeth, and Katherine Ketcham. 1994. *The Myth of Repressed Memory: False Memories and Allegations of Sexual Abuse*. New York: St. Martin's Press.

———. 1991. *Witness for the Defense: The Accused, the Eyewitness, and the Expert Who Puts Memory on Trial*. New York: St. Martin's Press.

Longino, Helen. 1994. "The Fate of Knowledge in Social Theories of Science." In *Socializing Epistemology: The Social Dimensions of Knowledge*, ed. Frederick Schmitt. Lanham, MD: Rowman and Littlefield.

Mackenzie, Catriona, and Natalie Stoljar, eds. 2000. *Relational Autonomy: Feminist Perspectives on Autonomy, Agency, and the Social Self*. New York: Oxford University Press.

Makin, Kirk. 1998a. "False Memory's Victims Languish in Jail." *The Globe and Mail* (Toronto), May 9, A1.

———. 1998b. "'Recovered Memory' Losing Its Value." *The Globe and Mail* (Toronto), May 8, A8.

Malcolm, Norman. 1963. "Memory and the Past." In *Knowledge and Certainty: Essays and Lectures by Norman Malcolm*. Englewood Cliffs, NJ: Prentice Hall.

Malebranche, Nicolas. 1674/1997. *The Search after Truth*. Trans. by T. M. Lennon and P. J. Olscamp. Cambridge: Cambridge University Press.

Mandeville, Bernard. 1711/1976. *A Treatise of the Hypochondriack and Hysterick Passions . . . in Three Dialogues*. New York: Arno Press.

McCluskey, Marsha T. 1994. "Transforming Victimization." *Tikkun* 9 (2): 54–56.

McInnes, John, and Christine Boyle. 1995. "Judging Sexual Assault Law against a Standard of Equality." *U.B.C. Law Review* 29 (2): 341–81.

McLoughlin, David. 2000a. "Is This an Abuse of the Truth?" *The Dominion* (Wellington), August 29.

———. 2000b. "Therapists in Sex Abuse Cases Could Be Sued." *The Dominion* (Wellington), August 28.

McNaron, Toni, and Yarrow Morgan. 1982. *Voices in the Night*. Minneapolis: Cleis Press.

McPhedran, Mary Lou. 1995. "The Legal Assault on Physician-Patient Privilege." *Canadian Medical Association Journal* 153 (10): 1502–6.

Menchú, Rigoberta, with Elisabeth Burgos-Debray. 1984. *I, Rigoberta Menchú: An Indian Woman in Guatemala*, trans. Ann White. London: Verso.

Merskey, Harold. 1997. "Evaluating Memory." *Health Care Analysis* 5 (2): 132–35.

———. 1995. "What Is a Syndrome?" *FMS Foundation Newsletter* (June): 6.

Meyers, Diana Tietjens. 1997. "The Family Romance: A *Fin-de-siecle* Tragedy." In *Feminism and Families*, ed. Hilde Lindemann Nelson. New York: Routledge.

———. 1989. *Self, Society, and Personal Choice*. New York: Columbia University Press.

Middleton, David, and Derek Edwards, eds. 1990a. "Introduction to *Collective Remembering*." London: Sage Publications.

———. 1990b. "Conversational Remembering: A Social Psychological Approach." In *Collective Remembering*, ed. Middleton and Edwards. London: Sage Publications.

Mills, Charles. 1997. *The Racial Contract*. Ithaca, NY: Cornell University Press.

Mitchell, Jann. 1993. "Memories of a Disputed Past." *The Oregonian*, August 8.

Morales, Aurora Levins. 1998a. "The Personal Is Political: How I Wrote This Book." In *Medicine Stories: History, Culture and the Politics of Integrity*. Cambridge, MA: South End Press.

———. 1998b. "False Memories: Trauma and Liberation." In *Medicine Stories: History, Culture and the Politics of Integrity*. Cambridge, MA: South End Press.

———. 1998c. "The Historian as Curandera." In *Medicine Stories: History, Culture and the Politics of Integrity*. Cambridge, MA: South End Press.

Morrison, Toni. 1987. "The Site of Memory." In *Inventing the Truth: The Art and Craft of Memoir*, ed. William Zinsser. Boston: Houghton Mifflin.

Murphy, Wendy J. 1997. "Debunking 'False Memory' Myths in Sexual Abuse Cases." *Trial* (November): 45–60.

National Association for Consumer Protection in Mental Health Practices. 1994. "A Proposal to Finance Preparation of Model Legislation Titled 'Mental Health Consumer Protection Act.'" Jointly sponsored by Illinois FMS Society, Ohio Parents Falsely Accused, Texas Friends of FMS, Minnesota Action Committee, Florida Friends of FMS.

Ofshe, Richard, and Ethan Watters. 1994. *Making Monsters: False Memories, Psychotherapy, and Sexual Hysteria*. New York: Charles Scribner's Sons.

———. 1993. "Making Monsters." *Society* (March/April): 4–16.

Olio, Karen, and William Cornell. 1998. "The Facade of Scientific Documentation: A Case Study of Richard Ofshe's Analysis of the Paul Ingram Case." *Psychology, Public Policy, and Law* 4 (4): 1182–97.

Parfit, Derek. 1984. *Reasons and Persons*. Oxford: Clarendon Press.

Park, Shelley M. 1999. "Reviewing the Memory Wars: Some Feminist Philosophical Reflections." In *Fragment by Fragment: Feminist Perspectives on Memory and Child Sexual Abuse*, ed. Margo Rivera. Charlottetown, PEI: Gynergy Books.

———. 1997. "False Memory Syndrome: A Feminist Philosophical Perspective." *Hypatia: A Journal of Feminist Philosophy* 12 (2): 1–50.

Pendergast, Mark. 1995. *Victims of Memory: Incest Accusations and Shattered Lives*. Hinesburg, VT: Upper Access.

Perry, Campbell. 2000. "Hypnosis and the Elicitation of Repressed and/or Dissociated Memories." *Hypnos* 27 (3): 124–30.

Philip, M. Nourbese. 1992. "A Long-Memoried Woman." In *Frontiers: Essays and Writing on Racism and Culture*. Stratford, ON: Mercury Press.

Pillemer, David B. 1998. *Momentous Events, Vivid Memories*. Cambridge, MA: Harvard University Press.

Poole, Debra A., D. Stephen Lindsay, Amina Memon, and Ray Bull. 1995. "Psychotherapy and the Recovery of Memories of Childhood Sexual Abuse: U.S. and British Practitioners' Beliefs, Practices, and Experiences." *Journal of Consulting and Clinical Psychology*, 63: 426–37.

Pope, Kenneth S. 1997. "Science as Careful Questioning: Are Claims of a False Memory Syndrome Epidemic Based on Empirical Evidence?" *American Psychologist* 52 (9): 997–1006.

———. 1996. "Memory, Abuse, and Science: Questioning Claims about the False Memory Syndrome Epidemic." *American Psychologist* 51 (9): 957–74.

Rachels, James. 1984. "Why Privacy Is Important." In *Philosophical Dimensions of Privacy: An Anthology*, ed. Ferdinand Schoeman. Cambridge: Cambridge University Press.

Raitt, Fiona E., and M. Suzanne Zeedyk. 2000. *The Implicit Relation of Psychology and the Law: Women and Syndrome Evidence*. London: Routledge.

Reiman, Jeffrey H. 1984. "Privacy, Intimacy, and Personhood." In *Philosophical Dimensions of Privacy: An Anthology*, ed. Ferdinand Schoeman. Cambridge: Cambridge University Press.

Rivera, Margo. 1999. "Introduction to *Fragment by Fragment: Feminist Perspectives on Memory and Child Sexual Abuse*." Charlottetown, PEI: Gynergy Books.

"Rock Must Modify Court's Rape Ruling." 1996. *The Toronto Star*, January 4, A16.

Rorty, Amelie. 1988. "Persons and Personae." In *Mind in Action*. Boston: Beacon Press.

Russell, Diana E. 1986/1999. *The Secret Trauma: Incest in the Lives of Girls and Women*. New York: Basic Books.

Schacter, Daniel L., ed. 1999. *The Cognitive Neuropsychology of False Memories*. Hove, East Sussex: Psychology Press.

———. 1996. *Searching for Memory: The Brain, the Mind, and the Past*. New York: HarperCollins.

Schechtman, Marya. 1994. "The Truth about Memory." *Philosophical Psychology* 7, 3–18.

Scheflin Alan, and D. Brown. 1996. "Repressed or Dissociative Amnesia: What the Science Says." *Journal of Psychiatry and the Law* 24: 143–88.

Scheman, Naomi. 2001. "Epistemology Resuscitated: Objectivity as Truthworthiness." In *Engendering Rationalities*, ed. Nancy Tuana and Sandra Morgen. New York: SUNY Press.

———. 1996. "Feeling Our Way towards Moral Objectivity." In *Mind and Morals: Essays on Cognitive Science and Ethics*, ed. Larry May, Marilyn Friedman, and Andy Clark. Cambridge, MA: MIT Press.

Scott, Sara E. 1997. "Feminists and False Memories: A Case of Postmodern Amnesia. Feminist Responses to the 'False' Memory Debate." *Feminism and Psychology* 7 (1): 33–38.

Sherwin, Susan. 1998. "A Relational Approach to Autonomy in Health Care." In *The Politics of Women's Health: Exploring Agency and Autonomy*, the Feminist Health Care Ethics Research Network (Susan Sherwin, coordinator). Philadelphia: Temple University Press.

Singer, Linda. 1993. *Erotic Welfare: Sexual Theory and Politics in the Age of Epidemic*. New York: Routledge.

Spanos, Nicholas P. 1986. "Hypnosis and the Modification of Hypnotic Suggestibility: A Social Psychological Perspective." In *What Is Hypnosis?* ed. Peter L. N. Naish. Philadelphia: Open University Press.

Spelman, Elizabeth V. 1977–1978. "Treating Persons as Persons." *Ethics* 88: 150–61.

Spence, Donald. 1982. *Narrative Truth and Historical Truth: Meaning and Interpretation in Psychoanalysis*. New York: W. W. Norton.

Stanton, Mike. 1997. "U-turn on Memory Lane." *Columbia Journalism Review* (July/August): 44–49.

Sutton, John. 2000. "Review of *Pillar of Salt.*" *Metapsychology Online Book Reviews*. http://mentalhelp.net/books/books.php?type=de&id=299. Accessed Jan. 29, 2002.

———. 1998. *Philosophy and Memory Traces: Descartes to Connectionism*. Cambridge, UK: Cambridge University Press.

Swindells, Julia. 1989. "Liberating the Subject? Autobiography and 'Women's History.'" In *Interpreting Women's Lives*, ed. Personal Narratives Group. Bloomington: Indiana University Press.

Tavris, Carol. 1993. "Beware the Incest Survivor Machine." *Montreal Gazette*, January 30, B1–2.

Taylor, Charles. 1991. "The Dialogical Self." In *The Interpretive Turn: Philosophy, Science, Culture*, ed. David R. Hiley, James F. Bohman, and Richard Shusterman. Ithaca, NY: Cornell University Press.

Thomas, Laurence. 1992–1993. "Moral Deference." *The Philosophical Forum* 24 (1–3): 233–50.

Underwager, Ralph, and Hollinda Wakefield. 1995. *Return of the Furies: An Investigation into Recovered Memory Therapy*. Chicago: Open Court Press.

Van Frassen, Bas. 1980. *The Scientific Image*. Oxford: Clarendon Press.

Van Gelder, Tim. 1995. "What Could Cognition Be, If Not Computation?" *Journal of Philosophy* 91: 345–81.

Vella, Susan M. 1994. "False Memory Syndrome: Therapists Are the Targets in New Sexual Assault Defence Theory." *National*, Canadian Bar Association (January/February): 36–39.

Vienneau, David. 1995. "Court Opens Rape Records to Accused." *The Toronto Star*, December 15, A3.

Villedieu, Yanick. 1999. "You Must Remember This!" *Enroute* (Air Canada), May, 34–43.

Waites, Elizabeth A. 1997. *Memory Quest: Trauma and the Search for Personal History*. New York: W. W. Norton.

Walker, Margaret Urban. 1998. *Moral Understandings: A Feminist Study in Ethics*. New York: Routledge.

Walton, Kendall. 1990. *Mimesis as Make-Believe: On the Foundation of the Representational Arts*. Harvard: Harvard University Press.

Warnock, Mary. 1987. *Memory*. London: Faber and Faber.

Waugh, Gordon. 2000. Letter. *Sunday Star Times* (Auckland), July 23.

Weininger Otto. 1906/1975. *Sex and Character*. Authorized translation from the 6th German edition. London: William Heinemann.

White, Alan R. 1990. *The Language of Imagination*. Oxford: Basil Blackwell.

Whitfield, Charles. 1995. *Memory and Abuse: Remembering and Healing the Effects of Trauma*. Deerfield Beach, FL: Health Communications.

Williams, Bernard. 1973. "Identity and Individuation." In *Problems of the Self: Philosophical Papers, 1956–1972*. Cambridge: Cambridge University Press.

Wilson, Elizabeth. 1999. "Something Happened: The Repressed Memory Controversy and the Social Recognition of Victims." In *Fragment by Fragment: Feminist Perspectives on Memory and Child Sexual Abuse*, ed. Margo Rivera. Charlottetown, PEI: Gynergy Books.

Wollheim, Richard. 1980. "On Persons and Their Lives." In *Explaining Emotions*, ed. Amelie Rorty. Berkeley: University of California Press.

Wray, K. Brad. 1997. *The Role of Community in Inquiry: A Philosophical Study*. Doctoral dissertation, University of Western Ontario.

Wright, Lawrence. 1993. "Remembering Satan." Parts 1 and 2. *The New Yorker* 69 (13): 60–81; 69 (14): 54–76.

Yabko, Michael. 1994a. *Suggestions of Abuse: True and False Memories of Childhood Sexual Trauma*. New York: Simon and Schuster.

———. 1994b. "Suggestibility and Repressed Memories of Abuse: A Survey of Psychotherapists' Beliefs." *American Journal of Clinical Hypnosis* 36 (3): 163–71.

CASES

A.(L.L.) v. *B (A.)*, [1995] 4 S.C.R. 536.

R. v. *Mills*, [1997] A.J. No.1036. (Alta. Q.B.), online: QL (AJ).

R. v. *Mills*, [1999] S.C.J. 68, online: QL (SCJ).

R. v. *O'Connor*, [1995] 4 S.C.R. 411, [1995] S.C.J. No. 98, online: QL (SCJ).

R. v. *Osolin*, [1993] 4 S.C.R. 595, [1993] S.C.J. No. 135, online: QL (SCJ).

INDEX

ABOUT THE AUTHOR

Sue Campbell is Associate Professor of Philosophy and Coordinator of Women's Studies at Dalhousie University. She has her doctorate from the University of Toronto. She is co-editor (with Susan Babbitt) of *Racism and Philosophy* (1999), and author of *Interpreting the Personal: Expression and the Individuation of Feeling* (1997) as well as numerous articles on emotion and memory. Her research, in feminist moral and political psychology, theorizes some of the complex relational, social, and political dimensions to psychological experiences that are, at the same time, deeply personal. She is currently at work on a project on memory and embodiment.

CPSIA information can be obtained at www.ICGtesting.com
Printed in the USA
BVOW040416301111

277149BV00001B/103/P

9 780742 532816